Cognitive Behavioural Therapy in Mental Health Care

Praise for the Book

'At last a text book about cognitive approaches to mental health that can be understood without the use of a dictionary or a scientific calculator. This book manages to bring to life both the theory of technique and the reality of practice. It is a must have book for anyone working in mental health.'

Ron Coleman, author, trainer and consultant based in Fife, Scotland

'This is a wonderful text – fresh, contemporary and practical, as well as subtly subversive! It manages to convey the essence of cognitive therapy in a clear, easy-to-read manner, while drawing the reader to re-consider some of the more questionable assumptions of mainstream approaches. In addition, it contains a number of innovative and important chapters – for instance, on assertive outreach, dual diagnosis, establishing cognitive behavioural work cultures, and critiquing evidence-based mental health. Somehow the authors manage both to embrace and overturn the established order – a remarkable achievement.'

James Bennett-Levy, Oxford Cognitive Therapy Centre

'Cognitive behaviour therapy is the ideal therapy for the modern NHS: it has a strong evidence base, it is focused and short term, and its collaborative, normalising approach is in keeping with the move to involve service users as much as possible with their treatment. Yet most textbooks on the subject pay little attention to the health service setting in which it is practised. This book is unique in presenting cognitive behaviour therapy in an accessible, contextualised way for mental health practitioners working in the NHS today. The chapters on specific areas are tailored to the needs of health service professionals, addressing disorders such as psychosis, borderline personality disorder, and dual diagnosis, as well as anxiety and depression. There are also valuable contributions on working in assertive outreach teams and forensic services. It is relatively easy to go on a basic training course, but much harder to find regular supervision and time to practise newly learned skills. There are chapters devoted to managing this "resistance" from managers, colleagues and organisations, with tips on how to establish cognitive behavioural work cultures. The authors have a great deal of experience of practising and teaching CBT and this richness is revealed in the many case examples throughout the text. This book will be particularly useful for community psychiatric nurses and other mental health workers who want to employ cognitive behavioural ideas in their everyday practice.'

Stirling Moorey, Head of Psychotherapy South London and Maudsley Trust

Cognitive Behavioural Therapy in Mental Health Care

Alec Grant
Jem Mills
Ronan Mulhern
and
Nigel Short

⑤ SAGE Publications
London ● Thousand Oaks ● New Delhi

First published 2004
Reprinted 2005, 2006

SAGE Publications Ltd
1 Oliver's Yard
55 City Road
London EC1Y 1SP

SAGE Publications Inc.
2455 Teller Road
Thousand Oaks, California 91320

SAGE Publications India Pvt Ltd
B-42, Panchsheel Enclave
Post Box 4109
New Delhi 110 017

British Library Cataloguing in Publication data

A catalogue record for this book is available from
the British Library

ISBN-10 0-7619-4141-X
ISBN-10 0-7619-4142-8 (pbk)

ISBN-13 978-0-7619-4141-5
ISBN-13 978-0-7619-4142-2 (pbk)

Library of Congress Control Number: available

Typeset by C&M Digitals (P) Ltd., Chennai, India
Printed in Great Britain by The Cromwell Press Ltd, Trowbridge, Wiltshire

Contents

Acknowledgements

We wish to thank Joe Curran, Ian Dyer, Dave Jones, Neil Kitchiner and Paul Rogers for their support of, and contributions to, this project. Warmest regards go to Christine Padesky and Robert Leahy for their inspirational leadership in the cognitive behavioural community and their great influence on our work. We are indebted to the following people for valuable feedback on the book: James Bennett-Levy from the Oxford Centre for Cognitive Therapy, Liam Clarke and Gail Louw from the University of Brighton and our friends Justine Chase-Gray, Eugenie Hobden and Jane Lever who gave us feedback on specific chapters. Finally, we wish to thank our clients and undergraduate and MSc Cognitive Psychotherapy students at the University of Brighton, who have taught us so much and without whom this book would not have been possible.

Foreword

Christine Padesky

In 1990 I was walking with Dr Aaron T. Beck, founder of cognitive therapy, when a colleague asked him where he hoped cognitive behavioural therapy (CBT) would be in 20 years. Without a pause he asserted that he hoped CBT no longer existed by the year 2010. His response startled me until he continued his reflective comments. Beck reminded us that the central importance Carl Rogers placed on warmth, empathy, and genuine human regard in psychotherapy was considered radical when first proposed. Rogers developed a new psychotherapy, client-centred psychotherapy, to embody these principles. This therapy approach competed with other therapy approaches for many years. Over time, Rogers' ideas proved so compelling that they were subsumed into almost all forms of psychotherapy. Few therapists call themselves client-centred therapists today. But almost all current therapies incorporate client-centred principles.

In the same way, Beck hoped in 1990 that the therapy principles and processes that characterise CBT would no longer need to be distinguished as a separate therapy in 20 years' time. He imagined by the year 2010 the word 'psychotherapy' would presume an active, collaborative therapy relationship in which client and therapist empirically examined beliefs, behaviours and emotional reactions. Further, he envisioned it would become the accepted standard of care for all psychotherapists to follow empirically based methods. In Beck's view, when these transformations of psychotherapy practice are achieved, there will no longer be a need to distinguish CBT as a separate school of therapy.

With 2010 rapidly approaching, there is still a need to educate therapists about CBT and the principles that account for its widespread success. In this text, the authors show how practitioners from all health disciplines can integrate CBT seamlessly into clinical practice in a variety of settings. They encourage practitioners new to CBT to experimentally introduce its methods into daily work with clients.

Cognitive behavioural therapy has proven its effectiveness and been adopted as an acceptable 'standard of care' for many problems. In the UK, governmental agencies and advisory boards make numerous recommendations for clinicians to employ CBT in the treatment of problems ranging from depression to psychosis. Despite mandates for use, institutional and practitioner bias have at times blocked dissemination and delivery of CBT treatments. Thus, it is a welcome contribution to the literature that the authors of this text directly address how CBT practitioners and students can manage institutional barriers and effectively interact with colleagues who dislike or misunderstand CBT.

In my personal teaching experience, when clinicians see cognitive behavioural therapy in action the reservations they hold about the therapy quickly drop away. And when therapists begin to practise CBT methods, positive client responses to these approaches dissolve any remaining barriers to practice. Thus, I encourage readers of this text to follow the recommended activities at the end of each chapter and experiment with the principles taught. Over time, you may or may not identify as a cognitive behavioural therapist. But both you and your clients benefit when you collaborate to identify and examine specific beliefs, emotional reactions, and behaviours using the methods taught in this book.

Will all psychotherapies embody these principles by the year 2010? Increasingly, treatment users and health payers ask for and even demand the features provided in CBT: a clear identification of goals, use of empirically proven methods to achieve those goals within a brief time period, skills building, ongoing measurements of progress, a high probability of success, and low relapse. These demands would have seemed daunting just a few decades ago when I began my career as a psychologist. Today, we know they can be satisfied for many clients and problems. Thus, I believe Beck's vision will be realised. In our lifetime, the CBT skills and principles taught in this text will be considered as fundamentally integral to psychotherapy as offering clients warmth, empathy, and genuine human regard.

Christine A. Padesky, PhD
Center for Cognitive Therapy
Huntington Beach, California USA
www.padesky.com

Foreword

Robert L. Leahy

Thirty years ago the cognitive behavioural approach to therapy was limited to the treatment of major depressive disorder and a very limited treatment for some anxiety disorders. Most practitioners at that time viewed this approach as rather simplistic – but admittedly effective for a small range of problems. The 'deeper' and more 'challenging' cases would be the focus for 'depth' therapies of various kinds. Although those 'depth' therapies provided little evidence of any effectiveness, they were seen as addressing the 'real underlying problems'.

Well, we have come a long way since then.

As this volume illustrates, the cognitive behavioural approach to therapy provides an effective treatment modality for the full range of psychiatric disorders. This approach empowers the clinician to provide effective treatment for depression, generalised anxiety, panic disorder, obsessive-compulsive disorder, social anxiety disorder, PTSD, bipolar disorder, schizophrenia, eating disorders, body dysmorphic disorder, couples problems and family therapy issues. Indeed, where medication is part of the treatment approach, CBT increases medication compliance, resulting in a better outcome for patients with severe mental illness. The emergence of case conceptualisation – and schematic models of personality disorder – have provided the clinician with the tools to help patients with long-standing, apparently intractable personality disorders.

Although psychodynamic theorists may still argue that CBT does not address the deeper issues, we would argue that we do deal with the deeper issues – only, we do it more rapidly and more effectively. New research that indicates that CBT can be effective with patients suffering from borderline personality disorder illustrates the power of case conceptualisation within a structured proactive approach.

Moreover, the treatment approaches described in the current volume are not simply derived from clinical lore and convenient anecdotes. Each structured treatment modality is supported by significant empirical research demonstrating its effectiveness. The structured and highly accessible presentation of these treatment approaches in the current collection of chapters will help the clinician to readily apply these interventions to patients who will benefit from the latest advances in cognitive-behavioral therapy.

Indeed, cognitive-behavioral therapy – as described in this volume – represents the empowerment of both clinician and patient. Both are given the tools and the understanding to collaborate in active and effective treatment. The current volume moves this respectful endeavour forward.

Robert L. Leahy

Preface

Influenced strongly by the Beckian tradition, this text is, unashamedly and inevitably, a selective perspective on cognitive behavioural knowledge and practice. It is aimed at readers wishing to acquire knowledge and skills at foundation and intermediate levels of cognitive behavioural practice and so provides, hopefully, the minimum amount of theory to make the skills understandable and coherent.

Research support for the utility of the cognitive behavioural approach in helping people with anxiety and depressive difficulties is longstanding, well established and robust, and is growing steadily in helping individuals with hearing voices and false beliefs and, so-called, personality disorders. It is therefore not our intention to extensively review the evidence bases for the approach in this text, although Part II of the book will, where appropriate, describe both the empirical and theoretical foundations for the problem areas discussed.

We aim for broad appeal, in terms of including the main areas of adult mental health work where the cognitive behavioural approach is useful. We also aim to guide practitioners in establishing cognitive behavioural work cultures. In this context, we thought it essential to help readers gain a basic understanding of some of the main factors at play concerning organisational resistance to change and the uptake of the approach.

Structure

Chapters 1 to 5 have a broad focus, introducing the reader to the need for the approach, its key central principles and skills, and the idea of organisational preparation. Chapters 6 to 14 illustrate the practice of these principles and skills in a range of specific contemporary work and problem settings, utilising case studies that illustrate the dynamic nature of the approach in its application. All case examples are taken from the clinical work of the authors, with clients having given their permission to be represented in the texts under pseudonyms.

Chapters 15 and 16 return to a broad focus, selectively critiquing the relationship between cognitive behavioural psychotherapy and evidence-based mental health, and organisational difficulties regarding the uptake of the approach. Finally, in the Epilogue, we briefly reflect on some of our ongoing concerns about our cognitive behavioural community.

Terminology

The terms 'cognitive therapy' and 'cognitive behavioural therapy' should be seen as synonymous throughout the text and, as a general rule, 'they' and 'theirs' are substituted for gendered pronouns, except where specific case illustrations merit otherwise. Reflecting both contemporary British mental health and cognitive behavioural parlance, the term 'client' denotes persons seeking help and, assuming a multidisciplinary mental health readership, the generic term 'practitioner' is used in most cases.

Ownership

Finally, it is important to point out that the views conveyed above and in the Epilogue are shared by the four main authors of this text – we make no assumption that they are held by the invited authors who have generously given of their time in contributing Chapters 8, 9, 10 and 12.

Alec Grant
Jem Mills
Ronan Mulhern
Nigel Short

ONE An Introduction to the Cognitive Behavioural Approach and Why it is Needed

Alec Grant, Jem Mills, Ronan Mulhern and Nigel Short

Learning objectives

After reading this chapter and completing the activities at the end of it you should be able to:

1   outline the cognitive behavioural approach to helping people with mental health difficulties in terms of the following key concepts:

   • the role of meaning, emotion and behaviour in mental health difficulties
   • problem and goal identification
   • the therapeutic alliance and case formulation, in relation to cognitive behavioural intervention strategies.

2   identify the significance of cognitive behavioural interventions in relation to:

   • the need for evidence-based mental health care internationally
   • problems concerning the dissemination of the cognitive behavioural approach internationally
   • problems regarding the dissemination of the cognitive behavioural approach in the UK
   • how the UK picture compares with that of other countries.

The cognitive behavioural approach

The role of meaning, emotion and behaviour in mental health difficulties

All cognitive behavioural (CB) interventions rest on the assumption that any of us may develop mental health difficulties if the meanings we give to specific events are sufficiently upsetting. When we are aware that something very pleasant is about to happen to us we usually feel happy and excited. However, if we attach distressing meanings to events we are equally likely to experience distressing emotions. For example, following the death of a partner, someone may feel continual and extreme sadness because of a deeply held belief that they have lost their *only* source of happiness in life (Greenberger and Padesky, 1995). Another individual who hears personally abusive and critical voices, and thinks that they are true, is likely to experience both low mood and anxiety (Mills, 2000).

Distressing meanings and emotions are, in turn, likely to influence changes in behaviour. Someone who feels continual sadness and believes that life holds no further happiness will very likely avoid doing activities previously experienced as pleasurable. Another who both fears and believes the voices they hear may increasingly hide away from contact with relatives and friends. From a CB perspective, the linkage of thoughts and emotions with behaviour serves to keep individuals with mental health difficulties stuck in a 'vicious circle', within which *what they do* both follows from, and serves to confirm, *what they believe* (Hawton et al., 1989).

Some, but certainly not all, of those individuals may also interpret events as more threatening or personally harmful than they really are because of deeply ingrained beliefs and rules for living learned at a much earlier stage in life. In a relatively 'silent' or tacit way, these influence how individuals make sense of their day-to-day experiences, the world and other people (Persons, 1989; Greenberger and Padesky, 1995; Mills, 2000).

Identifying problems and goals

The CB approach provides an empowering, person-centred and structured framework for collaborative working between practitioners and clients. The approach aims to enable mental health service users to make better sense of their difficulties by means of a journey of personal discovery and consider more useful ways of dealing with those difficulties. To this end, during the process of assessment, it is important that people are assisted in making explicit both the problems they want help with and the goals they want to work towards (Hawton et al., 1989; Fox and Conroy, 2000).

The therapeutic alliance and case formulation

With the practitioner ever mindful of the quality of, and threats to, the therapeutic alliance between both parties in the relationship, a developing case formulation emerges from the assessment process (Persons, 1989; Mills, 2000). The formulation is a written, usually diagrammatic, representation of clients' difficulties (this is discussed in detail in Chapter 2). It clarifies the links between troubling events and circumstances and how the client thinks, feels and behaves towards those, and takes into account the quality of the therapeutic alliance between practitioner and client (Hubble et al., 1999a; Leahy, 2001).

Based on a trusting relationship, the case formulation should be thought of as an evolving, rather than static, device that provides a continual and developing intervention reference point for practitioner and client. Enabling clients to contextualise their difficulties and develop strategies for feeling more in control of them, it also helps in the process of achieving informed consent for each stage of the intervention. This is because frequent explanation and discussion are necessary in its development, often combined with guided reading relating to specific points. The case formulation thus provides a clear rationale and guide for practitioner and client in making problem-solving decisions at all stages in the process.

As is discussed in Chapter 2, it may be relevant in some circumstances to include in the formulation the ways in which core beliefs and rules for living, developed earlier in life, seem to be impacting on current difficulties. However, it must be stressed that developing the case formulation in this way should only occur following careful consideration and supervision discussions about the impact this may have on the client's sense of themselves and their ability to progress with a CB approach. In unskilled hands, a focus on core beliefs and associated rules for living can disempower individuals and make them feel worse than they did before seeking help (James, 2001). We are of the opinion, after Persons (1989), that a good case formulation should use the minimum necessary explanatory elements to account for someone's difficulties.

CB intervention strategies

In our view, *appropriate* intervention strategies only emerge from a case formulation that tries to explain how the individual's difficulties hang together in the simplest way possible and takes full account of their relationship with the practitioner. These strategies should aim to help individuals tackle their problems and move forward with their lives, so are always goal-related. Interventions take the form of collaboratively negotiated 'experiments' that enable the person seeking help to 'test out' the extent to which the thoughts underpinning their difficulties can be supported or whether it might be more productive to try out new ways of behaving in relation to perceived and actual difficulties. The overall aim is to help each individual work towards their goals and, with an eye to the future, develop more helpful, adaptive ways of being with themselves, and others, in their worlds.

Why CB interventions are needed

The need for evidence-based mental health care

We live in an era when, internationally, it is becoming increasingly difficult to justify the provision of non-research-based forms of mental health intervention. The CB approach to helping individuals with mental health problems is thoroughly evidence-based. In recent years, support for its provision can be seen in an ever-growing range of mental health problems where it has been found to be helpful (Barlow et al., 1999; Nathan et al., 1999). This range includes anxiety-based problems and depression (Hawton et al., 1989; Wells, 1997; Leahy and Holland, 2000; Department of Health, 2001a) and the severe and enduring psychoses (Gamble and Brennan, 2000; Jones et al., 2000; NHS Centre for Reviews and Dissemination, 2000).

However, in spite of the evidence for the effectiveness of CB interventions, many individuals suffering from mental health difficulties are unable to access the help that they require (Andrews and Henderson, 2000). Undoubtedly, this is in large part because of the increasing costs of healthcare internationally (Rachman, 1996). Aside from economic problems, however, prejudice contin-ues to abound in mental health care with CB approaches often seen as pre-scriptive, mechanistic or, indeed, brutal (Clarke, 1999; Duncan-Grant, 1999). It is also likely that, both in clinical practice and education, many mental health professionals worldwide operate on the basis of 'custom and practice' or theo-retical orientation rather than empirical research. In Chapter 16 we argue that mental health provider organisations tacitly collude with this trend in the ser-vice of maintaining a status quo that disadvantages service users (Grant and Mills, 2000). A final problem is that many mental health workers are under-standably distrustful of the claims made in the name of evidence-based practice (Barlow et al., 1999; Bolsover, 2002; Brooker et al., 2002; Holmes, 2002) because of particular controversies associated with the concept. We share some of those concerns and Chapter 15 addresses selected key issues in evidence-based mental health care and CB practice.

CB provision – the UK scene

In concluding this chapter, it may be useful for readers to consider a brief example of some local problems concerning the dissemination of CB knowledge and skills. Practitioners in the UK desperately need training and education in this area because, reflecting the global picture, the public-sector provision of effective interventions for users of mental health services has been grossly inadequate to date. In this context, the National Service Framework for Mental Health stresses the urgency of expanding the provision of evidence-based training and education in mental health care generally to include CB interventions specifically (DoH, 1999a). Such provision would enable practitioners to respond appropriately to individuals with 'common' mental health problems encountered in primary care, including people with anxiety-related and mood disorders, and those people who suffer from psychotic problems.

In 1998, the Department of Health called for a greater investment in staff training to support this modernising agenda to ensure that effective interven-tions would be offered where they were most needed and would be likely to achieve the most impact (DoH, 1998). In line with this policy, a study conducted by Brooker et al. (2002) aimed to map university-accredited, post-qualifying training and education for mental health professionals in England, to equip them to work with people with serious mental health problems. Sadly, among a raft of other findings, Brooker and his colleagues reported that, in university mental health teaching departments, the provision of training and education in evidence-based practices generally, and in CB approaches specifically, seemed to be the exception rather than the rule.

SUMMARY

- Meaning, emotion and behaviour play a significant role in mental health difficulties.
- During assessment of such difficulties, problems and goals are made explicit.
- The therapeutic alliance and case formulation are pivotal in the CB approach.
- CB intervention strategies proceed from a developing case formulation.
- There is a need for evidence-based mental health care internationally and the CB approach has a strong research base.
- There is a gap between mental health need and effective, CB interventions throughout the world.
- This can be accounted for by increasing costs of healthcare provision, negative perceptions of CB interventions and evidence-based practice and professional and organisational resistance to change.
- The modernising agenda of mental health care in the UK calls for evidence-based training, education and practice.
- Evidence-based mental health training and education is the exception rather than the rule in the UK.
- This picture may usefully be compared and contrasted with provision in other countries.

Activities

- Identify and make contact with CB practitioners locally.
- Explore attitudes towards the CB approach in your organisation.
- Explore the gap between the need for, and provision of, CB interventions in your area.

Further reading

Greenberger, D., Padesky C.A., 1995, *Mind Over Mood: A Cognitive Therapy Treatment Manual for Clients.* New York: Guilford Press.
An excellent self-help manual that would be of great help to mental health workers who wish to learn about the approach by working through their own difficulties in a structured and sequential way.

Gamble, C., and Brennan, G. (eds) 2000, *Working with Serious Mental Illness: A Manual for Clinical Practice.* **London: Ballière Tindall in association with the Royal College of Nursing, Harcourt.**
This book is a lively and informative text for mental health workers who are trying to help individuals with psychotic difficulties.

Nathan, P.E., Gorman, J.M., and Salkind, N.J., 1999, *Treating Mental Disorders: A Guide to What Works.* **New York: Oxford University Press.**
This book provides a brief overview of the main features of all mental disorders, along with a summary of empirically supported treatments.

TWO The Therapeutic Alliance and Case Formulation

Alec Grant, Jem Mills, Ronan Mulhern and Nigel Short

Learning objectives

After reading this chapter and completing the activities at the end of it you should be able to:

1 outline key aspects of the historical significance of the therapeutic alliance in the CB approach
2 describe the main alliance issues related to maximising the potential of the approach
3 understand the historical development and significance of the case formulation concept in CB work
4 describe the relationship between thought, emotion, behaviour, physical reactions and environment in case formulation
5 outline models of case formulation used in the CB approach
6 describe the main issues involved in enhancing client motivation for the approach.

The therapeutic alliance in the CB approach

The notion that the CB approach fails to attach importance to the quality of the therapeutic relationship (sometimes called 'therapeutic alliance') is an enduring myth (Leahy, 2001). A brief and highly selective look at the relevant literature of the last decade suggests that authors and practitioners have been increasingly concerned about factors in the therapeutic alliance that may negatively impact on CB interventions.

Warmth and friendliness versus control

Wright and Davis (1994), summarising relevant contemporary research, argued that the therapeutic relationship and techniques were integrated aspects of a

Forms of resistance	Appropriate considerations for practitioners
• The client fails to complete agreed homework tasks.	• What function does the client's resistance serve?
• The client reacts to improvement with scepticism.	• How does the specific form of resistance fit into the client's developmental/historical pattern of resistance?
• The client shows high levels of expressed emotion towards the CB practitioner.	• What specific beliefs are influencing the client's resistance?
• The client subtly avoids things within sessions.	• What does the client fear might happen if they comply with the intervention?

single process rather than separate domains in the CB approach. The authors asserted that the quality of the client's involvement is crucial to the outcome of therapy, which, in turn, is dependent on the warmth and friendliness displayed by the practitioner. They stressed that overly controlling practitioners who, for example, coerce clients into case formulations or engaging with techniques were highly likely to experience client drop-out or poorer therapeutic outcomes.

Wright and Davis stressed that problems in the therapeutic alliance can and should be viewed as opportunities to explore and develop the case formulation and relationship rather than as irritants. In short, a technique-oriented approach to CB practice that minimises or trivialises the importance of the therapeutic alliance is likely to lead to poor client compliance and a high drop-out rate (Raue and Goldfried, 1994).

Client resistance

A useful way to begin to explore and deal with problems in the therapeutic alliance is to consider the ways in which client resistance to engaging in the CB change process has been conceptualised in the literature. Newman (1994) outlined four high-frequency forms of client resistance and appropriate responses, as shown in the table above.

Newman argued that, after an exploration and understanding of the above four questions, CB practitioners could usefully use the following interventions for reducing client resistance and increasing motivation:

- providing education about the approach, to increase the client's understanding
- using the Socratic method – sometimes referred to as guided discovery (see Chapter 4)
- providing the client with choices rather than one fixed approach
- reviewing the advantages and disadvantages of change
- collaborating and compromising with the client
- providing accurate empathy for the client's resistance.

Client's beliefs about practitioner	*Victimiser:* She will hurt, reject or abandon me. **Collaborator: She will work with me to help me.** *Saviour:* She will protect and save me.	Practitioner's beliefs about client	*Hostile aggressor:* He is trouble and a threat to me professionally. **Collaborator: He is capable of working collaboratively with me.** *Helpless victim:* He is incapable of helping himself.
Client's beliefs about self	*Victim:* I'm helpless and vulnerable. **Collaborator: I can work with someone towards my goals.** *Caretaker:* I don't deserve help; others do.	Practitioner's beliefs about self	*Victim:* I must protect myself so that others don't see my incompetence and inadequacy. **Collaborator: I'm competent and capable of working with this client to help them.** *Saviour:* I'm the only one who can help this client.
Client's beliefs about the intervention	*Hopeless:* This approach won't help me. *Maintenance:* This approach will keep me just as I am. I won't change. **Productive: This approach can help me improve and solve problems.**	Practitioner's beliefs about intervention	*Hopeless:* This approach won't help them. *Maintenance:* This approach will keep them just as they are, but won't help them change. **Productive: This approach can help them to improve and solve their problems.**

In addition to the above, Newman suggested that, in the interests of improving client motivation, it is important for the practitioner to repeatedly discuss the evolving case formulation with the client, in the client's own language. Finally, he argued that it is useful for the practitioner to gently and persistently help 'stuck' clients locate their own sense of self-direction.

Cognitive factors

More recently, Rudd and Joiner (1997) explored the ways in which the 'therapeutic belief systems' of both practitioner and client influence the therapeutic alliance. The main thrust of their argument was that both parties in the relationship may experience beliefs about themselves, each other and the intervention that effectively act as hindrances to progress. Forms of maladaptive therapeutic belief systems outlined by Rudd and Joiner are illustrated in the table above, with adaptive beliefs highlighted in bold type.

It clearly emerges from the table that practitioners using the CB approach would do well to monitor the quality of their relationships with their clients in terms of maladaptive and adaptive beliefs at play, during the course of interventions. An essential vehicle for this task is ongoing clinical supervision from more experienced CB practitioners (see also Chapter 5).

Task	Skills needed
Elicit the client's view of their relationship with the practitioner On the basis of available research, the client's perspective is most predictive of positive outcome of an intervention. However, the client's and practitioner's views of the relationship are often different.	Practitioners need to constantly monitor the quality of their relationships with their clients. This can be achieved by seeking feedback on a regular basis from clients and using client ratings of the relationship. Using clinical supervision to focus on the quality of the relationship is also essential (see Chapter 5).
Use the therapeutic relationship to generate hope Hope for positive change is an essential factor in psychotherapeutic work generally.	Practitioners should encourage clients to believe in the possibility of change in interventions that are oriented towards the future (see this chapter).
Use cognitive skills to establish a good therapy relationship A central overriding skill is the development of a collaboratively agreed case formulation.	From the basis of the formulation, practitioners can employ any of the specific skills mentioned later in this chapter, and throughout the book, to explore the quality of the relationship. Guided discovery and thought records, for example, may be useful tools (see Chapter 4).
Attend to ruptures in the therapeutic relationship Attendance to ruptures in the relationship is critical to outcome.	Instead of viewing problems that emerge in the relationship as an irritant, practitioners would do well to explore the significance of them in the ways described in this section.
Aim for positive therapist characteristics The personal adjustment of the practitioner is related to positive outcomes.	Practitioners will benefit from working on their own personal issues. Two useful texts to aid this process are Persons (1989) and Greenberger and Padesky (1995).
Attend to generalisation from the therapeutic relationship The relationship the practitioner has with the client should be viewed as a template for exploring the client's relationships with others.	Practitioners can explore the extent to which issues, ruptures and positive features of the relationship happen with other individuals in the client's life. This exploration may be useful in helping the client both modify their perceptions of, and improve the quality of, their relationships with others.
Attend to individual client issues in the therapeutic relationship Again, this points to the need for a carefully and collaboratively developed, individualised case formulation.	In addition, practitioners should explore and attend to the client's view of the specific ways in which they feel that the worker has been helpful.
Use clinical supervision to monitor the practitioner's relationship skills The importance of the client's satisfaction with the alliance suggests the need for supervision to provide a strong focus on relationship issues.	The factors identified in this section can be used as a basis for focusing on relationship issues in clinical supervision.

Maximising the therapeutic potential of the relationship

To complement the discussion so far, and round off this section of the chapter, the work of Waddington (2002) is briefly mentioned. In the conclusion of an extensive review of the therapeutic relationship in cognitive psychotherapy, Waddington provided eight tasks for practitioners keen to maximise the therapeutic potential of their relationships with clients. Regarding each task, we suggest the skills that need to be developed are as set out above.

Case formulation and the CB approach

Historical development and specific assumptions

The roots of case formulation can be traced to the mid-1960s. This marked the beginning of an era that has continued to date, within which psychological formulations to account for mental health difficulties have been offered as an alternative to psychiatric diagnosis and medical models of conceptualising emotional distress (Tarrier and Calam, 2002). Reflecting the development of CB approaches over the last 40 years, early versions of case formulation were concerned with the relationship between an individual's problems, expressed as 'problem behaviour', and environmental factors that were assumed to play a triggering and maintaining role in these (Tarrier and Calam, 2002). In contrast, more recent years have seen CB practitioners and writers being much more concerned with the pivotal role of thinking and information processing in the maintenance of mental health difficulties (Hawton et al., 1989).

Two specific assumptions underpin contemporary CB case formulation construction (Wells, 1997). These are that:

- emotional disorders arise from an individual's interpretation of events
- the way in which an individual behaves in relation to how they interpret events plays an important role in the maintenance of their problems.

It follows from these assumptions that all CB change methods used to help clients should proceed from a well-developed case formulation and constitute experiments to challenge beliefs (Wells, 1997). This is an important issue to stress as too many practitioners routinely and uncritically overuse strategies such as progressive muscle relaxation, distraction and thought stopping – frequently in the absence of a case formulation (Short et al., 2004). Another major problem is that, although they may be subjectively experienced by clients as helpful, the routine use of 'relaxation and distraction techniques are unlikely to produce optimal changes in belief in misinterpretations since patients could attribute the non-occurrence of catastrophe to use of their relaxation strategy' (Wells, 1997: 43). In other words, clients may use these strategies to feel safer each time they worry about something. By *doing* such 'safety behaviour', clients fail to find out that what they worry about either doesn't come true or is out of proportion to what actually happens (see Chapter 14).

Case formulation in practice: the interaction between thoughts, emotions, behaviour, physical reactions and environment

When a person experiences a distressing problem, it often feels like an overwhelming, complicated tangle of reactions. The involvement of others, such as family and friends, means that mental health problems affect more than just the individual. One way in which the CB approach first seeks to reduce this confusion is by mapping out the problem.

This usually involves following a recognised structure, based on psychological theory, to piece together various aspects of a person's difficulties. The result should be a clearer understanding of the problem, which then becomes a central source of information in the helping process. Approaches to case formulation can be usefully considered on a continuum from simple to complicated. Simple approaches include the use of naturally emerging 'vicious circle' formulations (see Chapter 8) and the three systems approach.

The three systems approach to case formulation

This approach, originating in the 1970s (Rachman and Hodgson, 1974), is useful for understanding emotional problems in terms of three linked areas (Hawton et al., 1989). These are:

- behavioural – what the individual does
- cognitive/affective – how the individual processes information and how this affects changes in mood
- physiological – the physical sensations the individual experiences, from head to feet.

All three areas relate to each other in that what someone does when they are emotionally distressed will correspond to how they think about events, themselves and others on a day-to-day basis. Each part of the system has an influence on each other part, and all in turn are triggered by events that are current or have occurred in the past. It is important to emphasise that environmental triggering events are significant to the individual in terms of activating emotional distress, so that events seemingly trivial or unimportant to others can be experienced as hugely upsetting by the person concerned. It is convenient to consider such events as either 'external' or 'internal' to the individual, which are anticipated (events that are coming up) or remembered (events that have happened). External events are day-to-day encounters with others, tasks, social events and the like, whereas internal events include triggering thoughts/mood, physical sensations and behaviour.

Once the three systems are activated, how an emotionally distressed individual thinks and behaves will, in turn, influence the kinds of (often distressing) physical sensations that they experience. It should be stressed that, as well as thoughts influencing behaviour, the reverse can occur. For example, an agoraphobic man who avoids busy public places for a period is likely to think more distressing thoughts about the possibility of collapsing in public if he has a panic attack in a supermarket than would be the case if he went into them on a regular basis and found that what he feared failed to happen. Similarly, just as how someone thinks and behaves will affect the physical sensations they experience – for example, fearful thoughts and avoidant behaviour triggering physical sensations of anxiety – such sensations will in turn influence fearful thoughts and avoidant behaviour. The panic feelings the agoraphobic man experiences when he gets close to a supermarket may well trigger thoughts such as 'I'm bound to have a panic attack and make a fool of myself if I go inside.'

As with more complicated examples of case formulation, the three systems approach is best expressed diagrammatically, as shown below.

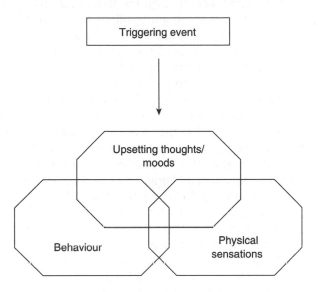

To illustrate the approach in action, we will consider the experiences of a client.

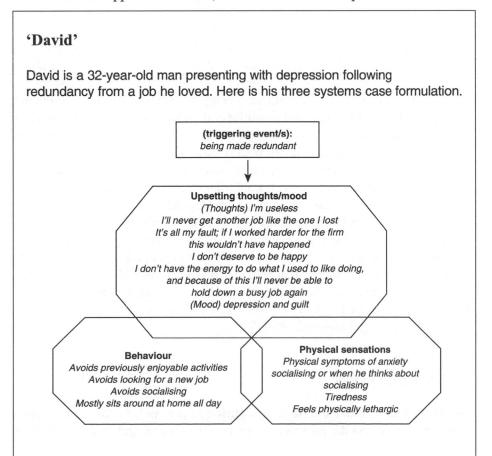

'David'

David is a 32-year-old man presenting with depression following redundancy from a job he loved. Here is his three systems case formulation.

It will hopefully be clear at this stage that David's presenting problem of depression is neatly summarised using the three systems approach. Prior to seeking help, he has already found solutions to his problems based on how he thinks about them. The trouble is that these solutions serve to maintain his problems in a vicious circle. Because he believes it was his fault that he was made redundant, and that he'll never find a job equal to the one he lost, he avoids looking for one. By avoiding, he never finds out whether his beliefs are true or not. Equally, because he believes that he doesn't deserve to be happy, he has stopped doing the kinds of activities that previously gave him pleasure. This results in him feeling unhappy, which, in turn, confirms his beliefs that he is undeserving of happiness. The fact that his activity levels have greatly reduced contributes to his low mood, tiredness and lethargy, and this strengthens his belief that he doesn't have the energy to do the kinds of things that he used to enjoy or cope with a demanding job in the future. Because he does very little, he has a lot of time on his hands to think self-damning and guilty thoughts. He feels anxious when out with other people as he fears that they may be judging him in exactly the same way he judges himself. He therefore avoids old friends, believing that they must feel contemptuous of him, but, by avoiding them, never finds out if this is true or not.

Some advantages and disadvantages of the three systems approach The three systems approach has proved useful in accounting for the experiences mental health service users report (Hawton et al., 1989), and is often a sufficient basis for providing CB help. As with more complex examples of case formulation, the approach helps the client and practitioner develop a shared understanding of the client's problems. This understanding can be tested out for accuracy by introducing behavioural experiments (to be discussed more fully in Chapter 4). For example, David, the depressed client mentioned above, could be helped to consider finding out whether or not his old friends *really* feel contemptuous of him by meeting them again. This would, of course, depend on a successful therapeutic alliance within which David feels reasonably comfortable with this task.

Having experienced and worked with the three systems approach to case formulation, practitioners may begin to realise that it fails to adequately capture the shifting environmental factors that help to explain the onset of emotional distress in one particular period rather than another. In view of this criticism, it is appropriate to next explore Padesky and Mooney's (1990) five aspect model as published in Greenberger and Padesky (1995).

The five aspect model

The five aspect model is also a straightforward structure for developing a conceptualisation. As the following diagram (Greenberger and Padesky, 1995: 4) illustrates, this model can be extremely helpful in achieving a clearer understanding of how elements of difficulties experienced in the here and now interact and is a useful way in which to introduce some key CB skills.

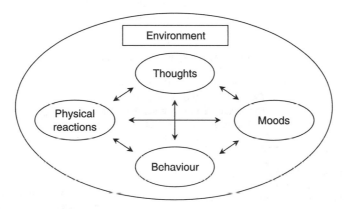

© 1986 Center for Cognitive Therapy

Environment

The environmental aspect is the overall context in which other aspects are experienced. This context refers to both specific and more abstract meanings of the term 'environment', including past and present influences. For instance a person's ethnicity, sexual orientation, family upbringing, socio-economic, accommodation and work status may all count as environmental aspects of life in this model. More specific environmental aspects of a problem would include being alone or in a crowd, darkness or being close to or far from home.

Thoughts, moods, behaviour and physical reactions

'Thoughts' includes memories, attitudes, images and beliefs (and, as in the example below, heard voices), as well as everyday conscious 'automatic' thinking (described below). 'Moods' refers to emotional experience, such as fear, sadness, guilt, anger and shame. 'Behaviour' refers to the person's specific actions in the problem situation and will often include avoidance or repeated patterns of behaviour. Physical reactions might well take the form of anxiety experiences, such as a churning stomach or more chronic experiences, such as lack of sleep or symptoms of substance misuse. The example below of 'Jane's' problem with cutting herself shows the vicious cycles that can result from the interactions between these five aspects.

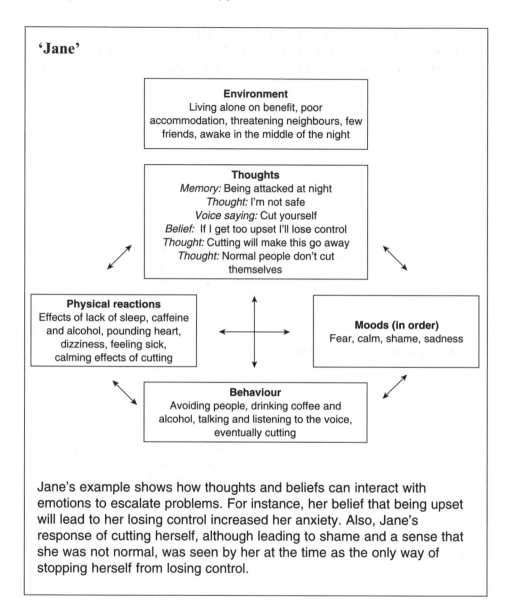

'Jane'

Environment
Living alone on benefit, poor accommodation, threatening neighbours, few friends, awake in the middle of the night

Thoughts
Memory: Being attacked at night
Thought: I'm not safe
Voice saying: Cut yourself
Belief: If I get too upset I'll lose control
Thought: Cutting will make this go away
Thought: Normal people don't cut themselves

Physical reactions
Effects of lack of sleep, caffeine and alcohol, pounding heart, dizziness, feeling sick, calming effects of cutting

Moods (in order)
Fear, calm, shame, sadness

Behaviour
Avoiding people, drinking coffee and alcohol, talking and listening to the voice, eventually cutting

Jane's example shows how thoughts and beliefs can interact with emotions to escalate problems. For instance, her belief that being upset will lead to her losing control increased her anxiety. Also, Jane's response of cutting herself, although leading to shame and a sense that she was not normal, was seen by her at the time as the only way of stopping herself from losing control.

Three levels of cognition – core beliefs, assumptions and thoughts

The cognitive model of mind describes three levels of related thoughts and beliefs. These are presented by Padesky (1998) in the form shown below.

The target model illustrates several key points. The outer ring of the target points to the form of mental activity that people have most access to. It represents the streams of consciousness that enter our minds in response to everyday events, including the negative automatic thoughts that become the focus of many CB interventions. There are exceptions to this as, for example, some people become aware of very strong and negative core beliefs with distressing

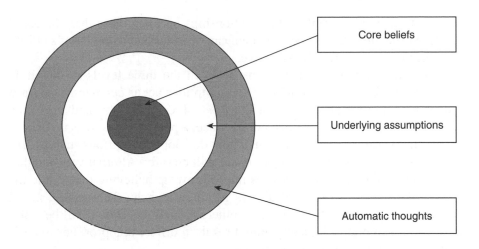

regularity. However, most people are more likely to be aware of, and find it easiest to tune into, the thoughts represented by the outer ring.

The middle ring represents a set of often less accessible and more general beliefs – referred to as underlying assumptions. These are tacitly held, apply to all situations and can be conveniently thought of as 'rules for living'. They are associated with patterns of responses in the ways that people act towards themselves, other people and the world in general. For instance, a person who holds the assumption 'unless I do things 100 per cent right, then I am a failure' may show a pattern of perfectionist behaviour or avoiding challenges.

In the centre ring of the target are core beliefs – also sometimes referred to as schemas or schemata. As the least accessible level of thinking, core beliefs represent the fundamental views we hold about other people, the world and ourselves in general. These beliefs arise from our early life experiences – mostly from the first and enduring lessons that life has taught us.

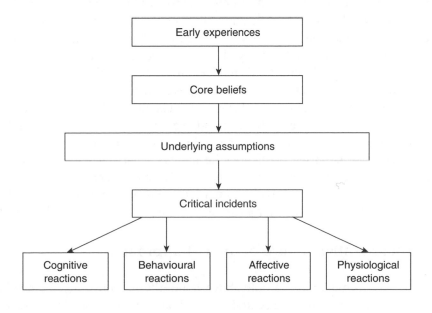

The target model also points to the relationships between these three levels of cognition. The interactions between them can be described using Beck's (1995) linear formulation model, shown above.

The diagram highlights interactions between the three levels of cognition described thus far. Beck describes how assumptions act as *compensatory* ways of dealing with life perceived via the lens of core beliefs, and are often expressed in 'if … then …' terms. For instance, a person who grows up believing that the world is a dangerous place may develop assumptions such as '*If* I carefully assess situations for danger, *then* I will be safe.' Alternatively, another person with different life experiences might grow up believing that, while the world is dangerous, others will always be there to help. This person might develop assumptions such as '*If* I have others around me, *then* I will be safe.' These two assumptions, logically, might result in different approaches to dealing with potentially dangerous situations.

The often compensatory nature of underlying assumptions in relation to core beliefs may be seen in individuals with core self and other beliefs such as 'I am vulnerable and others are abusive' that are compensated for by the assumption 'If I avoid getting close to people, I will not be abused.' Such assumptions often function as a way of protecting the person from the emotional distress of having core beliefs activated. The linear model shows how particular life events referred to as critical incidents can breach these defences to produce the cognitive, behavioural, affective and physiological reactions constituting mental health problems. Taking the earlier example, someone believing that the world is dangerous but others are helpful would probably find being alone in a dangerous situation very frightening. The assumption or rule that 'If I have others around me, then I will be safe' would effectively have been broken, leading to thoughts of danger and feelings of anxiety.

Continuing the earlier example of David's reactions to being made redundant, the linear model (see page 19) is initially helpful in two ways. First, it shows how some of David's core beliefs and assumptions were activated by the redundancy and also sheds light on the relationship with his practitioner. Second, it helps the practitioner to understand why David seemed reluctant to engage with the CB approach and why he avoids talking about his reluctance. The practitioner uses the formulation adapted from Beck's model to make links to David's early experiences. The resulting conceptualisation suggests calculated guesses about the significance of David's avoidant behaviour that can then be gently explored with him. The practitioner takes care to avoid blaming David for his behaviour. Indeed, using the linear model, they are able to agree that his avoidance seems entirely sensible given the predictions he has been making. Once David feels more comfortable discussing these issues, he is gently supported to move on using CB strategies. Later, David's somewhat tempered drive to do a good job becomes an asset in solving his problems and helping him work towards his goals.

The collaborative nature of the CB approach

David's case formulation example above hopefully demonstrates the need for clients to assume an equal and central role in their own progress. People seeking

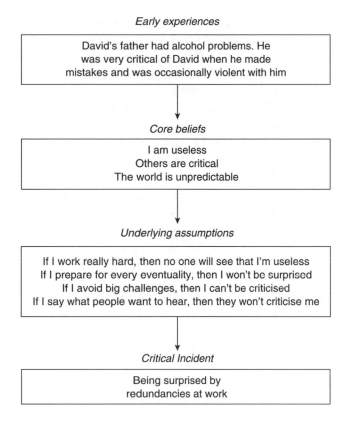

Early experiences

David's father had alcohol problems. He
was very critical of David when he made
mistakes and was occasionally violent with him

Core beliefs

I am useless
Others are critical
The world is unpredictable

Underlying assumptions

If I work really hard, then no one will see that I'm useless
If I prepare for every eventuality, then I won't be surprised
If I avoid big challenges, then I can't be criticised
If I say what people want to hear, then they won't criticise me

Critical Incident

Being surprised by
redundancies at work

CB help are sometimes surprised to find this out. Whether this is a daunting or exciting prospect, the collaborative nature of the approach will necessitate early discussion and preparation for the role. The relationship between therapist and client that lies at the heart of the approach implies a sharing of information and skills.

Enhancing client motivation

Inseparable from considerations concerning the quality of the therapeutic alliance and collaborative case formulation, it is important to highlight the important role for practitioners in enhancing client's motivation for change. Clients need to be helped to:

- be ready for change (Prochaska, 1999)
- achieve the hope that change is possible (Snyder et al., 1999)
- become change-focused – practitioner and client work together to create a context in which new or different perspectives, behaviour or experiences are welcomed and explored (Hubble et al., 1999a)
- potentiate change for the future – the practitioner helps the client see that any changes are a consequence of their own efforts (Hubble et al., 1999a)

- build on the client's competence – the practitioner helps the client identify and build on their own strengths and resources (Hubble et al., 1999a)
- tap into the client's outside world – the client is encouraged to identify the factors, people and resources in their own life that will be helpful in the change process (Hubble et al., 1999a)
- have a healing ritual – the practitioner should demonstrate that they believe in the CB approach (Hubble et al., 1999a)
- have a possibility focus – practitioners should encourage clients to believe in the possibility of change in interventions that are oriented towards the future (Hubble et al., 1999a)
- work in a structured and focused way – one of the best predictors of negative outcome in any form of psychotherapeutic intervention is a lack of focus and structure (Hubble et al., 1999a)
- experience the practitioner as flexible – practitioners should avoid 'hiding behind' models or techniques (Hubble et al., 1999a).

Several important interrelated issues emerge from this list. First, the onus is on practitioners to work to establish trust and confidence – not just in relation to the CB approach and specific techniques, but also in the relationship with their client. Frequently, people in receipt of CB help who may have dropped out because of, usually understandable, problems with engagement have received blanket labels, such as 'resistant' or 'poorly motivated'.

Second, it is important for practitioners to act as 'hopefulness role models' for people needing help. To achieve the client's trust and confidence – in addition to the requirement to demonstrate consistent respect, courtesy, warmth and friendliness – practitioners should display optimism that service users *can* work towards achieving their goals.

Third, service users should be encouraged to consider any progress made while engaging in a CB intervention as the result of their own efforts, rather than, for example, the specialness of practitioners.

Fourth, the problems and goals described by people seeking help should generally be taken at face value. In large part because of non-evidence-based aspects of mental health curricula (see Chapter 15), it is often the case that the problems clients describe are considered by practitioners to be indicative of deeper, unexpressed problems and their goals are thus trivialised or disregarded.

Fifth, people seeking help should be given accessible information about their difficulties. Guided engagement with different types of media – written texts, Internet sites, video and audio material, for example – on different types of specific problem areas, usually helps individuals feel that they are not unique or weird because of the emotional distress they experience. However, caution should be exercised in this area: it follows from what has been said so far that information should *in and of itself* inspire hope and optimism in readers. It would thus be unhelpful to give a (say, psychoanalytical) reading that either mystifies or suggests that the person's subjectively experienced problems are not their *real* problems and that there are deeper problems at play.

Some useful websites and sources of helpful guided reading are listed at the end of the chapter.

SUMMARY

- The therapeutic alliance has long been considered crucial to the success of CB interventions.
- There are clear tasks and skills that need to be developed in the maintenance of a good therapeutic alliance.
- The historical development of the case formulation concept in CB work is associated with key assumptions.
- In practice, case formulation maps out the relationship between thought, emotion, behaviour, physical reactions and environment.
- Models of case formulation used in the CB approach range from simple to complicated.
- There are key issues to be considered in relation to enhancing client motivation for the approach.

Activities

- Consider the attention paid to the therapeutic alliance in your own work organisation. How could the situation be improved using the information from this chapter?
- Reviewing the case notes of clients in your organisation, explore the extent to which case formulation is used. Are records ever kept in case formulation diagrammatic form? If not, discuss with your colleagues whether or not doing so might enhance record-keeping.
- Explore with clients the factors that they think keep them motivated within the mental health system. Compare and contrast their responses with the motivation discussion in this chapter.

Useful websites

www.octc.co.uk
The website of the Oxford Cognitive Therapy Centre. Several useful self-help books have been prepared by members of the centre for specific problems, such as social anxiety and low self-esteem.

www.babcp.com
The website of the British Association for Behavioural and Cognitive Psychotherapies. A comprehensive array of informative leaflets is available from this website, both for specific disorders and to explain the CB approach.

www.padesky.com
This excellent website contains a comprehensive list of the latest recommended textbooks for those interested in the CB approach, as well as audio and video resources for its application.

Further reading

Leahy, R.L., 2001, *Overcoming Resistance in Cognitive Therapy.* New York: Guilford Press.
In a considerably detailed way, Leahy provided a comprehensive overview of forms of, and ways to overcome, resistance in CB work. This emphasises the importance of the practitioner addressing their own distorted thinking about their relationship with the client.

Hubble, M.A., Duncan, B.L., and Miller, S.D., 1999, *The Heart & Soul of Change: What Works in Therapy.* Washington, DC: American Psychological Association.
This highly important text brings together the evidence for the common factors at play in the success of psychotherapeutic and counselling interventions.

Greenberger, D., and Padesky, C.A., 1995, *Mind Over Mood: Change How You Feel by Changing the Way You Think.* New York: Guilford Press.
This excellent self-help workbook is recommended for practitioners. It will enable them to work through and gain experience of case formulation and interventions, using their own difficulties as a reference point.

THREE Key Skills of Assessment

Ronan Mulhern, Nigel Short,
Alec Grant and Jem Mills

Learning objectives

After reading this chapter and completing the activities at the end of it you
should be able to:

1 outline the aims and principles of CB assessment, including face-to-
   face interviewing as a main, but not sole, strategy
2 explain the features of problem and goal lists, as well as capsule
   summaries
3 understand the importance of achieving a detailed description of the
   problem or problems and expressing this in case formulation terms
4 understand the relevance of co-constructing a case formulation as part
   of the assessment process
5 describe the role of measurement and evaluation in the assessment
   process
6 appreciate the importance of structure and agenda-setting in the CB
   approach
7 understand the role of the case formulation in structuring subsequent
   interventions.

Aims and principles of assessment

The processes of case formulation and assessment are interlinked in CB practice. Following Wells (1997), the principal objectives of assessment are to:

- establish what the person's problems are in clear, specific and measurable
  terms
- access factors that serve to maintain both the problem or problems and the
  person's vulnerability
- determine the impact of the problem or problems on the person's life
- construct a continually developing case formulation
- establish a baseline against which to evaluate the progress and impact of the
  intervention.

With these in mind, it is important that practitioners adopt flexible, structured and sensitive approaches to assessment. The aim of it is not only to gain insight into a person's distress, but also build the foundations for a therapeutic alliance (see Chapter 2). The form of the assessment can vary according to the nature of clients' problems, their complexity and, most importantly, the meanings attached to them by clients.

In combining flexibility with structure, practitioners would do well to utilise different forms of information-gathering, including:

- face-to-face interviewing
- client self-monitoring (keeping detailed records of the occurrence of the problem)
- reports on the client's problem or problems from significant others (such as their partner)
- behavioural tests of the problem or problems (that is, observations of the client experiencing the problem)
- standardised and person-specific measures of their problem or problems.

Because face-to-face interviewing is perhaps the most common mode of assessment, it is the main focus of discussion in this chapter. However, it should be stressed that combining different forms of information-gathering facilitates the development of a more comprehensive understanding of both the client's problems and the contexts within which they occur.

Face-to-face interviewing

Pre-interview preparation by the practitioner, such as ensuring a relaxed physical environment, is helpful in putting the service user at ease. Information provided in referral letters and existing clinical records can help in the process of developing an outline structure for the interview. However, the practitioner should be flexible in this regard, as users may disagree with the way that they have been represented (or misrepresented). In our experience, referral letters are often unreliable and inaccurate.

People seek assistance from mental health services for differing reasons, with differing expectations of what help they need or will receive. They may well have been aware of their problems for a considerable time and will have tried to address them prior to seeking help on the basis of the meaning the problem has for them. For example, someone who is fearful of panic attacks will probably have avoided situations where they believe panic attacks may occur. From a sophisticated case formulation standpoint (see Chapter 2), such avoidance can be labelled as a maintaining factor in panic disorder. However, from the subjective point of view of the panic attack sufferer, it may seem a sensible form of problem-solving.

At the commencement of the interview, it is important to allow the client to express their anxieties and concerns – and not just about their problems and their meaning for the client, but also about the meanings concerning their presenting for help. For example, an individual who is referred for the first time may fear that they are going crazy or their problem is so severe that they are 'beyond help'. Equally, they may have had helpful or unhelpful previous contact with mental health services and believe that either they or their problems will not be taken seriously.

Developing the problem list

The use of a problem list (Persons, 1989), collaboratively developed and agreed from the case formulation, is essential. Problem lists guide the choice of desired goals (see below) and in which order goals are best tackled. For example, if someone is afraid of heights and likes apples it will probably help them to try and pick an apple from a lower branch of a tree rather than attempting to climb a ladder and pick one from the top branch. Once a problem list has been developed, it should be prioritised according to which problem is most distressing or most disabling.

Obtaining a detailed description of the problem

By this stage, the practitioner will have encouraged the client to 'debrief' concerning the ways in which they have been represented, currently and in the past, and voice their expectations of, and anxieties about, seeking help. The problem list will have been constructed and prioritised and the practitioner will be reasonably clear on how the client has previously tried to cope with their difficulties. It now becomes important to develop more of a focus on how the client describes their problems. Kirk (1989) provides the following series of useful questions to obtain more focused information.

- What is the problem or problems?
- When does it occur?
- With whom does it occur?
- How often does it occur?
- How frequently does it occur?
- How does it range in intensity (mild to severe)?
- How long does it last when it occurs?
- When, and in what circumstances, did it start?

Expressing the problem in case formulation terms

Having established how they view their problem using the questions above, it is then useful to try to help the client to understand it in case formulation terms by discussing a recent example of its occurrence. The five aspect model described in Chapter 2 is useful in this regard. This model informs the questions asked, as set out below.

Problem domain	Useful questions to ask
Behavioural	• How did you escape the problem? • When the problem was at its worst what changes to your usual day-to-day behaviour did you notice? • Using the example you've just described, what did having the problem cause you to do and how did it interfere with what you might otherwise have done? • If you didn't have this kind of problem, what sorts of things would you be doing that you're not doing now?
Cognitive	• At its worst, what kinds of thoughts went through your mind? • Are these typical of the kinds of thoughts you normally have with the problem? • I guess that made you have thoughts you rather wouldn't have? What were they?
Emotional	• How would you describe your feelings when you were in the thick of the problem? • If that were me, I'd have felt scared/sad/panicky ... How about you?
Physical	• When it was at its worst, what physical sensations did you have, from head to feet? • What's the worst physical sensation you experienced?
Environmental	• What triggered it off (current)? • Having given me an example, what was happening around the time your problem started (historical)?

Capsule summaries

During the course of the assessment process, it is helpful for the practitioner to reflect back to the client the information that they have heard. Useful ways of doing this include saying, 'Just to make sure I've got this right, how about I summarise what you've told me so far?' or 'Perhaps it might be helpful at this stage to recap on what you've told me in the last few minutes?' So-called 'capsule summaries' aid both the important task of structuring sessions (see below) and demonstrating to the client that they have been heard and are being taken seriously.

Co-constructing the case formulation

Once their difficulties have been assessed, the practitioner will be in a position to help the client consider the early case formulation in the spirit of, 'What sense do you make of this?' (Padesky, 1993). Whatever model is chosen, case formulations are best expressed diagrammatically. To ensure the client's active involvement, it is recommended that practitioners use either a white board to draw the early conceptualisation with the client or employ Padesky's 'shoulder-to-shoulder' strategy – sitting beside the client and drawing out the formulation as the assessment conversation progresses (Padesky, 2003). This not only allows for the problem to be seen and considered by both parties, but also begins to allow the client to feel more in control of their problem, by seeing how all the elements of it are interconnected. The use of case formulation diagrams is especially helpful in enabling the client to see the ways in which what were previously regarded as solutions or natural reactions – what they are doing or thinking – may be maintaining their difficulties.

Goal-setting

In the context of early case formulation development, it is helpful to focus on goals the client wants to achieve, as their participation and motivation in the process of change plays an important role in successful outcomes (Hubble et al., 1999a). Some CB writers recommend eliciting short- and long-term goals. This provides an opportunity for short-term goals to be set up for early success, which in turn may provide the client with hope for future goals.

As with problems, goals are best described in very specific terms. Clients may, for example, describe very vague goals, such as 'I just want to feel better about myself.' As this statement needs to be translated into the specific and concrete, practitioners have to help clients express in what ways they wish to feel better by asking questions such as, 'What would you be doing if you felt better about yourself?'

Standardised and person-specific measures

The concept of measurement is central to the CB approach, as it enables both client and practitioner to evaluate the impact of interventions. Measurement occurs at all levels of practice, from the largest of randomised controlled research trials measuring population outcome (see Chapter 15) to the minutiae of individual experiences within sessions. Within the context of a CB intervention for an individual, measurement may still operate at various levels, as illustrated below.

Standardised measures

Standardised measures are those that have been researched to show, among other things, that they effectively measure what they claim to (validity) and that the results are not affected by the measuring process (reliability). Such measures have been developed to assess mental health problems at different levels of focus. For instance, the brief psychiatric rating scale (BPRS) (Overall and Gorham, 1962) is a fairly broad measure of the severity of various mental

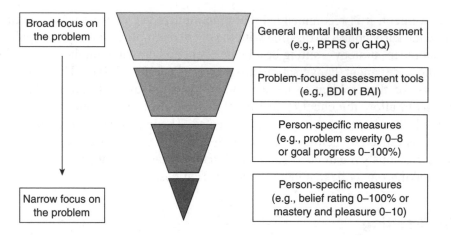

illness symptoms. The general health questionnaire (GHQ) (Goldberg and Hillier, 1978) is broader still in its focus, including more general indices of stress. However, standardised measures exist for more specific mental health problems. For instance, the Beck anxiety inventory (BAI) (Beck and Steer, 1990) restricts its focus to feelings associated with anxiety, while the Beck depression inventory (BDI II) (Beck, 1996) measures depression-related experiences.

Person-specific measures

Although standardised measures do allow for the comparison of an individual's level of distress (for example, in depression) within populations sharing the same disorder, they can often fail to adequately capture the unique nuances of someone's experience of their problem or problems. For instance, clients sometimes feel that items on the BDI II do not quite describe their feelings of sadness. For this reason, it is important that person-specific measures of problems and goals are used to complement standardised measures. Person-specific measures can be achieved using a simple rating scale, as shown below.

Evaluating the success of an intervention

It is useful to repeat person-specific and standard measures regularly. This can help the client and practitioner accurately monitor the progress of the intervention. In keeping with the principles of motivation enhancement, and developing hope and a possibility focus, repeated measurement may also enable both practitioner and client to gain an understanding of the most helpful components of the intervention.

It is important to note that sometimes the score of some self-report instruments may initially increase. For example, if someone has been deliberately avoiding a situation, their score prior to engaging in that situation may be low in terms of anxiety experiences. If they then begin to gradually confront their difficulty, their

Problem statement	Rating scale – Severity				
	(0 none	**2 slight**	**4 moderate**	**6 great**	**8 extreme)**
			Date		
	25 Nov 04	1 Jan 05	6 Mar 05	13 May 05	
Client A 'I feel depressed, resulting in me not eating and a reduction in my activities.'	7	4	3	1	
Client B 'I feel unable to leave my property because I think I will faint.'	8	7	4	2	
Client C 'I do not seem to be able to manage any housework.'	6	4	3	0	
Client D 'The voices I hear frighten and anger me to the extent that I've lost trust in most people.'	8	6	4	2	

Goal statement	Rating scale – progress towards goal				
	(0 none	**2 slight**	**4 moderate**	**6 great**	**8 goal achieved)**
			Date		
	25 Nov 04	1 Jan 05	6 Mar 05	13 May 05	
Client A 'To eat more and increase previously enjoyable activities.'	0	2	4	5	
Client B 'To be able to leave my property with increased comfort for a period of time determined by myself.'	0	1	5	7	
Client C 'To explore ways to tackle and feel more in control of my housework.'	0	3	4	6	
Client D 'To explore ways in which I can feel less frightened and angry about the voices I hear and regain trust in people.'	0	2	3	5	

anxiety may understandably increase initially. No change in measures may provide an opportunity to look at the difficulties that may be blocking progress. This may be simply due to the client having insufficient time to attend to specific activities. Alternatively, it may be that there has been a misunderstanding between practitioner and client regarding what was expected. Whatever the reason, it will be important for both to revisit, and possibly revise, the case formulation while taking account of relevant issues in the therapeutic alliance.

Structuring sessions

As was stressed in Chapter 2, one of the defining characteristics of a CB approach is the use of structure. In interventions, this can take several forms, including:

- working from a list of goals
- working from an agenda in sessions
- using measurement and evaluation regularly
- having key tasks that are repeated during each session, such as weekly measures of mood level
- following a planned programme
- following a self-help resource, such as books or computer packages.

Structure can be flexible, using the individual case formulation for guidance. The collaborative and educational nature of the CB approach seeks to involve the client in planning for, and monitoring progress towards, their independent use of CB change interventions. With this in mind, parts of the intervention are often structured on the basis of helping the client to learn new skills.

Using agendas

Often the first step in structuring a CB session is the construction of an agenda (Leahy 2001), occurring at the start of each session. This necessarily emerges from a collaborative initial discussion between the practitioner and client. In the initial stages of CB work, the client will have less knowledge of the approach than the practitioner and may have less to contribute to the agenda. However, following the illustration below, it is often helpful to clearly discuss how this should change over time as the client becomes more expert in the approach.

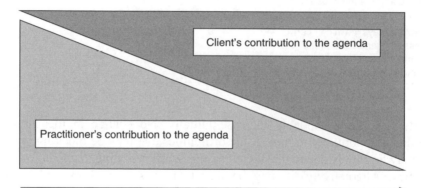

Course of intervention

Example of an agenda-setting discussion

Practitioner: Would it be helpful if I said a little bit about what we might do today?

Client: Yes, OK.

Practitioner: Well, I generally find it useful to start by making a list of things to discuss in the session. That way we can make best use of our time and make sure that we cover everything we set out to cover. How would that be?

Client: OK.

Practitioner: So, what do you most want to get out of today's session?

Client: I need to know whether or not you can help me.

Practitioner: OK. I was going to say something similar. I suppose today is about you and I making some decisions together. We need to know if you can work with me using a cognitive behaviour therapy approach. Also, we need to think about whether or not the problems that you're going through might respond to that approach. So I guess that you need to hear a bit about what I do and I need to hear a bit about what you've been going through. How does that sound?

Client: That sounds all right. Shall I start by telling you about what's happening at the moment?

Practitioner: That would be really good.

Note how the language used from the start of this session emphasises the collaborative nature of the CB approach. The next example took place later in the intervention with the same client. The practitioner encouraged the client to reflect on how their understanding of the case formulation might help in setting the agenda.

Practitioner: So, what do you want to cover today?

Client: Well, I want to tell you about the results of the survey we planned last week. My wife has been getting me down all week. I had a confusing session with my psychiatrist and there's an issue that has come up about my return to work.

Practitioner: That sounds like quite a lot, especially as I was expecting quite a bit to come out of the survey. As we know from our case formulation, you have a tendency to try to get things done very quickly. I'm wondering if there is any way in which we could prioritise those things.

Client: Well, the work thing and the session with the psychiatrist could wait until next week, but I really need to address this issue with my wife before we go away at the weekend or I'm afraid the trip might be ruined.

Practitioner: OK, how long do we need to spend on the issue with your wife?

Client: Let's say 25 minutes.

Practitioner: OK and can we spend the rest on the survey?

Client: Sure. Which shall we do first?

Structure and the case formulation

The case formulation can be a useful resource when collaboratively planning the structure of subsequent interventions. It can, for instance, be helpful when using a linear formation as a means to encourage the client to decide the point at which to intervene first. For example, a client may choose to tackle life rules followed by troublesome negative automatic thoughts. The practitioner's role in this process is to describe what might be involved at each stage, what the likely effects on the client's life might be and how long it might take.

SUMMARY

- The assessment process in the CB approach has key aims and principles.
- These include face-to-face interviewing as a main, but not sole, strategy.
- Key to assessment is the development of problem and goal lists, and capsule summaries.
- A detailed description of the problem area should be sought and expressed diagrammatically as a case formulation.
- The case formulation should be collaboratively constructed with the client.
- Measurement, evaluation, structure and agenda-setting are central to the assessment process.
- The case formulation is a crucial resource in structuring subsequent interventions.

Activities

- Explore the ways in which mental health service users are assessed in your clinical area.
- Consider the ways in which CB assessment might enhance this process.
- Practise some of the assessment strategies detailed in this chapter.

Useful website

www.padesky.com
The audiotape *Case Conceptualization: An In-session Collaboration* (audiotape code CC), which can be obtained from this website, is an excellent resource to develop the skills needed in co-constructing case formulations in the assessment process.

Further reading

Hawton, K., Salkovskis, P.M., Kirk, J., and Clark, D.M. (eds), 1989, *Cognitive Behaviour Therapy for Psychiatric Problems: A Practical Guide.* New York: Oxford University Press.
The sections on relapse prevention in this book are important further reading.

Kirk, J., 'Cognitive behavioural assessment', in Hawton, K., Salkovskis, P.M., Kirk, J., and Clark, D.M. (eds), 1989, *Cognitive Behaviour Therapy for Psychiatric Problems: A Practical Guide.* New York: Oxford University Press.

Readers will find it useful to compare and contrast this chapter, along with Wells' description of assessment in the book mentioned below, with the information we have provided in this chapter. Doing so will help readers consolidate and develop knowledge and skills of assessment.

Wells, A, 1997, Cognitive Therapy of Anxiety Disorders: A Practice Manual and Conceptual Guide. Chichester: John Wiley.

FOUR Cognitive Behavioural Interventions: Understanding Techniques in the Context of Theory

Jem Mills, Alec Grant,
Ronan Mulhern and Nigel Short

Learning objectives

After reading this chapter and completing the activities at the end of it you should be able to:

1 describe what is meant by 'emotional hijacking'
2 understand the links between 'emotional hijacking', attribution style and cognitive distortion
3 outline the rationale for reattributional cognitive interventions
4 describe a method of tuning in to thoughts and feelings
5 describe what is meant by the 'cognitive content specificity of emotion'
6 rate the strength of emotions and belief, understand the process of uncovering the meaning behind emotion and generating more helpful thoughts
7 understand the role, function and process of behavioural experiments.

The analogy of the broken vase

Imagine you are alone, sleeping in an unfamiliar house, when you wake to the sound of breaking glass. What thoughts, images and emotions might you experience? What would you do about the situation? You might well plan to either face the threat, flee from the situation, hide or try to get help. Continuing the story further, imagine that you then heard a scratching sound followed by a 'meow'. You summon the courage to investigate this and find that a cat has knocked over and smashed a vase. How would your reactions differ after discovering this? Most people would have a sense of relief as the thoughts of an intruder and feelings of anxiety dissipated.

This analogy can demonstrate some underpinning principles of the CB approach, and lead to some interesting and complicated theoretical questions. How does someone wake automatically to the sound of breaking glass but not to other sounds of equal volume, such as traffic noise? Why do they not instantly recognise non-threatening possible explanations? Finally, why do actions such as fleeing seem to present themselves before the situation has been fully considered?

Emotional hijacking

Goleman's (1996: 13) term 'emotional hijacking' refers to the brain's capacity for responding to different life situations by switching between different modes or styles of thinking. We tend to be aware of thinking processes under our conscious control, such as preparing a shopping list. This is obviously useful when we consider the amount of information available to our senses on a moment-by-moment basis – the temperature of a room, background sounds of neighbours' activity, feeling of sitting in a chair, internal bodily sensations. All these sources of information would be very distracting to a person making a shopping list if they were treated with equal priority. Hence, the brain has ways of selecting which information is dealt with automatically and which is brought to our conscious attention.

Some types of information are given higher priority – especially those relating to the safety of our self and loved ones. Our automatic attention processes scan our environment for various types of information and the analogy of the broken vase demonstrates that such scanning occurs even when we are sleeping. Switching to an automatic thinking process, outside of conscious awareness, is a hallmark of emotional hijacking. A clear example of this is the way in which our brains deal with threat. Once a potential threat has been identified, the brain activates what might be described as an emergency thinking mode, prioritising focusing on and responding to the threatening situation. Memory systems are adjusted to access only the most relevant recollections and attention focuses on the most pressing information, such as ongoing signs of threat and escape routes. Hormones are released that help the body to prepare for action.

When applied to the scenario of the broken vase, this perspective offers a more detailed description of what might be occurring. The sound of breaking glass is detected by the sleeping person and recognised as a sign of potential threat as the brain starts switching to wakefulness. At the same time, emotional hijacking occurs and a stream of relevant memories are analysed. These memories include times when the person has felt alone and threatened, stories read in media and seen in films of people detecting and dealing with similar threats and the memory of locking doors and windows in the house before going to bed. The brain releases hormones that help to make the senses more acute. The house is scanned for further sounds and the direction of the threat is ascertained. The person's breathing quickens and blood pumps to the major muscle groups in preparation for action. By the time the person has sat up in bed with an image of an intruder in mind, breathing heavily but quietly, less than a second of time has passed.

The analogy demonstrates that emotional hijacking allows for a very fast reaction to threat. This speed is achieved by bypassing many other processes. The major drawback of this bypassing effect is its tendency to lead to mistakes. From the perspective of evolutionary theory, survival is less likely with a slow but accurate threat-detection system, which accounts for what Goleman (1996: 22) describes as the 'fast and sloppy' nature of emotional hijacking.

The example so far has involved threat appraisal and the emotional response of anxiety. However, Goleman points out that emotional hijacking occurs with all types of emotions. In support of this position, Mathews' (1997) review shows how these types of processes play a pivotal role in mental health problems such as anxiety and depression. It is difficult to counter the effects of emotional hijacking, but the role of a practitioner using a CB approach is to do just that. This involves helping a client to realise that many thoughts or beliefs that *seem* true are actually inaccurate conclusions derived from useful, but imperfect, processes. These unhelpful effects on thinking are referred to by Burns (1989: 96) as 'cognitive distortions'.

Attribution style and cognitive distortions

Attribution theory in relation to mental health problems is concerned with how emotional disorders influence conclusions people make about events. The patterns in the way people are influenced are referred to as 'attribution style'. One way to describe attribution style uses the three dimensions listed below:

```
internal-----------------------------external
stable-------------------------------unstable
global-------------------------------specific
```

The internal/external dimension refers to the extent to which a person attributes an event to factors within his or her self or to factors outside of personal control. The stable/unstable dimension relates to whether the attribution represents a regular or irregular occurrence. The global/specific dimension refers to whether the attribution is made to a broad or narrow range of conclusions. A clearer way to explain these categories is with specific examples (their names have been changed).

> 'Paul' was depressed when he tried to do some mechanical work on his car. He was unable to fix the problem he was working on and concluded that he was a failure as a person. He told himself he had always been a useless mechanic because he was a failure at everything he did.

In this example, Paul blamed himself (internal attribution) for not being able to fix the car when, on further examination, it transpired that he was missing a vital piece of equipment. He thought he had always (stable attribution) been a useless mechanic because he was a failure at everything he did (global attribution). Paul's thinking arose from a common attribution style in depression – a tendency towards making internal, global, stable attributions about events.

Distortion	Example
All-or-nothing thinking Seeing things in black-and-white categories.	Paul has the thought that he is a failure when he cannot fix his car without help.
Overgeneralisation Seeing a single negative event as a never-ending pattern of defeat.	Becca tells herself that she is unemployable after an unsuccessful job interview.
Mental filter Picking out a single negative detail and dwelling on it to the exclusion of other details.	Sally thinks that her week has been awful because she spent a day in bed.
Disqualifying the positive Rejecting positive experiences by insisting they 'don't count'.	Jon concludes that he is unlikeable despite having friends, thinking that they only spend time with him because he has money.
Jumping to conclusions Mind reading – arbitrarily making conclusions about what others are thinking. Alternatively, fortune telling – predicting that things will turn out badly.	Marie assumes that her practitioner thinks she is lazy when she is late for an appointment. Cyril concludes that his psychiatrist will make him go to hospital if he attends a meeting with him.
Magnification (catastrophising) or *minimisation* Exaggerating or shrinking the importance of things inappropriately.	Adam believes his shortness of breath is a sign that he is having a heart attack, while simultaneously discounting his high level of physical fitness.
Emotional reasoning Thinking that negative emotions reflect the way things really are.	Lucy thinks that her flat is a very unsafe place to be because she feels anxious there.
Should statements Criticising oneself and others using unfair rules and standards.	Anne-Marie feels angry when her room-mate doesn't keep things as tidy as she thinks they *should* be.
Labelling Calling oneself names in response to events.	Craig has the thought that he is a 'useless fool' when he forgets someone's name.
Personalisation Blaming oneself or others for something without accounting for other factors that were involved.	Carrie has the thought that her friends did not enjoy their night out because of her depression rather than the poor restaurant they went to.

Bentall et al. (1991) argue that people experiencing paranoia have an external, stable, global attribution style. For instance, 'David' believed that his head pains were the result of secret agents tampering with his brain while he slept (external attribution). He felt that they were always doing things like this (stable attribution) and that they had the power to insert bugs anywhere about his person or in his flat (global attribution).

The list given in the table above can be seen as a summary of ways in which attribution style is affected by strong emotions. Identifying the particular distortions at play can be a useful first step when dealing with unhelpful thoughts.

These cognitive distortions represent the effects of unhelpful attribution styles. The cognitive interventions below can be described as reattribution techniques. They literally encourage the person to reflect on attributions they have made and to re-evaluate them in order to generate more helpful alternatives.

Cognitive interventions: reattribution techniques

A classic cognitive intervention is the use of a thought diary technique (Fennell, 1989; Greenberger and Padesky, 1995; Leahy and Holland, 2000). This encourages reflection on the negative automatic thoughts a person experiences when emotionally hijacked. The ultimate aim is to re-examine the often negative meaning underpinning unhelpful feelings about an event and generate a more helpful view. The thought record has a number of key aims – namely, helping a person to:

- recognise emotions and thoughts as they happen
- recognise how events, thoughts, emotions and responses interact
- become aware of how emotional hijacking can produce plausible but inaccurate conclusions
- re-examine the conclusions reached about an event
- generate less debilitating ways of viewing events
- ultimately, use the technique habitually in order to reduce emotional distress.

The intervention can be seen as comprising two related stages. The first focuses on becoming aware of emotions and the particular meaning behind them. The second is concerned with analysing that meaning and generating more helpful alternatives.

Stage 1: tuning into thoughts and feelings

For most people it is unusual to be aware of thoughts and feelings during very emotional experiences. For this reason a period of learning to recognise and reflect on them is useful. This can be done using a thought diary made up of four columns:

Date	Description of the event	Emotions experienced	Thoughts or images experienced

We each have a unique way in which we experience and describe emotions and thoughts and it can be helpful to pay attention to this when helping a person to reflect more fully on them. For instance, it is common for people to describe an emotion in terms of its physical effects. In these instances, the person can be encouraged to use attention to particular physical feelings in the early detection of emotions. Once emotions are recognised, the person can be encouraged to concentrate on reflecting on the meaning associated with them.

A first step in detecting meaning is to become aware of negative automatic thoughts as they occur. This is often described as 'listening to the running commentary' we produce during times of distress. However, people have varying degrees of awareness of these thoughts and it can take time to home in on the ones involved with unhelpful reactions to events. The table below lists some common difficulties and helpful solutions reported by people trying to become aware of negative automatic thoughts for the first time.

Difficulty	Example	Possible explanation	Possible solutions
Little awareness of thoughts.	Person reports negative feelings but denies having thoughts.	Thoughts are there, but are being mislabelled or not recognised for some other reason.	Use the person's own language, such as worries, feelings, little voice inside. Ask questions, such as 'What was bad about that situation for you?' 'What did you tell yourself about that?' If appropriate, role-play the situation, stopping at hot spots and asking the same sorts of questions as above.
		Person may be experiencing mental images rather than verbal type thoughts.	Ask the person to describe any mental pictures in detail and identify the meaning it holds for them.
Little awareness of emotions.	Person has a sense of feeling generally bad, but cannot distinguish particular emotions or feel emotionally blunted.	Long-term avoidance of bad feelings, including little opportunity for discussion about emotions with others. Some problems, such as post-traumatic stress disorder, lead to blunted emotions.	Hypothesise particular emotions using specificity of thoughts (see below). Detect particular patterns of physical feelings associated with types of events. For example, analyse loss events and help the person to associate physical feelings, such as the 'sinking feeling' associated with sadness.
Recorded thoughts and emotions don't seem to match.	Person reports anxiety and thoughts such as 'it will be OK' or 'you're strong.'	The person is having a stream of thoughts, but tuning into them at a later point, thereby missing the initial ones.	With positive self-talk-type thoughts, use a telephone analogy, which involves describing the person on both ends of a telephone conversation. The 'you'll be Ok' end of the conversation has been recorded well. Ask 'What were these thoughts replying to?'
	The person reports feeling anxious, but has thoughts such as 'I'm so unhappy.'	The person is reporting bits of a cycle of thoughts and emotions – such as having a thought about danger and feeling anxious followed by a thought about being weak and unlovable and feeling sad.	When other thoughts seem not to match, use the specificity of emotion model below to ask emotion-specific questions, such as (with anxiety) 'Did you feel as if something bad might happen?' or 'What was the danger there for you?' or, with depression, 'Did you feel that you had lost out on anything? What was that?'

The cognitive content specificity of emotion

Wells (1997) reminds us that the style of thinking relates to the types of moods experienced by individuals. The following table describes the link between emotion, thematic meaning and automatic thinking.

Emotion	Theme	Example thought
Anxiety	Perceived threat, prediction of danger.	'If I speak up I'll be criticised and I won't be able to cope.'
Depression	Perceived loss.	'My future is hopeless, I'll never work again.'
Anger	Perceived transgression of personal rules by others.	'The doctor should never have told my husband that I wasn't coping.'
Guilt	Perceived transgression of personal rules by self with negative consequences for others.	'I'm such a terrible mother – I can't look after my children properly. They will be permanently damaged by this experience.'

Rating strength of emotions and belief – what's the meaning of this emotion?

As mentioned above, a key aim in the process of keeping a thought diary is to encourage people to become aware of the plausible, but inaccurate, conclusions that often underpin periods of emotional hijacking. On becoming more aware of emotions and thoughts, people often end up with a number of recorded thoughts from a particular event. It is crucial to the success of the thought diary technique to focus on the meaning most strongly associated with the distress.

Many initial attempts at using a thought diary are thwarted by re-examining a conclusion that does *not* lie behind that distress. One way to focus in on the appropriate conclusion is to rate the strength of emotion and belief in the associated thoughts using a 0–100 per cent scale. Greenberger and Padesky (1995) describe these underpinning conclusions as 'hot thoughts', indicating that most of the time a person's strength of belief in an underpinning thought matches the level of distress that they are experiencing.

'Dan'

Event	Emotion 0–100 per cent	Thoughts 0–100 per cent
Getting ready to introduce myself during a round of introductions in a new project group meeting at work on Monday morning.	Fear 75 per cent.	'My throat is closing up' – 50 per cent. 'My voice will sound shaky' – 60 per cent. 'People will see that I'm anxious' – 75 per cent. 'Everyone in the project group will think I'm lacking in confidence and they'll have no respect for me' – 75 per cent.

Following on from this example, if Dan had proceeded to the next stage of the thought diary – focusing on the thought 'My throat is closing up' – he probably would have had little or no relief from his fear. This is because his underpinning conclusion about people losing respect for him would have remained intact. Using the downward arrow technique (Greenberger and Padesky, 1995), Dan was able to identify the hot thought by repeatedly asking himself questions such as 'What would that lead to?', 'What would be so bad about that for me?' or 'What would that mean about me?' In this way he was able to home in on, and see the significance of, the threat that he associated with the feeling of his throat was closing up.

Below is an example of the downward arrow technique, as applied to Dan's thought record.

'I might appear anxious as I introduce myself to the group.'

↓

'What would be so bad about that?'

↓

'They might start to judge me in a negative way.'

↓

'OK. If that were true, what would be bad about that for you?'

↓

'They'd see me as lacking in confidence and lose respect for me.'

↓

'And in your wildest fears, what would that mean about you as a person?'

↓

'That I'm useless! No good! A failure!'

Stage 2: generating more helpful thoughts

The ultimate aim of this stage is to reach a new conclusion about the problematic event in order to reduce distress. This stage involves three key tasks:

- reflecting on the accuracy of conclusions or thoughts
- generating an alternative, more helpful conclusion
- evaluating the effects of the new conclusion on the original feelings of distress.

Reflecting on the accuracy of conclusions or thoughts

Before attempting to generate alternative thoughts, it is helpful to understand how the original one was reached. To this end, asking questions such as 'What tells me that this is true?' or 'What am I basing this on?' can be useful.

Reflecting on the list of thinking errors described earlier can also be helpful with this. For instance, people who have an 'emotional reasoning' style of reaching conclusions will often deny any specific evidence for a conclusion. In this case they are concluding that a thought is accurate because it feels that way. One example is when a person believes a situation is going badly because it feels emotionally distressing.

Another method for identifying sources of evidence is to consider patterns of attention. People pay particular attention to aspects of their environment that concur with their beliefs (Goleman, 1996). For instance:

- someone worried about being followed will notice people travelling in the same direction
- a person with a core belief 'I'm a failure' will notice upcoming challenges and all his or her mistakes
- holding the belief 'Nobody respects my rights' will lead to noticing more examples on having rights infringed.

With this in mind, asking questions such as 'Were you looking out for anything in particular?' or 'What did you notice about that situation?' may help people to reflect on the evidence for their conclusions.

An individual's descriptions of events also tends to highlight their attentional patterns. For instance, listening to and discussing someone's description of walking into a room to give a presentation could reveal quite different patterns of attention. The table below illustrates how a particular belief might affect attention which would consequently influence someone's description of an event.

Description	Attending to	Unhelpful belief
'I stepped into the room and all eyes were on me.'	First reactions of the audience.	'The people in the audience are apprehensive because they think that I won't be able to present properly.'
'I opened the door to the room and I could have cut the atmosphere with a knife.'	Emotional felt sense of the environment.	'The audience don't want to be here. They have been forced to listen to me.'
'When I entered I saw that the room was set up perfectly for my presentation.'	Everything but the reactions of the audience.	'The audience must have great respect for me.'

Sometimes tracking down the processes that have led to a particular set of unhelpful thoughts can seem like detective work. Listening to a person's description of events, asking about particular things he or she noticed and keeping the specificity of emotions model in mind are three ways in which to assist people in that detective work.

Collecting the evidence for an unhelpful thought then becomes a summary of how that thought was reached. This in itself can be helpful, as it can demonstrate how emotional hijacking has led to an inaccurate thinking style or an over-reliance on particular sources of evidence. It can also show how habitually biased patterns of attention lead to conclusions that *seem* plausible as they help to build an incomplete picture of events. These features become central to the next stage of the process – focusing on evidence against the unhelpful thought.

Reflecting on evidence against unhelpful thoughts

At this point the collaborative nature of the CB approach becomes crucial. Having thoughts subjected to this kind of scrutiny can seem very critical. For instance, when first presented with this technique, it is not unusual for people with depression to conclude that they are bad at thinking as well as everything else. In order to avoid ruptures in the therapeutic alliance, the practitioner should continually share ideas behind the technique and help the person to understand that the process of emotional hijacking is a normal human occurrence.

How good is the evidence for the unhelpful thought

The first and often most productive question to ask during this part of the thought record process is 'How is the evidence I've collected in support of the conclusion flawed?' This re-examining of evidence for the thought helps to reveal gaps in the thinking process.

It can be useful to take each piece of evidence in turn and subject it to scrutiny. It is at this point that people often have difficulty as they are attempting to break out of habitual styles of thinking. For this reason, the first reviews of this type are usefully shared with the practitioner, as two heads are better than one when undertaking this work. Reflecting on the evidence in support of the thought takes the form of asking questions such as:

- 'Am I making any thinking errors such as all or nothing thinking?'
- 'If so, what is the middle ground view of this situation?'
- 'Is this evidence based on a particular thing that I've noticed to the exclusion of others?'
- 'What might I have missed, discounted or forgotten about?'
- 'If I had to state this as evidence in a court of law, what objections might there be to my conclusions?'
- 'Does this evidence justify my conclusion or am I making a leap of some sort?'

After re-examining the evidence in this light, further evidence against can be generated in discussion and reflection on questions such as those posed by Greenberger and Padesky (1995), which include:

- 'Have I had any experiences that show that this thought is not completely true all the time?'
- 'When I am not feeling this way, do I think about this type of situation differently? How?'
- 'Are there any strengths or positives in me or the situation that I am ignoring?'

In summary, this review of the evidence helps the person to identify how conclusions about an event have been affected by emotional hijacking. It encourages a reflective process that seeks to go back and fill in gaps left by this 'fast and sloppy' emergency style of thinking. Once these gaps have been located and filled, an alternative, more helpful, conclusion about the event can be generated.

Generating a new, more helpful, thought and testing it against the original distress

This last part of the process acts as a summary of the argument so far and presents a new conclusion about the event. In order to be helpful, the new conclusion must be believable and, as such, it is useful to measure this in the same way that the original thought was, using a 0–100 per cent scale with 0 signifying no belief in the thought and 100 complete belief in it. This rating is the first indication of how successful the process has been.

If the level of emotional distress is not reduced by reflecting on the new conclusion, then the process has been derailed somewhere along the line. In this case, going back over the thought record and considering the issues above should lead to the desired effect. If the thought record is still unsuccessful after this, it may be that the event has activated deeply held core beliefs in the person (see Chapter 2).

'Walter'

Walter came for help with his long-term problem of lack of confidence and low self-esteem. He spent time recording his thoughts in situations where he felt anxious.

After a few weeks of writing down the evidence for and against his unhelpful thoughts, he noticed a pattern. He discovered that entering social situations invariably led to negative thoughts about what others were thinking of him. He also noted that he had a tendency to mainly notice negative and ambiguous body language in others. By reflecting on this, he realised that his anxiety was associated with a 'mind-reading' style of thinking and a tendency to ignore or discount friendly responses from others.

Once he discovered this, he used it to help him see alternative ways of viewing situations. At times when he felt anxious, he was able to catch his unhelpful thoughts and ask himself questions such as, 'Could I be doing that mind-reading thing again?', 'How do I know this is true?', 'Is there any evidence that these people around me do not think badly of me?'

Using this method, he was able to reach alternative conclusions and predictions about events soon after spotting the initial feelings of anxiety, thus making events less distressing for him.

Below is an example of a typical thought record completed by Walter.

Situation	Emotions	Thoughts	Evidence for	Evidence against	Helpful alternative	Emotions
Standing outside a restaurant thinking about entering and joining Dave's birthday party.	Anxious – 70 per cent.	'I can't go in' – 50 per cent. 'It's too much' – 60 per cent.	'People always look at others when they enter a room.'	'Looking up is an automatic response – it doesn't mean they are unfriendly.'	'People look up automatically when others enter the room.'	Anxious – 20 per cent.
		'Everyone will see that I'm anxious as I enter and decide not to talk to me' – 70 per cent.	'Dave noticed that I was anxious when I visited him at work.'	'Dave knows me very well – his colleagues didn't notice my anxiety.'	'Only those who know me well spot my anxiety. I will find it difficult to mix and chat, but Dave's friends are all nice people and I've managed things like this before.'	
			'I find it hard talking to people when I'm anxious.'	'I always feel more anxious than I look.'		
			'There are people here I don't know.'	'I find it hard talking to people, but they don't always find it hard to speak to me.'		
				'Dave said his friends are similar to him in that they are quite caring.'		

Behavioural experiments

Behaviour and beliefs

The reciprocal relationship between beliefs and behaviour forms a central part of the CB understanding of emotional problems. Experience moulds our beliefs and beliefs mould our attention patterns and behavioural responses. Behavioural responses and attention patterns, in turn, shape much of our experience.

As discussed earlier, underlying assumptions or rules for living are sets of beliefs lying behind repeated patterns of behaviour. Much of the time these beliefs are beyond our awareness. What we tend to notice first is our habitual responses to different situations in life. For instance, students of CB therapy often find themselves doing many alternative activities when faced with written assignments (Worthless et al., 2002).

One student on our degree course found himself cleaning parts of his house he had previously neglected on a day that he had planned to begin work on an essay. On further reflection, he noticed that he repeatedly undertook more domestic tasks when faced with written assignments. His thought record revealed an anxious prediction: 'If I sit down to write, I'll find out that I have nothing to say and I won't be able to complete the assignment.'

Using the downward arrow technique, the student identified a rule for living: 'If I leave challenging tasks until the last minute, then I can blame low grades on lack of time rather than my lack of ability.' He found that, looking back, he had operated according to this rule for a long time and, with rare exceptions, he had achieved only average grades. Years of applying this rule and achieving average grades served to confirm his prediction that he would find himself lacking if he gave himself enough time to undertake his best attempt. Hence, what we do is intricately bound up with what we think.

Experience is the currency of conviction

Conviction in beliefs, such as our rules for living, is directly related to how much experience we have to back them up. Considering that rules for living shape our life experience, it becomes clear that this situation can produce self-fulfilling prophecies. This process often follows a kind of reverse logic as behavioural responses to our unhelpful beliefs lead to a lack of disconfirmation (Wells, 1997). For instance, the student mentioned earlier who had always acted on his rule about leaving assignments to the last minute had had years of experience of not discovering that his best attempts were poor, leaving him believing that the rule was accurate. Of course the reverse is also true, in that he had not found that his best attempts were actually very good. However, we all tend to perceive our life experience from the perspective of our most strongly held beliefs. Repeated patterns of unhelpful behaviour are often part of an emotionally distressing problem and are generally associated with unhelpful beliefs. These beliefs generate, and are underpinned by, relevant life experience. Consequently, the most helpful interventions for developing new beliefs, such as rules for living or assumptions, are experiential ones – commonly referred to as behavioural experiments.

Planning and conducting behavioural experiments

Descriptions of behavioural experiments generally divide the process into five stages (Fennell, 1989; Wells, 1997). These can be described as:

1 identifying the unhelpful belief to be worked on
2 discussing the nature of the unhelpful belief
3 identifying more helpful alternative beliefs
4 planning a test to explore which of the two beliefs is more accurate
5 discussing the results of the test and ways of putting any new knowledge into practice.

Identifying the unhelpful belief to be worked on

Once beliefs and unhelpful behaviours have been identified, decisions about which ones to work on can be made collaboratively.

Behavioural experiments seem to work best with beliefs at the 'rules for living' or 'assumptions' level, and such beliefs may become apparent at any stage in the intervention, as shown in the following example.

'Sarah'

Sarah wanted to work towards a more open relationship with her parents. When the practitioner helped her to explore this goal in more detail, she identified a pattern of not telling them about any difficulties or problems she experienced in life. Sarah thought about this and realised that she felt anxious, guilty and angry when thinking about discussing this subject with them. She would have thoughts such as, 'They will be upset', 'They won't be able to cope', 'They will worry too much' and 'They will think less of me.' Using the downward arrow technique, Sarah and the therapist found three of her rules for living that applied to the problem:

- 'If I show people that I'm vulnerable, then they will think I am weak and think less of me'
- 'If I burden my parents, then they will get ill and it will be my fault'
- 'People who are close to me should support me through hard times'.

Each of these three rules triggered an emotional reaction when Sarah thought about sharing her feelings with her parents. Unsurprisingly, she felt quite confused about this. The beliefs behind her difficulty were incorporated into the conceptualisation of her overall problem and were highlighted for later work as, for the moment, Sarah wanted to prioritise working on her panic attacks.

Sometimes rules for living emerge later in therapy as the conceptualisation continues to develop.

'Jon'

Jon experienced this when discussing his prolonged recovery from depression. He had been hoping to feel better sooner and had found using thought records quite useful. However, his mood stayed consistently mildly low. He reported strong feelings of loneliness, despite having a close relationship with his family.

By means of more detailed discussion, Jon found that he was missing the contact he used to have with friends and work colleagues – especially a small group he used to go to a comedy club with. Jon identified an assumption that, 'If I go out with my friends, then they will find me boring and I will feel terrible, which will lead to a relapse in my depression.' This explained to him why he was avoiding a significant activity in his life that used to bring him great pleasure.

Unhelpful beliefs that might be addressed using behavioural experiments arise from a variety of sources. The generic 'cognitive model' (Beck, 1995: 18) describes how unhelpful assumptions or rules for living can operate in compensation for negative core beliefs. They lie behind unhelpful patterns of behaviour and underpin themes in unhelpful thoughts and feelings. Consequently, they can emerge during discussion or work on any of these areas. Once emerging beliefs are incorporated into a shared conceptualisation of the problem, interventions can be planned collaboratively.

Discussing the nature of the unhelpful belief

This stage aims to generate a shared rationale for working on the unhelpful belief. This is central to maintaining a collaborative approach to the belief-testing process. It involves examining positive and negative consequences of holding on to the belief and also helping the person to reduce their conviction in it (Leahy, 2001).

The person's conviction in the belief can be rated using a 0–100 per cent scale and this can be a useful tool for structuring the discussion. For instance, if the conviction rating is 80 per cent, one can ask questions such as, 'What does the other 20 per cent say about this?', thus leading the client into exploring alternative perspectives. If conviction is very high, the belief will be experienced as a fact rather than as a belief that may or may not be true, so a gentler approach may be needed in order to avoid ruptures in the therapeutic alliance.

The shared conceptualisation should show how the belief impacts the person's difficulties. Often, negative impact takes the form of unhelpful behavioural consequences, such as overworking, alienating people or self-isolation. Also, this type of discussion can and should identify helpful consequences of having the belief. Often a cost–benefit analysis (examining the pros and cons) of the belief provides a good summary of its relative merits (Leahy, 2001). The conceptualisation also shows how the belief has been maintained by the person acting as if it were true and, consequently, never having had it disconfirmed. This is especially useful for people who have very strong convictions about their assumptions or rules for living. They may find it difficult to see the belief as anything other than fact, but they can generally see that it has never been put to the test.

Other ways in which practitioners can help people to re-examine their conviction in beliefs include:

- examining the internal logic of the belief – for example, with the belief 'If other people reject me, then I am unlikeable', asking questions such as 'What if there are two people and one thinks you are wonderful and the other doesn't?'
- examining the evidence for and against the belief
- asking trusted people about their beliefs on the subject.

If conviction in the unhelpful belief is reduced and its negative consequences are identified, then the person holding that belief will feel more confident about testing it out.

Identifying more helpful alternative beliefs – guided discovery

At this point, it is useful to introduce the dialogue approach of cognitive therapy known as 'guided discovery' (Padesky, 1993, 1996a). Based on the principles of Socratic dialogue, the client is helped to explore issues by means of sensitive and gentle questioning. Guided discovery has four main elements:

- *information questions* aimed at encouraging the client to describe their problem
- *empathic listening* to the struggle that they have with it
- *summarising* the main elements of the described problem
- *synthesising* the problem with future possibilities for dealing more constructively with it or seeing it in a different way by developing different rules for living related to it (see under the heading 'Synthesising questions' below).

Developing alternative rules for living This is a relatively simple but important aspect of behavioural experiments and the overall process of change. Identifying alternative beliefs, along with goal-setting, enables people to develop their vision of how things might be different, which, in turn, is an important part of helping people to prepare for change (Hubble et al., 1999a).

Some people will find thinking of alternative rules for living fairly straightforward and, indeed, may have already begun the process. For instance, people sometimes come to therapy saying such things as, 'I would like to be able to disagree with people without shouting at them' or 'I need to let go of a project without it being perfect.' Guided discovery around these types of statements can reveal current rules for living, such as 'If people disagree with me' then they don't respect me as a person' or 'If I finish a job perfectly, people will not see that I am a failure.' Once uncovered, people often link their desired outcomes to alternative beliefs, such as, 'People can disagree with me and still respect me' or 'If I finish some jobs to a 75 per cent standard, then I won't be so hard on myself and other people; sometimes it is more successful to get things done to an OK standard.'

Synthesising questions   When people find it more difficult to think of alternative beliefs or ways of responding, it can be helpful to start by thinking of alternative ways in which to react by asking constructive, future-directed questions (Mooney and Padesky, 2000; Padesky, 2003), such as, 'How would you like to respond in these types of situations?' or 'What do others do about this?'

It can also be useful for the person to consider a specific role model, or icon, for the problem area (Padesky, 2003). Role models can be drawn from real life, from the person's own group of family and friends or fictional characters. Whichever, they represent for the client a more helpful way of responding to the situations under discussion.

Once an alternative belief has been identified, the process moves on to planning a test.

Planning a test to explore which of the two beliefs is more accurate

This crucial stage of the process can be usefully guided by the following principles:

- maintain collaboration
- encourage a 'no lose' attitude
- encourage cynicism now rather than later
- encourage clear, specific and detailed planning.

Maintaining collaboration involves encouraging people to make the test their own, helping them to foster a sense of curiosity and sometimes fun.

When first using this technique, practitioners can find themselves developing tests of their own beliefs rather than the client's. Practitioners often report automatic thoughts, such as, 'If I can just show the client this is true, then they will feel much better.' Working closely to the conceptualisation and firmly within the client's perception will help to avoid this and, ultimately, provide a more meaningful result.

Encouraging a 'no lose' attitude is related to reattribution and problem-solving. Reattribution techniques – such as experiments and thought records – are useful for addressing problems associated with inaccurate or exaggerated thoughts and beliefs. Alternatively, problem-solving methods are employed when clients face practical difficulties, such as skills deficits or financial problems. Much of the time, the CB approach involves balancing these two domains. Behavioural experiments allow for the exploration of whether a problem is associated with an inaccurate belief or a practical difficulty.

Cultivating this attitude also helps the practitioner develop a sense of naïveté towards the test, so that it remains a process of discovery rather than a demonstration to the client that the practitioner has the correct view (Padesky, 1993). It can be useful to state this openly as part of the rationale for the test. For instance, people often ask, 'But what if I discover that my belief is true?', to which a useful reply might be, 'In that case, rather than this being a problem to do with unhelpful beliefs, we will find out that you have a practical difficulty that needs to be dealt with. Either way, we will work on a solution together.'

Practitioners helpfully play 'devil's advocate' during the planning stage by discussing all possible outcomes – positive and negative – and what they might mean to the client. For instance, while planning her test, Sarah (described above) found herself thinking that if she showed her vulnerability to her parents, then they would try to hide their disappointment in her to avoid hurting her feelings. She then worked with her practitioner to make sure that the test covered this possibility.

Clear, specific and detailed planning ensures that the client is aided in conducting a meaningful experiment. Leahy (2001) asserts that being clear about exactly what needs to be done and how the results are going to be recorded helps the client to feel more confident about undertaking these difficult tasks. With this in mind, it can take several sessions to plan, carry out and discuss the results of a behavioural experiment.

Discussing results and putting new knowledge into practice

This part of the process can involve three types of activity:

- problem-solving and action planning around practical difficulties
- helping the client to understand the CB model more fully
- maximising the benefits of any new discoveries.

Practical difficulties are regularly discovered in the course of behavioural experiments as people gain a more accurate view of problem situations. For instance, someone testing beliefs such as, 'If I let my guard down, then I'll be hurt', may discover that, while some people will take advantage of their vulnerabilities, others can be trusted. In this case, the client can be helped to identify ways in which to address this problem, such as finding ways in which to work out who can be trusted and remaining guarded in some situations.

People are often quite surprised when they discover inaccuracies in their beliefs. This can be a useful time to revisit the CB theory as it relates to real life. For instance, helping a person to recognise that beliefs can seem like facts and remember the feelings associated with changes in strongly held beliefs can be a valuable experience when it comes to addressing other problems. This is especially useful when helping a person to address a set of beliefs. The least distressing experiment is often opted for and this can provide a crucial confidence boost for moving on to more strongly held beliefs.

Maximising the effects of the experiment involves re-examining all the ways in which the person was acting on the old belief. In effect, the experiment can be repeated many times over in as many situations as the person sees fit. For instance, a person addressing beliefs about avoiding conflict might initially conduct a test with a trusted friend or partner before moving on to other situations, such as work colleagues or strangers. In this way, the initial experiment paves the way to developing an ongoing action plan for change.

SUMMARY

- A useful way in which understand the links between emotion, behaviour and thinking is the notion of 'emotional hijacking'.
- This notion can, in turn, help us to understand attribution style and cognitive distortions.
- In this context, it is helpful for practitioners to use reattributional cognitive interventions to help people to tune in to their thoughts and feelings.
- Specific emotions relate, in turn, to specific themes and associated automatic thoughts.
- The strength of emotions and beliefs can be measured.
- It is important for practitioner and client to try to understand the meaning behind emotions and work at generating more helpful thoughts.
- Behavioural experiments are an immensely powerful tool in this context.

Activities

- Practise keeping a thought and mood diary for a week and explore the meanings behind the emotions uncovered.
- Try to construct your own case formulation, using one or more of the models discussed in Chapter 2.
- Identify a personal development need from your own formulation and generate a behavioural experiment concerning it.

Further reading/watching

Bennett-Levy, J., Butler, G., Fennell, M., Hackmann, A., Mueller, M. and Wesbrook, D., 2004, *The Oxford Guide to Behavioural Experiments in Cognitive Therapy*. Oxford: Oxford University Press.
This excellent, groundbreaking text will introduce readers to both the theory and the 'how to do it' of behavioural experiments. Numerous illustrative case vignettes are provided to help new and experiences practitioners alike.

Greenberger, D., and Padesky, C.A., 1995, *Mind over Mood: A Cognitive Therapy Treatment Manual for Clients.* **New York: Guilford Press.**
In a step-by-step way, the authors skilfully encourage readers to review the evidence for and against their automatic thoughts. This is then summarised to create a more helpful view of a distressing situation.

Leahy, R.L., and Holland, S.J., 2000, *Treatment Plans and Interventions for Depression and Anxiety Disorders.* **New York: Guilford Press.**
Leahy and Holland describe 46 methods for re-examining unhelpful conclusions.

Padesky, C.A., 1996a, *Guided Discovery Using Socratic Dialogue.* **Newport Beach, CA: New Harbinger Publications and Center for Cognitive Therapy.**
This excellent training video – available from www.padesky.com – takes the viewer through the four key stages of guided discovery in relation to several role-played client examples.

FIVE Establishing Cognitive Behavioural Work Cultures

Alec Grant, Jem Mills,
Ronan Mulhern and Nigel Short

Learning objectives

After reading this chapter and completing the activities at the end of it you should be able to:

1   describe the features of personal, interpersonal and organisational obstacles to acquiring expertise in the CB approach
2   outline the elements of developing a 'possibility of change', 'change' and 'stages of change' focus
3   recognise and use in your own work setting:

- categories of distorted thinking at play regarding specific obstacles to the development of CB work cultures
- CB strategies to 'unblock' such specific obstacles

4   describe the importance of clinical supervision with regard to both the welfare of the client and its role as a learning process aiding self-development in terms of specific recommendations for practitioner, clinical supervisor and service manager.

Introduction

Practitioners aiming to acquire expertise in the CB approach will quickly realise that developing skills in this area does not take place in a vacuum. There are many obstacles to the effective implementation of the approach, and these will be more fully discussed from the perspective of selected organisational change literature in Chapter 16. For the moment, it is sufficient to argue that it is useful to consider obstacles ranging from the personal, through to interpersonal and organisational.

Although not necessarily insurmountable, because of the existence of such obstacles to change, it is extremely important that individuals interested in developing CB skills do some preparatory work beforehand. This chapter aims to provide readers with the necessary tools for this task. After a brief exploration of the forms that barriers to the development of a CB approach can take, we develop this picture and suggest specific ways in which individuals can build and sustain a focus on organisational change. We hope that this will provide readers with a framework for the careful assessment of existing levels of workplace support and resources in relation to likely obstacles to progress. Finally, to round off the chapter, we will explore the meaning, function and purpose of applying clinical supervision for practitioners using the approach. Illustrative points will be made throughout, from our own experiences as CB psychotherapists working in the British National Health Service, private practice and in graduate and postgraduate education.

Personal obstacles

From a CB perspective, personal emotional and behavioural barriers sometimes follow from the belief that the approach is easy to learn and need not involve the practitioner in extended self-reflection, self-development and clinical supervision. In both the academic and mental health practice fields, we occasionally encounter individuals who claim to be 'doing' CB work on the basis of little or no training in the area, with no supervision and, on further questioning, without a clear grasp of the approach. Equally, we meet individuals who think that the approach is far too difficult for them to learn and believe it to 'belong' solely and exclusively to professions having advanced psychological training. Clearly, neither of those polarised positions is helpful in the urgent need to disseminate knowledge to underpin the safe and supervised practice of CB knowledge and skills.

Interpersonal obstacles

In many work settings, interpersonal barriers are likely to include resistance from staff who feel threatened by change and voice distorted automatic thoughts to individuals whom they perceive to be challenging their existing work practices. Work groups, in a relatively 'silent' or tacit way, also tend to exert pressures on individuals to conform to group preferences concerning working and thinking about work. Individuals actively challenging such group norms constitute a threat to the integrity of the group and can quickly find themselves on the receiving end of corporate hostility, gaining the label 'troublemaker'.

Organisational obstacles

Personal and interpersonal barriers to change may, in turn, be influenced by broader organisational cultural factors. These include aversion to risk-taking and conformity to traditional structures of rank informing clinical practice. Professional rank ordering in many mental health settings results in a culture within which practitioners at or near the bottom of the hierarchy are encouraged to 'know their place'. Unless they are personally and collectively tenacious and resourceful, all of the above forms of resistance are likely to inhibit practitioners potentially interested in learning the approach from taking the necessary first steps.

Developing a 'possibility of change' focus

Despite such obstacles, we believe that, by observing some key principles and guidelines in order to establish supportive networks, practitioners can increase their confidence in being able to create a work climate sympathetic to the goal of collective expertise in the safe practice of the approach. We do not claim robust research support for adopting these principles and guidelines. However, in research parlance, we do claim 'face validity' for their utility, drawing as they do on both key factors in the nature of organisational change and some broad and specific psychotherapeutic strategies for achieving personal goals that do have a strong basis in research.

Perhaps the first principle that should be emphasised is don't go it alone! In a classic organisational change text, Georgiades and Phillimore (1975) argued against the idea of individuals single-handedly attempting to alter work cultures. In their words (p. 315), in response to such attempts 'Organisations … will, like dragons, eat hero-innovators for breakfast.' Following the advice of the authors, instead of such individualistic, misdirected enthusiasm, it would be better to do the following.

- *Follow the path of least organisational resistance* Begin to think about introducing changes in ways that are most likely to mobilise support from organisational members, rather than alienate them from your ideas.
- *Don't focus on lost causes* Avoid trying to introduce change with people who are extremely antagonistic to the approach or to the notion of changes in work practice. Instead, do the following.
- *Identify allies* Begin to meet and talk with individuals in your organisation whom you perceive to be most welcoming of your ideas for change. Then begin to do the following.
- *Work in teams and small groups* A team approach to CB change initiatives confers many advantages, including solidarity, moral support, problem-solving at difficult moments and the development of a good practice culture. Then, collectively, do the following.
- *Check out authority* On the basis that some individuals will be most influential – either because of their position in the organisation or their inter-personal style – try to identify and recruit people with clout to your change initiative. Having done this, do the following.
- *Proceed on a realistic timescale* Change in organisations is a lengthy business and results cannot be achieved hastily. Think in terms of two to three years rather than two to three months.

Developing a 'change' focus

Having established the preliminary organisational conditions for development of collective expertise in the CB approach, it then becomes necessary to home in on some of the specifics of organisational change. In Chapter 14 of their groundbreaking text, Hubble, et al. (1999a) provide the practitioner with several areas to guide the development of their work with clients. Some of these areas have implications for the preparatory process of the organisational development of the CB approach. The first relates to the need to develop a change focus in interpersonal relationships, involving the following key principles.

- *Working together to create new workplace contexts to explore and try out CB strategies and methods that build on and improve existing strengths and resources of the work setting* Grant has had some success in this area with students on his courses who have subsequently, for example, persuaded their colleagues that developing case formulations for clients on wards or community caseloads results in a better understanding of clients' experiences and behaviour previously seen as simply 'troublesome'.
- *Tapping into supportive resources and facilities outside of the work setting* Extending Georgiades and Phillimore's advice on developing allegiances, this will involve seeking the help of local, experienced CB psychotherapists and joining national and international associations. Membership of the British Association for Behavioural and Cognitive Psychotherapies (www.babcp. com) provides practitioners with regular journals and frequent local and national conferences and workshops. Dr Padesky's website (www.padesky. com) is an excellent resource for current recommended reading, audio and videotapes on specific aspects of CB practice and residential workshops. Both of these websites provide links to other important sites, including the International Association of Cognitive Psychotherapy and the Beck Institute.

Developing a 'stage of change' focus

A second area described by Hubble and his colleagues is attention to the readiness for change of the client. By analogy, practitioners championing the CB approach would do well to assess the likely stage of change of their work setting and broader organisation. Because of some of the thought processing errors at play in resistance to the approach (described under 'Specific obstacles to progress' below), work groups may fall into one of the following four change stages.

- *Pre-contemplation* At this stage, the people in the work group have not begun to consider the possibility of incorporating the approach into their work practices. It is really important that the points of view and concerns of work group individuals are listened to with respect and courtesy, but also that information is provided to help them begin to explore and find out more about the approach. This may take the form of reading, visual or audio material.
- *Contemplation* At this stage, work group members will have read some literature, and perhaps watch videotapes or listen to audiotapes, about the approach in practice, yet will continue to express ambivalence about adopting

the approach in the form of 'Yes, but …' In response to this, it is important for practitioners who believe in the value and potential of the approach to continue, gently, to explore the advantages and disadvantages of changing. This may take the form of, for example, discussions about specific problem areas or building on areas of good practice in the work setting without resorting to pressure or urging people to take action.

- *Preparation* Work groups who are at this stage will be ready to take the approach on board, but will continue to require help to explore the need to develop organisational goals in relation to clearly specified problems, and the CB strategies to aid this endeavour. As described in Chapter 3, simple measurement scales will be useful at this stage to give a 'baseline' rating of problems and goals for later evaluation.
- *Action* At this stage, the work setting has incorporated the approach within its existing culture and will need help to maintain, and fine-tune, the necessary focus and structure of the approach in practice. Regular meetings in relation to problem and goal statements and rating scales will aid this process.
- *Maintenance* By now, there will be no doubt but that the approach has been helpful and discussions should turn to how the work setting, and individuals within it, have learned from the process – including mistakes made and forms of resistance initially encountered. This constitutes a blueprint for future development, which may include extending the approach to other areas of the organisation or turning to new problems and goals within the work setting.

Specific obstacles to progress

In the above discussion, we considered three phases in the change process: possibility for change, change and stages of change. It is important to point out that these phases may not happen in a neat, sequential way and, in reality, may appear 'messier', with overlaps between phases and considerable backtracking. This parallels client change work in the use of the CB approach and should be expected rather than seen as an irritant.

Difficulties in the maintenance of continual progress relate to specific obstacles in establishing CB practice cultures in organisations. In an equally circular way, these will directly correspond to both readiness for change and stage of change in work settings. It is to these specific obstacles that we now turn. The framework we use for exploring them is drawn directly from the practice and knowledge base of CB psychotherapy, specifically the range of categories of distorted automatic thinking (Leahy and Holland, 2000) and strategies for working through problems relating to such distortions (Greenberger and Padesky, 1995; Leahy, 2001).

We believe that this framework has tremendous utility in the business of changing perspectives on work practice, as distorted thinking is a feature of being human rather than solely to be associated with mental ill health. On this basis of there being only one side of the fence, we hope that the examples and unblocking strategies (which may be worked through in both group and clinical supervision contexts) provided alongside the following distortion categories will help change-orientated groups in the diagnosis and resolution of blocks to the development of CB organisational cultures. Groups can map their progress, or lack of it, against this framework and the change principles described above and use the examples and unblocking solutions below as a flexible guide for further difficulties not covered.

Categories of distorted thinking	As possible examples of obstacles to progress in the organisational development of CB approaches
Mind-reading The assumption of clear knowledge of what others think, in the absence of supportive evidence.	You, and others, are enthusiastic about the approach, but you all assume that other individuals in the ward you all work in will be against its development.
	Unblocking strategy Arrange to do some gentle and informal survey work (via day-to-day conversations) in order to get a more informed sense of opinions.
Fortune-telling A negative prediction of the outcome of future events, in the absence of supportive evidence.	You work in a ward or community team that, collectively, predict CB strategies won't work before the approach has even been used.
	Unblocking strategy With the help of your clinical supervisor, after exploring with staff what they mean by 'It won't work', set up a small, low-risk experiment based on a very modest goal and collect baseline and post-experiment measures.
Catastrophising A belief that the outcome of something may be totally unbearable rather than, say, unpleasant but tolerable.	You, and others, are enthusiastic about the approach, but you are scared to begin the process described earlier in this chapter for fear that 'it will be terrible if I/we fail.'
	Unblocking strategy Explore, as a group, the possible outcomes in two columns: positive and negative. In each column, order the outcomes from most to least positive and most to least negative. Then, subject each item in the negative outcome column to the question, 'Would this be totally unbearable and, if so, in what ways?'
Labelling Assigning global, stereotyping, negative traits to individuals or groups, without considering redeeming or contradictory information.	You, and others, are enthusiastic about the approach, but label the work setting or organisation as too backward-looking or institutionalised or other negative terms to adopt the approach.
	Unblocking strategy As a group, look for historical information that contradicts such labelling. This may include times when the organisation has been innovative or adopted different ways of working. Consider also the pay-offs (motivating factors) for the organisation at times of such innovation or different ways of working. Could your group use this information to their advantage in trying to generate enthusiasm for the development of the approach?

(Continued)

(Continued)

Categories of distorted thinking	As possible examples of obstacles to progress in the organisational development of CB approaches
Discounting positives Positive features of an event or process are filtered out as 'not counting' so that negative features are treated as if they constituted better-quality information.	Your group has had some small successes in mobilising organisational support for the approach, but these are discounted by the group in the face of 'stronger' messages of resistance.
	Unblocking strategy Draw a straight line with 0 at one end and 100 at the other. Divide the line up into intervals of 10 – 0, 10, 20, 30 and so on. At the '0' point, write the absolute statement 'No compliance' and at the '100' point write 'Total compliance'. Plot all examples of compliance and resistance on this continuum.
	Bear in mind that anything put at point '0' would have to be characterised by 'absolutely no evidence of compliance whatsoever'. Similarly, anything put at point '100' would have to be characterised by 'absolutely no evidence of resistance at any period in the process'. After doing this, as a group, re-evaluate whether or not you still feel the same way towards both the previously negative and positive information.
Negative filtering An almost exclusive focus on negative events at the expense of seldom noticing positive things that happen.	The energies of your group are consumed with the difficulties involved in developing the approach and little account is taken of positive events.
	Unblocking strategy As a group, after defining what count as 'positive' events, maintain a positive data log. This could be kept in the form of a simple, two-column diary, with 'date' and 'event' recorded. The group should review this diary at regular intervals.
Overgeneralising The perception of a global pattern of negative events made on the basis of a single incident.	You work in a ward or community team that, on the basis of one unfortunate thing happening following the inception of the approach, predict that bad things will always happen as a result of using it.
	Unblocking strategy Maintain an events diary, again in columns fashion, with a bias towards looking for positive events that happen in relation to using the approach.
Dichotomous thinking Viewing events, people or issues in polarised terms, such as wonderful/awful, black/white or all/none. Processing information in this way undermines more balanced thinking.	The group of CB enthusiasts to which you belong takes the attitude that 'Unless we can develop this approach *perfectly*, it's not worth doing at all.'
	Unblocking strategy As a group or individuals feeding into the group process, list all the major things that you all do in your working lives. Give all tasks a rating from '0' (totally imperfect) to '100' (totally perfect). Then, collectively, reflect on how many items are scored as perfect.

(Continued)

(Continued)

Categories of distorted thinking	As possible examples of obstacles to progress in the organisational development of CB approaches
Shoulds Interpreting events, issues or people in terms of an idealised view of how they *should* be, rather than how they *are*.	Some members of your group express the view that work settings within the organisation should want to change, on the basis of the evidence for the approach, in spite of their resistance.
	Unblocking strategy As a group, conduct a discussion experiment to consider the number of things that group members think should happen in life actually do happen. Having done this, consider all the reasons for things not working out in life as they should. In this regard, consider whether or not everyone has the same standards and where standards come from.
Personalising Attributing a disproportionate amount of blame to yourself for negative events, failing to see that others, and unforeseen circumstances, have contributed to this.	You give yourself almost exclusive blame for the fact that you have not been able to mobilise the change process in your group of CB allies without considering the contribution of other factors, people and circumstances.
	Unblocking strategy Construct a 'responsibility pie'. This is a simple device that begins with you drawing a large circle on a piece of paper. Imagine this circle as a pie, within which you will draw imaginary pieces (by drawing straight lines from the centre to the periphery of the pie). On a separate piece of paper – perhaps with the help of your supervisor – list all the factors, people and events contributing to the negative event. In this list, include yourself and your actions. Now give a responsibility percentage score for each item on your list (bearing in mind that the total of all items on the list should not exceed 100 per cent!) Finally, draw out the unequal portions of the pie, reflecting each of the items on the list and its percentage score.
Blaming A focus on the other person or group as the sole cause of your negative feelings, rather than looking at your own contribution to, or interpretation of, events.	You and your CB allies have been described as 'too aggressive' by people in your work setting and wider organisation for your attempts to push through change. As a group, you are resisting discussing compromising or changing your approach.
	Unblocking strategy As a group, conduct a cost–benefit (pros and cons) analysis of maintaining your current stance versus adopting a more accommodating one. Consider what you fear that you may lose and what you may, in fact, have to relinquish by changing your current style and whether or not there are, thus, sunk costs (investments, more or less hidden) embedded in your current style. These may be, for example, investments in a group identity as 'special', having the 'moral high ground' or more tangible and less abstract, such as a wish to achieve greater job satisfaction in using evidence-based approaches. Finally, as a group, it may be useful, to consider what new investments and opportunities are apparent if you change your approach.

(Continued)

Categories of distorted thinking	As possible examples of obstacles to progress in the organisational development of CB approaches
Unfair comparisons Interpreting events in terms of unrealistic standards – for example, in terms of other people or groups more advantaged than you in terms of training, natural abilities or experience and perceived as performing better than you or your group.	You and your colleagues have started to use CB principles and methods in your work setting. As a result of supervision, you realise that you are making some fundamental errors in the practice of the approach. You berate yourselves for these mistakes, comparing yourselves negatively with more experienced practitioners, without focusing on the implcations emerging from the fact that they *are* more experienced. *Unblocking strategy* As a group, and with supervision, try to make fairer comparisons. Consider the ways in which you've each achieved mastery of a task or skill in the past, such as learning to drive or swim.With these tasks in mind, think about what you would expect from a learner driver or swimmer at an equivalent stage in their development to that which you now are as a practitioner of the approach.
Regret orientation A focus on the idea that you could, and should, have done better in the past, rather than on what you could do now.	On the basis of mistakes made in the practice of the approach, you and your work group fail to focus on how you can learn from these mistakes to improve on your current and future performance. *Unblocking strategy* As a group, list what has gone wrong in your practice of the approach so far and specifically, identify, how you will use those experiences to improve the quality of your work now and in the future.
'What if ...?' An overpreoccupation with asking 'What if ... (something dreadful happens)' questions in relation to intended action, which stops you from carrying through the intended action.	You are part of a group that has developed and been influential in shaping the climate of the organisation in ways favourable to the uptake of the approach. Your group has been given permission to pilot the approach in a particular setting, but you are all aware of using delaying tactics to start the project, because of a group tendency to 'What if ...?' *Unblocking strategy* As a group, break the pilot project down into a series of tasks related to the different parts of the project, from start to finish. Then, identify all the 'What if ...?' fears associated with the first task of the project, run the first task and compare what actually *did* happen with the feared 'What if ...? ideas.' Repeat with all parts of the project.
Emotional reasoning Interpreting reality solely on the basis of experienced emotions, while simultaneously discounting the possibility of any alternative interpretation.	As part of a group trying to influence the uptake of the approach in your organisation, you have met with staff from a particular ward whose responses to your ideas triggered feelings of anxiety on your part. Instead of considering other options, including the possibility that you felt anxious because of the way in which you interpreted their responses, you assume that you felt anxious therefore they were hostile – and not just to the ideas you put forward, but also to you as a person. *Unblocking strategy* In the group and clinical supervision, begin to consider other possible

(Continued)

Categories of distorted thinking	As possible examples of obstacles to progress in the organisational development of CB approaches
	reasons for the responses of the staff, including their possible fears that may warrant further sensitive exploration. It may also be useful for group members to consider other occasions when interpretations of reality were made, falsely, on the basis of feelings alone. For example, consider the consequences for a man and his family when he decides that his marriage is over solely on the basis of feeling depressed.
Inability to disconfirm The unwillingness to consider, and the rejection of, any evidence or arguments that may disconfirm negative thinking.	The staff from a particular work setting consistently respond with 'Yes, but ...' to your challenges to their negative responses to the idea of incorporating CB principles into existing practice. *Unblocking strategy* Patiently and sympathetically listen to the concerns of the staff and document them. Encourage the staff to be as specific as they possibly can with their 'Yes, but ...' predictions. Then, when their concerns are exhausted, help the staff rank order them along a continuum of most to least likely to happen (alternatively, encourage staff to give a 0–100 rating for each item). It might then be possible to subject the 'Yes, but ...' item ranked as least likely to happen and test it out using a small experiment that the staff are willing to engage in.
Judgement focus Viewing others, issues, events and yourself in morally evaluative terms, including good/bad, worthwhile/worthless, superior/inferior. By continually evaluating in this way, you ensure that you and others often fall short of these arbitrary standards.	You would like to be part of the burgeoning CB interest group in your organisation, but have thoughts such as 'If I join, I won't do well at it' and 'Other people will be successful, but not me.' *Unblocking strategy* Think about other situations, events and issues when you define yourself and others in terms of polarised and extreme moral worth. Make a list of each situation, event and issue, then write down the advantages and disadvantages of this style of thinking for each item on the list. Then, take each item on the list and the polarised terms you originally associated with each. Draw a line and write your polarised terms down at each end of the line (for example, success-------failure), with '100' at the 'success' pole and '0' at 'failure'. Now, predict your likely place on this line in terms of level of success in joining the interest group. Next, consider what 'success' will mean, for membership of the group, in very specific terms (for example, success = consistently and punctually turning up for meetings, reading relevant literature and so on). Now, rerate yourself for each of these newly defined items using the 0–100 scale (for example, likely success at 'consistently and punctually turning up for meetings'), 100 representing 'absolute success'. Add up all your ratings for your newly defined 'success' items and divide the total by the total number of items. Finally, compare that number with your original rating on the success – failure continuum.

Clinical supervision

In the report of a survey of clinical supervision in practice among CB psychotherapists accredited by the British Association for Behavioural and Cognitive
Psychotherapies, Townend et al. (2002: 486) argue, on the basis of consensus
in the literature, that:

> ... the primary focus of supervision is the welfare of the client and ... supervision is a learn-
> ing process in terms of knowledge attainment, attitude refinement, and skills development.
> Through supervision the supervisee is able to develop him or herself with the help of another.

The welfare of the client

In addition to applying appropriate interventions, practitioners engaged in the
CB approach constantly need to reflect on the therapeutic interpersonal boundaries between themselves and their clients. Useful questions to ask constantly
in relation to this issue include:

- 'What are the distinct characteristics of my helping relationship with this client?'
- 'How does this compare with other relationships I have in my life, including,
  familial, collegiate, social and sexual?'

While maintaining appropriate warmth and 'naturalness' (described in the
therapeutic alliance section of Chapter 2), practitioners should always be able
to see clear distinctions between the answers to these two questions.

All human beings have blind spots in their awareness and filter reality
(Goleman, 1985). With regard to the importance of clinical supervision, these are
likely to be played out in practitioners' relationships with clients. They include
such things as feeling dislike for a client because they remind you of a teacher
who gave you a hard time at school or processing a neutral comment made by a
client as critical of you. Equally, although intending to maintain appropriate
boundaries (Leahy, 2001), both practitioners and clients sometimes become
confused between fantasy and reality in relationships. Without fantasies, including
sexual thoughts and images, human beings would fail to thrive and develop.
However, vulnerable individuals – clients and practitioners alike – can often
become confused about this distinction, risking acting on the basis of fantasy as
if it were reality. This is especially the case if individuals have no support facility
to aid them in expressing and working through confusion. For practitioners, this
takes the form of clinical supervision, which, to paraphrase Barker (1992) exists
to protect clients from practitioners and practitioners from themselves.

Supervision as a learning process aiding self-development

To conclude this chapter, the lists that follow have been derived from advice
specifically aimed at fully trained CB psychotherapists (Townend et al., 2002).
However, we have adapted it to provide a standard appropriate to practitioners

generally who are interested in developing supervised expertise in this area, thus maintaining fidelity with best, evidence-based, practice in developing high-quality CB clinical supervision.

Recommendations for practitioners

- In the process of seeking a supervisor, investigate their level of training and experience in both the CB approach and clinical supervision. Also check out whether or not they follow a specific model of CB supervision (Padesky, 1996b, for example).
- Negotiate with your supervisor the structure, form, frequency and duration of supervision sessions so that they are appropriate to your needs.
- Ensure a balance between case discussion and rehearsal and role-playing of therapeutic techniques.
- Only with the written consent of clients, video- or audiotape CB sessions to allow for the proper evaluation of the quality of the interventions actioned by yourself and your supervisor.
- Consult the paper by Milne and Gracie (2001), which addresses how you can contribute to the facilitation of the clinical supervision process.

Recommendations for clinical supervisors

- Establish a supervision contract (see Scaife, 2001, for guidance).
- Set agendas at the beginning of each supervision session.
- Make supervision an active process, with role-playing and other enacted methods, such as guided discovery.
- Encourage audio- or videotaping of supervisee's interventions with their clients. Also, give the option of including audio- or videotapes of your own work in the process.
- Include reviews of audio- or videotapes that illustrate a particular intervention or difficulty.
- Review your current competency with regard to supervision and think about whether or not further training would be helpful.
- Discuss supervisory roles with peers and establish systems and processes for supervision for the supervisor.

Recommendations for service managers

- Effective supervision of the CB approach requires access to tapes, preferably videotapes. It would thus be helpful for those seeking to develop expertise in the approach to have access to, and support for, using video cameras.
- Ways of supporting and funding supervisor training and supervision should be explored and considered.
- Set standards with practitioners of the approach and their supervisors, to reflect the advice given in this list.

- Establish audit and benchmarking systems to establish whether or not supervision of practitioners in the CB approach is contributing to improvements in practice.

SUMMARY

- Acquiring expertise in the CB approach does not take place in a vacuum.
- There are likely to be personal, interpersonal and organisational obstacles to acquiring expertise in the approach.
- However, these are not necessarily insurmountable and can be engaged with by using principles and guidelines relating to a 'possibility of change' focus, a 'change' focus and a 'stage of change' focus.
- Specific obstacles to the development of CB cultures may result from cognitive distortions of both change agents and those whom they wish to convince.
- These may be worked through in supportive work groups and in supervision, using methods drawn directly from the CB literature.
- The primary focus of clinical supervision is on the welfare of the client.
- Clinical supervision is essential because of the imperfections in practitioners' information processing about their work with clients.
- Specific recommendations are made for practitioners, their supervisors and service managers about clinical supervision practice.

Activities

- Consider what possible blocks to the development of the CB approach may be present in your own work setting.
- Think about who your allies might be with regard to taking the approach forward within your work setting.
- Show this chapter to a 'friendly manager' and arrange to meet with them later to hear their responses to it.

Further reading

Goleman, D., 1985, *Vital Lies, Simple Truths: The Psychology of Self-deception.* New York: Touchstone, Simon & Schuster.
This book provides excellent coverage of the ways in which human beings process information in selective, protective and socially distorted ways – excellent supplementary reading to clinical supervision.

Leahy, R.L., 2001, *Overcoming Resistance in Cognitive Therapy.* New York: Guilford Press.

This book constitutes a superb guide to establishing good therapeutic interpersonal boundaries to aid the clinical supervision process. In particular, Part III of the book discusses specific forms of boundary-breaking and ways to respond to those.

Padesky, C.A., 1996b, 'Developing cognitive therapist competency: teaching and supervision models', in Salkovskis, P.M. (ed.), 1996, *Frontiers of Cognitive Therapy*. New York: Guilford Press.
An excellent 'how to do it' chapter, combining experiential CB teaching and supervision models.

SIX Working with People Who Hear Voices and have Strange Beliefs

Jem Mills, Ronan Mulhern, Nigel Short and Alec Grant

Learning objectives

After reading this chapter and completing the activities at the end of it you should be able to:

1 describe the current picture of the evidence base for CB interventions in this area
2 identify problems inherent in an illness model of psychosis and the ways in which voices, unusual beliefs and strange thoughts can be thought of as understandable human phenomena
3 describe the ways in which individuals may become over-involved with voices and strange beliefs to the extent that they are caught up in vicious circles
4 outline the link between stress and vulnerability factors in the development of psychotic experiences and how individuals may be helped on the basis of the stress vulnerability model
5 describe the ways in which individuals may be helped to normalise their experiences
6 identify the relationships between hearing voices, strange beliefs and low self-esteem
7 describe the relationships between the CB approach and the recovery process
8 identify the opportunities afforded by compassionate case formulation and behavioural experiments.

Introduction – the evidence base for the CB approach

CB interventions for voices and strange thoughts are yet to become part of mainstream mental health practice in Britain, despite governmental agencies asserting its helpfulness in reducing admissions and preventing relapse (NHS

Centre for Reviews and Dissemination, 2000). Interestingly, given the underdeveloped evidence base in this area, the CB approach is recommended for *all* people with a diagnosis of schizophrenia who still experience symptoms after psychopharmacological treatment (NICE, 2002). The updated Cochrane library review of the CB approach for 'schizophrenia-like illnesses' (Cormac et al., 2003) yielded 13 studies for review. However, the interventions in these studies shared common elements but were ultimately directed at different client groups, for different durations, with different aims, in different settings, which was acknowledged in the cautious note: 'Currently, trial-based data supporting the wide use of CB therapy for people with schizophrenia or other psychotic illnesses are far from conclusive' (Cormac et al., 2003: 1).

Far from implying that the data are of no use, this simply suggests how new, and therefore undeveloped, the research base is. Indeed, the individual studies have important implications for clinical practice. The Kemp et al. (1998) study into the effects of a six-session intervention on medication compliance in schizophrenia has helped to illuminate the positive effects of engaging in full and frank discussions of all issues surrounding medication as opposed to a benign insistence that the client should comply with a medication regime.

Key issues surrounding cognitive behavioural interventions for voices and strange thoughts

As is discussed further in Chapter 15, the most cursory view of much of the CB literature reveals a strong tendency towards the use of medical terminology and diagnostic classifications. The fact that contemporary social policy and evidence-based literature advocates the CB approach no doubt increases funding opportunities for research and training, so the approach has much to gain from its association with the medical model.

However, an interesting paradox has emerged from the CB research and therapy focus on schizophrenia. Bentall (1990) argued that the net result of over 100 years of research into schizophrenia only served to demonstrate its lack of credibility as a scientific concept. The in-depth assessment and formulation methods that form part of a CB approach continually show how voices and strange beliefs are just as much a result of normal meaning-making processes as automatic thoughts and beliefs (Chadwick et al., 1996; Fowler et al., 1995).

Bentall's (1990) response to the questionable validity of the schizophrenia concept was to propose that CB research focuses on the individual experiences that cause distress and disruption to peoples' lives. In a complementary way, Kingdon and Turkington (1994) presented a 'normalising' approach to the 'symptoms of schizophrenia'. Their demonstration that, in certain circumstances, many people will have experiences like these, placed phenomena such as voices, strongly held beliefs and paranoia on a continuum of normal human experience.

Problems with the illness perspective for voices and strange thoughts

Mental health services have traditionally understood voices and strange thoughts as falling within the category of chronic and disabling illness. People who have such experiences are labelled in such a way as to suggest a line between what is normal and abnormal, sane and mad, acceptable and unacceptable – a viewpoint strongly resisted by key individuals within the user movements who have experienced such phenomena (see, for example, Coleman, 1999, 2000).

Voices and strange thoughts can be understood

The style of many mental health services is to invalidate and pathologise the experiences of such individuals, thereby lessening their chances of inclusion within mainstream society. There is thus an urgent need for practitioners to understand people who experience voices and strange beliefs on a much more human and equal footing (Barker, 2000). Central to this acceptance is the principle of empathic concern for individuals within good and supportive relationships focused on human experiences rather than 'psychotic symptoms'.

When people begin to experience voices and strange beliefs they often have intense emotional experiences, including anxiety, which, in turn, provoke an automatic and rapid search for meaning (Garety and Hemsley, 1994). Thus, locking on to an explanation provides a much needed sense of relief, even if the explanation seems bizarre (Kingdon and Turkington, 1994). As discussed in Chapter 4, once a belief is established, normal attention and behavioural processes pick up information supporting the belief, while information contradicting the belief is screened out.

It follows that directly arguing against a strongly held belief can reinforce it as the person is then forced to state their case with more conviction (Watts et al., 1973). By the time people reach the attention of mental health services, they will probably have their own fairly well-established explanations of their strange experiences. Dismissing those explanations – either implicitly by imposing an illness label on them or explicitly by refusing to engage with the individual's explanation or by arguing directly against it – may well, understandably, provoke resistance. Sadly, this is likely to lead to a rupture in the therapeutic alliance before it has even had a chance to properly begin (Leahy, 2001). The following example shows how this happens.

'Adrian'

Adrian's first year at university was difficult as he had never been away from home before. The atmosphere at home had been critical as his parents had always found his quiet and isolationist style hard to cope with. Despite this, he felt dependent on the family for support and found being alone quite distressing.

Adrian had grown up with a sense that he was not good enough. His low self-esteem led to passive and unassertive behaviour, and he became a target for bullies at school. His compensatory response was to work very hard at his studies, which, although reducing parental criticism, incited more bullying.

Consequently, Adrian began his history degree feeling as if he was not up to the mark and worked long hours to ensure that he did not lose his place at university.

Adrian shared a room with a young man who tried to help him relax his pace of work by introducing him to cannabis. Adrian found that the drug helped him to sleep and soon began using it regularly. Eventually, the cannabis use affected his ability to study, which made him worry more, and, after a few months at university, he began to feel quite strange. He had a general feeling that something was wrong, but could not identify what it was. He kept these feelings to himself, hoping that they would pass, and stopped using cannabis.

Adrian's anxiety increased, however, and he started to feel as if his mind was leaking out of his head and reaching other people. One day, he entered a canteen to get some food and heard his name being called. Looking around, he noticed how other people were staring at him. As he watched their faces, he clearly heard voices commenting on his appearance, but noticed that the people in the canteen were not actually speaking. He found this terrifying and began to spend more time in his room, continuing to hear negative comments as people passed it.

Adrian's terror began to abate one day after he heard a voice saying, 'Do not be afraid; something wonderful is happening.' Over the coming weeks he listened and communicated with this voice, who explained that he had developed an age-old human capacity for telepathy and that he had been chosen by a community of telepathic people to teach these skills to others.

The university staff began to notice Adrian's absence from classes, so he was contacted by a welfare worker from the university who discovered that he was writing a textbook on extrasensory perception. Adrian felt good about having been chosen for this task and spent long hours writing with assistance from the voice.

The student counsellor arranged an appointment with a doctor, who in turn referred him to a psychiatrist, who suggested he take medication. In the three months since first encountering the student welfare worker, Adrian heard a variety of explanations for his experiences and had a variety of reactions to his own version of events.

- The student counsellor explained how university life was very stressful and that these kinds of experiences were surprisingly common, but would not be drawn into a discussion about telepathy.

- Adrian's family were concerned about him, but, after a while, became angry when he continually talked about his mission.
- The psychiatrist explained how stress and cannabis can cause a chemical imbalance in the brain that often leads to the mind playing tricks. He, too, would not be drawn into a discussion on telepathy.

Adrian consulted his voice, which explained that people are often afraid of the paranormal. He decided to stop taking the medication and, a few months later, was compulsorily admitted to a local psychiatric unit after barricading himself in his bedroom.

Taking Adrian seriously

Leahy's (2001) approach to overcoming resistance, along with Romme and Escher's (2000) advice about working with a person's explanation of voices and strange beliefs, would suggest a different response from that described above to Adrian and others like him. This would include:

- being interested in, and assessing, the details of the person's experiences
- exploring how the person reached their conclusions about the meaning and significance of their experiences
- taking note of how other people's reactions to them have affected the person
- reacting to direct requests for validation ('Do you believe this is true?' for example) by acknowledging that the person's conclusions, however unlikely, could be true but that more exploration is needed to make such a judgement
- understanding the life circumstances surrounding the onset of the person's experiences
- exploring how the person's reactions have interacted with their experiences, both helpfully and unhelpfully.

Becoming overinvolved with voices and strange beliefs

People react to their voices and strange beliefs in different ways depending on their explanations of what is happening. Some people believe that they have to pay close attention to them, while others avidly avoid them. A CB perspective sees such reactions as having potentially helpful or unhelpful consequences. As discussed in Chapter 4, unhelpful consequences include the prevention of the disconfirmation of unhelpful, inaccurate beliefs.

Adrian's reactions can be grouped into four main types, as shown below.

Type of reaction	Example	Unhelpful consequence
Cognitive	Adrian's preoccupation with his voices related to his beliefs about telepathy.	His perceptions of other people's reactions to his behaviour led to him becoming more isolated.
Behavioural	Adrian listened out for his voice and spent many hours conversing with it.	This made it more frequent.
Emotional	Adrian felt more relaxed and somewhat happy about his special status.	This added to his resistance to other explanations.
Physical	Adrian worked far too hard on his book.	This led to reduced sleep and a lack of attention to his nutritional needs.

The creation of vicious circles

Adrian's example above can help us to see how reactions to problems interact with the problem itself. Common unhelpful cycles relating to voices and strange thoughts include:

- a preoccupation with the beliefs increases the conviction that they are real – the more time people spend thinking about strange thoughts or listening to voices, the stronger their beliefs about them become
- having strong beliefs about voices or strange thoughts sets up attention patterns that lead to automatic and purposeful scanning for evidence that the beliefs are true
- scanning for one type of evidence leads to a biased view of the situation
- having negative beliefs about voices and strange thoughts can make them very frightening, and anxiety and stress exacerbate the situation.

Stress and vulnerability

The exploration of interactions between stressful life events and vulnerability factors has always been a central feature of CB approaches to voices and strange thoughts (Clements and Turpin, 1992; Kingdon and Turkington, 1994; Brennan, 2004). Such theories can be very helpful in generating a wider understanding of how people's reactions might impact on their difficulties, and the model below, proposed by Zubin and Spring (1977), has been described as a classic influence on this work (Clements and Turpin, 1992).

Although the model is presented as a graph, it is not intended to suggest that there is any mathematical relationship between the factors involved and, indeed, the diagram itself is often clinically cumbersome in this respect. However, discussion of the principles behind the model invariably lead to helpful practical interventions.

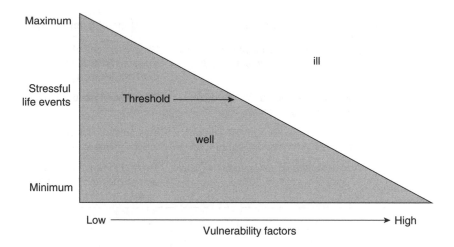

Another way in which the model is useful is in the construction of a case formulation (see Chapter 2). It provides an alternative, often more hopeful and compassionate, explanation than those previously experienced by people, such as 'I'm crazy, I have an incurable disease', or 'I'm being controlled by a higher power.'

From a CB perspective, the model suggests that all human beings have a degree of susceptibility (or vulnerability) to hearing voices or experiencing strange, worrying thoughts. Indeed, research shows that, in certain high-stress situations or highly vulnerable states, hearing voices or experiencing strange thoughts is by far the most common human reaction (Kingdon and Turkington, 1994; Romme, 1998).

Circumstances that can lead to almost anyone experiencing these kinds of difficulties include:

- extreme social isolation
- long periods of sensory deprivation
- bereavement
- periods of sleep deprivation
- prolonged interrogation
- experiencing torture.

The above suggests that experiencing voices or strange thoughts in these situations may be part of a naturally occurring, and in some cases protective, process. The difficulty for some people is when the process becomes overactive or oversensitive. Returning to the graph depicted above, as someone's vulnerability increases, so the level of stress required to push them over the well-being threshold, drops. This may explain why, for some people, a trivial argument or a wrong look from someone seems to tip the balance so that they then experience voices or strange thoughts.

Equally, experiencing extremely challenging life events or suffering an accumulation of several stressors at one time can have the same effect. Because of chaotic lifestyles or long-standing under-assertion, some individuals are

Reduce vulnerability	Reduce stressful life events	Increase resistance to stress
Improve financial security	Avoid breaking the law	Boost self-esteem and confidence
Learn to manage intense emotions	Improve communication in key relationships	Improve problem-solving skills
Improve physical health	Manage debts	Improve social networks
Get involved in sport	Learn to be more assertive	Improve family relationships
Improve sleep	Manage time – for example, by learning to keep a diary	Be part of a community
Eat a balanced diet	Have a balance between work, life and leisure	Use community resources
Deal with unresolved psychological issues	Have a structured day, including fulfilling activities	Manage ongoing stress using relaxation, meditation, yoga
Organise more stable housing	Maintain personal safety	Maintain personal spiritual beliefs

dramatically more susceptible to life events than others. Either way, Zubin and Spring (1977) describe how crossing the threshold at any point leads to the experience of hearing voices or having strange thoughts.

Practical measures arising from an assessment of stress and vulnerability factors seek to reduce individual vulnerability, decrease unnecessary life stressors and increase personal resistance to the effects of stress. Examples of these measures are set out in the table above.

Normalisation

The stress vulnerability model helps us to understand that voices and strange beliefs are not that unusual. The user literature suggests that people can experience phenomena such as voices yet experience little disruption to their lives. It is therefore more important in clinical settings to explore issues of meaning, distress and disability, as opposed to the presence or absence of 'symptoms'.

Putting normalisation into practice

The actions and attitudes of practitioners can have a major impact on how clients and carers understand and perceive voices and strange thoughts. Practitioners need to be aware of and address negative perceptions by means of educational and clinical supervision activity and create a future-directed possibility focus for clients by helping them to formulate voices and strange beliefs within the normal, if distressing, range of human responses (see Chapters 2 and 5). This process is made possible by gaining an understanding of people and their experiences as opposed to the 'symptoms' that they report.

However, engagement and establishing a therapeutic relationship with someone experiencing voices and strange thoughts is recognised as being a complicated and, at times, difficult process. As with all relationships, time is an important factor and it is imperative that the pace of the relationship is of the client's choosing. The process involves not only listening to the client's story, but gaining an emotional insight into the events that have shaped the direction of someone's life. The content of someone's voices or their unusual beliefs may seem nonsensical at first, but frequently make sense in the context of their own story.

'Rasheed'

Rasheed, a 28-year-old Asian man, was diagnosed as a paranoid schizophrenic from the age of 20. He lived at home with his parents and was referred for CB help for his 'treatment resistance'. During the previous eight years he had received antipsychotic medication, monthly outpatient appointments with a psychiatrist and weekly visits by a community psychiatric nurse. Both felt that the outlook was 'poor' and that the referral was made in an attempt to try something 'different'. He had been in hospital on one occasion, on a voluntary basis, and mainly coped by staying at home and avoiding contact with others.

In the course of his problems prior to referral, Rasheed had had repeated reassurances from others that he was not being spied on or likely to be murdered if he left the house, but he was well aware that the care team and his family viewed his behaviour as bizarre and abnormal. So, while tentatively engaging, Rasheed's mistrust of his new practitioner became apparent. He would be hyper-vigilant and overtly suspicious of gentle probing questions that were asked. However, as a direct result of him and his experiences being taken seriously, his suspiciousness reduced over time and he became noticeably more relaxed.

Rasheed's personal narrative highlighted several pieces of information absent from his case notes and his parents' recollections of his development.

- *Aged 5* Awareness of being the 'only brown-skinned person' in his class. Rasheed felt as if he stood out more than others and wanted to be close to his mother, with whom he felt a sense of belonging and being safe.
- *Aged 5–9* Rasheed always felt self-conscious and shy, fearing that others would reject him.
- *Aged 9–13* Almost daily Rasheed was bullied by others for being different. He felt that he would never be accepted. He kept away from others and stayed at home studying. He had feelings of shame and humiliation.
- *Aged 13–18* Rasheed became fearful of social interaction and felt depressed. He did not want to tell his parents due to the fear of being rejected or construed as odd.

- *Aged 19* Rasheed attend the local university where he was racially abused by others and physically assaulted twice – the second assault resulted in hospitalisation. His parents encouraged Rasheed to report the assault and return to university, which he did despite his fears. No charges were brought by the police. He felt 'depressed, trapped, alone and vulnerable'. At this time Rasheed heard derogatory statements directed at him ('Paki bastard'), but there was no one there when he looked around. He became increasingly preoccupied about finding the origins of the voices in order to prepare for the 'inevitable attack'. Rasheed missed tutorials and became convinced that he needed to stay at home. He felt depressed, a failure and a burden on his family. The family became concerned at his behaviour and, after a few months, called the family doctor, who prescribed antidepressant medication.
- *Aged 20* Rasheed barricaded himself in his room and played his music loud to drown out his persecutors. Rasheed believed that he had conclusive proof that he was to be killed by racist neighbours and that the police would do nothing to protect him. He was admitted to hospital on a 'voluntary' basis and suffered an assault by another resident. He was discharged home with the condition that he take antipsychotic medication. Rasheed remained at home in a state of constant fear and anticipation of assault. He was angry at others who did not believe him. There was tension in the family as their expectations of him were not being fulfilled.

From his story, it is difficult to diagnose Rasheed's responses as paranoid. The social realities of racism have become intertwined with his psychological development and need for protection. From his narrative account, it became obvious that his behaviour was not 'bizarre', but an exaggerated form of survival response. This information enabled both parties in the collaborative relationship to construct a shared understanding of his behaviour based on his psychological development and past traumatic events.

Voices, strange thoughts and low self-esteem

The stance taken in this chapter emphasises that voices and strange thoughts can be generated from normal meaning-making processes. In this way voices can be understood in the same way as thoughts in that they are deeply connected with emotions and underlying beliefs. As discussed in Chapter 4, our beliefs both arise from and mediate our experience of life. Thus, it becomes clear that voices and strange thoughts can be related to people's views of themselves, other people and the world in general.

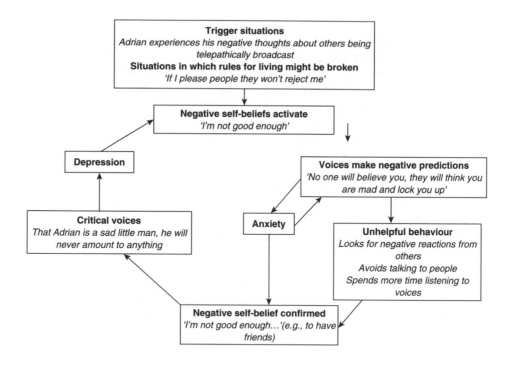

Fennell's (1997) model of low self-esteem describes how negative self-beliefs generate self-criticism and negative predictions about personal performance and or negative reactions from others. This negative thinking combines with unhelpful behaviour and emotional distress to ultimately confirm the person's poor self-esteem. As is shown above this was useful in formulating Adrian's difficulties.

The implication emerging from the above is that the CB approach to low self-esteem, which includes building up more helpful core beliefs and associated rules for living, could be useful for people experiencing voices and strange thoughts. This approach, currently underdeveloped in the mainstream CB literature, becomes more compelling when viewed alongside the life narrative approach described earlier and the recovery perspective, to which we will now turn.

Recovery and the CB approach

The CB relationship has always constituted a benevolent 'social laboratory' (Beck et al., 1979) within which people can test out new ways of being and doing. However, this is an area that may inevitably present a challenge to clients and practitioners as the experience of psychosis has long been associated with social isolation and problematic relationships. These are often compounded by intrapersonal factors, such as paranoia or suspiciousness and shame, interpersonal factors, such as high levels of expressed emotion and difficulties with trust, as well as more general factors, including stigma and discrimination.

The practitioner needs to help the client to develop a social environment despite these problems within which learning by means of behavioural experimentation can take place. A useful way in which to do this is to carry out case formulation and behavioural experiments.

CB interventions emerge from a compassionate case formulation

The compassionate case formulation pulls together an understanding of how life experiences and reactions to events have led to a person's particular view of voices and strange thoughts. It explains how, given this personal explanation, the person's reactions are understandable and justified in their eyes. Short-, medium- and long-term consequences are also mapped out in the formulation to show how the problem fluctuates over time. In practice, the client's level of understanding develops as time passes and formulations can be correspondingly simplistic or comprehensive.

In our experience, practical belief-testing methods (see Chapter 4) often have the most impact on these types of difficulties. The discussion surrounding the development of a formulation provides an essential rationale for undertaking the practical work, including the creation of doubt. Given that beliefs underpin both development and maintenance factors, belief testing can have a variety of objectives in this context, including:

- whether or not what might seem like a fact could be a belief
- the meaning of intense emotions about voices or strange thoughts – for example, 'because I hear this voice I am damned forever'
- beliefs about self, others and the world that underpin the problem
- beliefs associated with unhelpful reactions that maintain the problem – for example, a belief that neighbours are collecting information about you that leads to you screaming at them to stop, which, in turn, leads to further alienation.

Maintaining a collaborative relationship is essential to this work and decisions about the timing, focus and structure of behavioural experiments should be made on this basis.

To conclude this chapter, we describe some examples of experiments that we have undertaken with people, including one that went badly wrong!

Summary of case formulation	Summary of behavioural experiment
Del is a 23-year-old Afro-Caribbean man who had been a victim of mistaken identity by the police. Since that time, he would lock himself in his room and constantly listen out for sirens. Once his door had been locked, he would hide under the bed. Consequently, he had a poor sleep pattern that served to increase his suspicion. He would only make forays out to collect his benefits and food. When he saw police, he would run and hide in the nearest shop. Seeing this, the police would then give chase and, if they caught him, would check his identity. Del's name was well known to the police and, once he was recognised, they would take no further action. Del believed that the police were toying with him.	Del and his therapist discussed his behaviour in detail and agreed that it would be useful to observe what might happen if the therapist (a white male) acted in the same way. Del predicted that the police would show no interest in the therapist as they had no vendetta against him. This turned out not to be the case – the police gave the therapist a hard time, refusing to accept his story until he had been checked out at the police station. Del found this very funny and afterwards agreed to drop his evasive behaviour as a further experiment. This was repeated until his behaviour changed permanently and his suspiciousness decreased by 20 per cent. Del's belief is still present, but less distressing and he is able to get out much more than before.
Jonathon (See also Chapter 11) grew up carefully monitoring his emotional reactions to avoid falling foul of his mother's quick temper. When he started hearing voices after a period of prolonged stress and sleep disturbance, his spiritual beliefs led him to think that he was being attacked by spirits. He believed that, unless he performed the special tasks set by the spirits, he would be damned. Constant scanning and responding to voices maintained them. This interfered with his life, which, in turn, added to his distress in a variety of ways.	Jonathon made a list of consequences he believed might result from ignoring the voices. He acknowledged an alternative, but seemingly unlikely, consequence that the voices might subside on their own. He then practised ignoring the voices and found that, after a brief increase in their volume and, consequently, in his distress, they did indeed fade away. He discussed the nature of spirits with a trusted friend and decided that his voices might be hallucinations related to stress and his life experiences.
George is a 34-year-old man with a 12-year history of unusual beliefs. He was admitted to an acute inpatient unit, but believed that what the doctors called psychosis was actually a spiritual event. As far as he knew, he was God's son. This led to fights with other residents who refused to take up his call to follow him.	The therapist made the mistake of setting up what he thought would be a good experiment. He asked George to identify another client whom he trusted to adjudicate. The test was for George to turn water into wine and he readily agreed. A flask was filled with water and George prayed over it. The therapist predicted that it would still be water, while George thought that it would be wine. The adjudicator tasted the contents and declared that it was still water. The therapist, feeling pleased with himself, invited George to discuss the meaning of this outcome. George felt humiliated and, as he punched the therapist, told him not to 'tempt the lord thy God'! Experiments need to be negotiated and thoroughly thought out so that the person's self-esteem and sense of protection against psychological assault is minimised.

SUMMARY

- The evidence base for CB interventions in the area of hearing voices and strange beliefs is new and underdeveloped. However, clinical and research experience suggest that the approach has a lot to offer.
- There are problems inherent in an illness model of psychosis and the ways in which voices, unusual beliefs and strange thoughts can be comprehended as understandable human phenomena.
- Individuals may become overinvolved with voices and strange beliefs to the extent that they are caught up in various forms of vicious circles.
- There is a link between stress and vulnerability factors in the development of psychotic experiences and individuals may be helped on the basis of the stress vulnerability model.
- Individuals may be helped to normalise their experiences as psychotic phenomena can be explained in non-pathological or illness terms.
- The relationship between hearing voices, strange beliefs and low self-esteem offers opportunities for new forms of CB intervention.
- The CB approach is compatible with, and helpful in, the recovery process.
- Case formulation and behavioural experiments afford clients and practitioners great opportunities for recovery.

Activities

- Make a general assessment, case formulation and care plan for a client, based on stress vulnerability concepts.
- If you are helping someone who is experiencing voices or strange thoughts, consider how the content of those experiences might be related to their life story narrative.
- Consider what dilemmas and difficulties might emerge from adopting the perspectives described here in your own clinical setting.

Further reading

Coleman, R., 1999, *Recovery: An Alien Concept*. Gloucester: Handsell Publishing.
An excellent book from a leading figure in the mental health user movement.

Morrison, A. (ed.), 2002, *A Casebook of Cognitive Therapy for Psychosis*. Hove: Brunner-Routledge.
An excellent book for readers who wish to explore further the ways in which CB approaches can be of help for people with problems in this area.

Romme, M., and Escher, S., 2000, *Making Sense of Voices: A Guide for Health Professionals Working with Voice Hearers*. London: Mind.
An essential book for readers keen on depathologising the experience of hearing voices.

SEVEN Working with People Who have Complex Emotional and Relationship Difficulties (Borderlines or People?)

Jem Mills, Ronan Mulhern, Alec Grant and Nigel Short

Learning objectives

After reading this chapter and completing the activities at the end of it you should be able to:

1 describe the diagnostic view of borderline personality disorder (BPD) in the more general context of the psychiatric classification of personality disorder.
2 outline the developmental context for these clients' difficulties and psychological formulations emerging that would suggest the need for a more empathic and less distancing response than that related to psychiatric diagnoses
3 consider the implications of BPD as a label of social exclusion
4 demonstrate an understanding of 'schema maintenance', 'schema avoidance' and 'schema compensation', in turn related to possible early abuse
5 describe the emerging features of effective service provision for this client group
6 describe some of the main CB interventions in this context.

Introduction – the diagnosis of personality disorder

The *Diagnostic and Statistical Manual of Mental Disorders*, 4th edition (APA, 1994) – commonly known as DSM IV – views personality disorder as distinct from psychosis-, depression- or anxiety-based mental state disorders. Mental state disorders are placed in axis I of the classification system, with personality disorders appearing in axis II. A further subdivision results in the following three clusters of diagnosable personality disorder:

- *cluster A* paranoid personality disorder; schizoid personality disorder; schizotypal personality disorder
- *cluster B* antisocial personality disorder; borderline personality disorder; histrionic personality disorder; narcissistic personality disorder
- *cluster C* avoidant personality disorder; dependent personality disorder; obsessive-compulsive personality disorder.

Borderline personality disorder

Borderline personality disorder (BPD) appears in cluster B because service users within this group are said to share the following characteristics:

- impulsivity
- mood instability
- antisocial behaviour
- disturbed thinking.

The diagnosis of BPD is made if the client exhibits five of the following criteria:

- frantic efforts to avoid real or imagined abandonment
- a pattern of unstable and intense interpersonal relationships, characterised by alternating between the extremes of idealisation and devaluation
- identity disturbance – a marked and persistent unstable self-image or sense of self
- impulsivity in at least two areas that are potentially damaging to the self (such as sex, spending, substance abuse, dangerous driving, binge eating)
- recurrent suicidal behaviour, gestures or threats, or self-mutilating behaviour
- affective instability related to marked mood reactivity (such as intense episodes of unhappiness, irritability or anxiety that usually last only between a few hours or a few days)
- chronic feelings of emptiness
- inappropriate and intense anger or difficulty in controlling anger (frequent displays of temper, constant anger, frequent physical fights, for example)
- transient, stress-related paranoid thinking or severe symptoms of dissociation.

BPD as a developmental problem rather than a disorder

Whereas the diagnostic approach represents people in 'disordered' terms, psychological formulations tend to suggest a different picture – one of people whose difficulties are understandable in the context of their disadvantaged developmental backgrounds.

In Linehan's (1987, 1993) biosocial view, such individuals have difficulty in regulating their emotions, which is reflected in dramatic overreactions and impulsivity, and, while growing up, have repeated experiences of having their emotional reactions discounted by significant others in their life. As a result of these 'invalidating environments', they fail to develop emotional regulation skills. Further, because their emotional communication is consistently invalidated, they come to believe that they are expected to solve any difficulties by themselves without having the personal resources to do this. This leaves them with two extreme options in order to gain self-affirmation: either dramatic outbursts of emotion or avoidance of people and maladaptive ways of emotional and cognitive self-management.

From a complementary cognitive perspective, Young (1990; Pretzer, 1990) argues that 'early maladaptive' schemas (core beliefs) develop as a result of toxic childhood experiences that in a circular way, result in behaviour that reinforces schemas, making them increasingly more rigid and inflexible. Using Young's framework, the following schemas and related rules characterise such individuals (see also Chapters 2 and 4).

Early maladaptive schema	Related rule for living
Abandonment/loss	'If I don't take steps to prevent this, I will be alone forever and nobody will be there for me.'
Unlovability	'If people really got to know me, they would not love me or want to be close to me.'
Dependence	'If I'm on my own, I won't be able to cope.'
Subjugation/lack of individuation	'If I don't subjugate my wants and needs to the desires of others, then I'll be abandoned or abused by them.'
Mistrust	'If I don't protect myself, people will take advantage of me or hurt me.'
Inadequate self-discipline	'Because I can't control or discipline myself I must be reliant on others.'
Fear of losing emotional control	'If I don't control my emotions, something terrible will happen.'
Guilt/punishment	'Because I am a bad person, I deserve to be punished.'
Emotional deprivation	'I must constantly seek emotional support as no one is there to meet my needs or be strong and care for me.'

Schema maintenance, schema avoidance and schema compensation

Young identifies three major processes that help us to understand how schemas function with regard to thinking, mood and behaviour. These processes involve early maladaptive schemas that are central to the organisation of personality and, in order to maintain a sense of self-consistency in the face of a poor sense of self, people with the 'borderline' label will behave and process information in ways that fail to challenge such schemas.

First, schema maintenance is accomplished by processing information in ways that confirm the schema and minimising or failing to notice information that contradicts it. The behavioural equivalent of this is repeatedly engaging in self-defeating behavioural patterns. However, as early maladaptive schemas, when triggered, result in perceptions of unbearable levels of distress, some individuals may engage in the second process – schema avoidance. This may take several forms, including cognitive avoidance, which is automatic or motivated thought blocking, or 'tuning out' (Leahy, 2001). Affective, or mood, avoidance means automatic or motivated attempts to block feelings. A common example of this is the self-mutilation that many of these individuals engage in (discussed further below). Behavioural avoidance is the tendency to avoid the kinds of real-life situations that may trigger painful schemas.

Third is schema compensation, which is the phenomenon of clients adopting cognitive or behavioural styles that seem to be the opposite of what might be predicted from knowledge of their early maladaptive schemas. Young (1990) cites the example of someone who behaves in a narcissistic, exaggeratedly self-loving manner as an adult because of significant emotional deprivation in childhood.

BPD as a label of social exclusion

In contrast to the above psychological formulations, which describe and explain people in distress, 'personality disorder', subsuming BPD, is all too frequently the diagnosis of social exclusion from mainstream mental health services (Castillo et al., 2001).

This is ironic because, although practitioners rally against the causes of childhood abuse and neglect, they seem less willing to understand or engage with the longer-term consequences of it in practice. Sadly, clients' understandable, but maladaptive, responses tend to be negatively evaluated by workers, with the term BPD being used to make moral, as opposed to professional, interpretations of clients' behaviour and label it as inappropriate, manipulative and disruptive. This absolves practitioners from the professional responsibility to understand and contextualise such behaviour and from investing in the kinds of therapeutic alliances and helping processes with clients that are described below.

Implications for service provision

Promoting understanding and mutual support

Because of the negative labels given to this client group, it is frequently the case that practitioners with less experience and theoretical understanding are allocated to the task of 'caring' for them, despite this being counter-therapeutic. Equally, mental health services have a responsibility to care for not only the client but also the practitioner. Specialist training for practitioners in dedicated services within a benevolently managed environment may help to both reduce this risk and increase the level of understanding and mutual support within work settings. This is especially relevant given Linehan's (1993) assertion that this client group is best helped within the framework of a supportive team (which can, in turn, provide a good contextual basis for strengthening therapeutic relationships between workers and clients).

The need to establish a good working alliance

The establishment of a therapeutic relationship with this group of clients is a complicated and difficult long-term process. Because of their previous experiences and cognitive and emotional responses, establishing mutual trust and empathy can take much longer than usual and will probably also be more difficult to maintain.

The alliance will depend on three essential components: the practitioner, client and process. Practitioners need to ensure that they do not create the conditions that reinforce the person's unhelpful view of themselves and others. As argued above, this can prove to be difficult as the client is likely to process information in keeping with their schemas and rules, so they will be constantly on the lookout for confirmation of them (see also Chapter 4). Because their actions will constantly provide evidence to support clients' maladaptive beliefs, practitioners will need to:

- examine their attitudes and assumptions towards individual clients and have an adequate knowledge base of the characteristics and formulation of the client group broadly in order to move increasingly towards an empathic collaborative relationship with them
- accept that mental health services, and practitioners within them, can be invalidating, indicating a crucial need for exploration of workers' own unhelpful ways of processing events and feelings in regular, good-quality clinical supervision (see Chapter 5)
- encourage clients to take an active part in their own adaptive development (see below)
- remain calm and assured in response to hostility and resistance
- accept that resistance and ambivalence are inevitable components of the relationship, but can contribute towards learning for worker and client
- validate clients' attempts and willingness to change
- remain hopeful.

Related to the above, clients can be gently and sensitively encouraged to:

- make a commitment to invest in the therapy process for an agreed period of time or number of sessions
- accept that managing risk (of, say, suicide) is a priority and that risk reduction is an agreed aim of the intervention
- view the relationship process as part of the intervention when, for example, the dialogue in intervention sessions is about how client and practitioner interact and work together.

Finally, the process of engagement and establishing an effective working alliance requires both practitioner and client to do the following.

- Focus on the meaning of behaviour in context, which will, in turn, enable both parties in the therapeutic relationship to remain in emotional contact with each other. The decontextualised labelling of client behaviour as troublesome by practitioners inevitably leads to feelings of rejection, isolation and distress in the client.
- Encourage the development of the client's narrative. Relating a personal narrative can be extremely frightening and risky for clients, given their schemas and rules. Practitioners must allow time for this narrative to be built, using gentle and non-confrontational guided discovery (see Chapter 4). Due to clients' often poor or undeveloped sense of self, developing a personal narrative can help people begin to discover both who they are and who they want to become. Reconstructing the meaning of past events through guided discovery can help people emotionally connect with the biosocial, emotional, cognitive and behavioural factors which continue to influence their maladaptive ways of relating to others, and to consider new opportunities for growth and development

The need to understand the meaning of clients' unusual ways of achieving emotional and cognitive regulation

Schema avoidance – based on beliefs that emotions are dangerous and uncontrollable and others are likely to let them down and not to be trusted – can lead clients to engage in unusual solutions. Practitioners need to learn the meaning of such coping strategies within individual case formulations, tailoring them for each client (see Chapter 2 and below). Coping strategies such as cutting are usually developed and utilised when someone perceives that there is an absence of viable alternatives. Many who cope in this way do so in private to seek relief from distress, not to attract attention. Having established the meaning and function of these maladaptive coping strategies, the practitioner can then work collaboratively with the client to help them explore the accuracy of their beliefs.

The need to help clients identify maladaptive core beliefs (schemas)

Identifying core beliefs using guided discovery and the downward arrow technique (see also Chapter 4) is a sensitive area requiring practice, sensitivity and good supervision. James (2001) points out that the experience for clients can be quite traumatic and it is essential for the practitioner to have a clear idea of how to proceed.

Using a CB approach to help people deal with unhelpful care beliefs about themselves, others and the world in general has the following three main aims:

- to help individuals become aware of how core beliefs develop
- how they persist for so long
- how they are related to emotional distress, relationship problems and unhelpful behaviour.

People with rigidly held negative core beliefs often experience them as factual rather than potentially inaccurate. The effects that negative core beliefs have on attention and information processing can be summarised as shown in the table below.

Information processing effect	Examples for a core belief of 'I'm Useless'
Noticing information that supports the belief.	Selectively attending to mistakes or criticism from others.
Unconsciously ignoring information that contradicts the belief.	Failing to notice or acknowledge personal strengths.
Discounting information that contradicts the belief.	Thinking that a compliment from someone cannot be truthful and must contain a hidden agenda.
Distorting ambiguous information to fit the belief.	Helpful advice is judged to be criticism and, therefore, proof of uselessness.

Schema maintenance and confirmation information processing has implications for how the client will experience the CB intervention process, particularly their relationship with the practitioner (see the case example of 'Samina' later in this chapter). Beck et al. (1990) describe how clients' core beliefs impact on the therapeutic alliance so that the exploration of interpersonal issues as they occur within the therapeutic relationship can help to bring about positive change in the relationships the client has with others.

A complementary approach to developing awareness of the effects of core beliefs is to use Padesky's (1994) self-prejudice metaphor. This straightforward procedure involves the following four steps.

Step one	The client is asked to think of someone they know who has a deeply held prejudice against a particular ethnic, social or sexual group.	The client says when they have someone in mind, and tells the worker about the person and their prejudice, including how the prejudiced individual might justify or account for their prejudice in terms of the negative attributes they make about the group of people they don't like.
Step two	The client is asked to speculate on how the individual acquired their prejudice in the first place.	People usually answer this with the following phrases: 'from their parents', 'upbringing', 'formative development', 'cultural and social background'.
Step three	The client is asked to think about how the prejudiced individual maintains their prejudice.	A common answer to this is that the individual seeks out and attends to information that supports their prejudice while ignoring, failing to process, or discounting information that challenges it.
Step four	The client is asked to consider what the prejudiced individual would have to do to overcome their prejudice.	The answer for this tends to be that they would have to be willing to begin to attend to information that they previously avoided or discounted in order to find out whether it was reasonable or otherwise for them to maintain their prejudice.

In summary, the client is encouraged to consider how someone with strong prejudicial beliefs might think in various situations and how those beliefs might influence attention patterns, decision making and behaviour. A process of guided discovery is then used to explore how the prejudiced person might be helped to review and change their beliefs. The discussion then turns to similarities with the client's core beliefs: 'it seems as if your life experience has led to you become prejudiced about yourself.' Handled sensitively, this type of discussion can be quite illuminating as it helps clients to consider their core beliefs as potentially inaccurate rather than factual. This, in turn, often leads to explorations of practical ways forward.

The need to help people identify alternative, more helpful core beliefs

Sadly, many clients have had no opportunity to begin work on processing information in a more accurate and less distressing way. As will be described below, it is possible to help people to construct new core beliefs that facilitates their directing attention towards previously screened-out information.

The new belief feels strange at first, but, as the person builds up a bank of experience that accords with it, so conviction increases. As one of our clients put it, 'It feels strange to act differently at first, but the more you do it, the more it becomes a habit and, after a while, that habit becomes the norm.'

Interventions for developing new core beliefs

Continuum work

As discussed above, strong negative core beliefs are served by psychological processes that can heavily distort a person's perception of events. Black-and-white thinking is a common reaction that leads a person to judge situations on the basis of two categories alone, such as success and failure, good and evil or worthy and worthless. Information-processing problems described earlier lie at the heart of this tendency, as some information is ignored, discounted and distorted so it fits into either of the two categories. Interventions that help to widen a person's perspective beyond this restrictive view will, consequently, weaken those habitual information processing effects.

For instance, people who have strong conviction in the belief 'I am a failure' will judge any mistake as a sign of failure and routinely screen out anything other than 100 per cent success, tending to discount even the greatest of successes by pointing to a slight flaw.

Continuum work aims to help the person explore a less black-and-white view of failure. Several examples of this are described by Padesky (1994), including charting two continua together. The two continua method shown below could be used to explore a black-and-white statement such as 'failure is always bad'. This is done by plotting a 0–100 per cent 'Failure' continuum over another 0–100 per cent 'Helpful' continuum.

Questions arising from the model include, 'Can failure ever be helpful?' The resulting discussion can lead to a number of further interventions, such as:

- discussing the subject with other people to explore alternative perspectives
- conducting a more formal survey of a number of people – for example, asking ten people to judge whether the statement 'No failure is ever helpful' is true or false

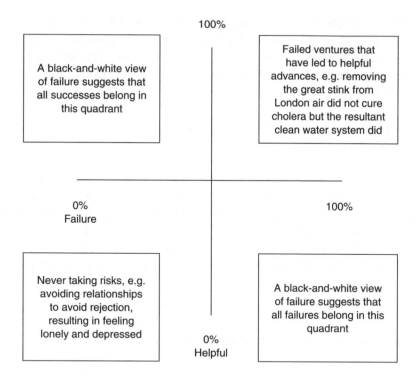

- planning experiments to explore if failure can ever be helpful
- identifying a more helpful attitude to mistakes and acting on this new belief.

Another example of a continuum method appears in the second case example below. 'Samina' defines a new core belief using a set of subcriteria and records evidence of her displaying these characteristics in a 'positive data log' (Padesky, 1994).

A crucial component of continuum work is patient and empathic discussion with the practitioner as people experiencing the unhelpful thinking styles associated with negative core beliefs require help over a long period. The experience of being unable to reach beyond habitual and rigidly held perspectives can leave people doubting their own intelligence. This, in turn, can activate the maladaptive core beliefs that both parties are trying to tackle.

Helping people to gain experience that builds up their new beliefs

As argued in Chapter 4, 'experience is the currency of conviction'. Someone able to act as if the alternative belief is true, will find it increasingly easy to recognise and acknowledge information that confirms it and, consequently, contradicts the old, unhelpful belief.

This process requires great courage as people put themselves in new situations while dropping defensive coping mechanisms that they have relied on for years. This phase thus involves acquiring new knowledge and skills. It also calls for regular monitoring and reflection as new rules for living associated with the new core belief are developed. For instance, someone who has never been assertive may need to learn assertive techniques as well as more sophisticated ways of judging different conflict situations. A trial-and-error approach to these new experiences is advisable, along with plenty of discussion concerning likely reactions to unexpected outcomes.

Using icons and role models and acting as if the new belief is true

This method begins with the client being encouraged to think of someone whose actions suggest that they embody the new belief (Padesky, 2003). Images of this iconic role model are then accessed by the client in situations where alternatives to habitual, maladaptive reactions are hard to think of. For instance, one of our clients believed that she was weird and was anxious much of the time, especially when she felt judged by others. Because of this, she would try so hard to fit in that her behaviour had the opposite effect, alienating her from other people. After identifying her maladaptive belief and understanding how it developed and was maintained, she felt able to explore alternatives that would help her gain experiences to support her new belief.

She was a fan of contemporary art and decided that her new belief – 'I am a unique, interesting individual' was exemplified by the controversial artist Tracy Emin. She paid attention to Emin's media appearances to gauge how she dealt with people who found her strange. She then practised having what she called 'Tracy moments', which, in effect, were examples of her acting as if the new belief were true, and found, as a pleasing result, that her repertoire of reactions to social situations increased. The more experience of social success she had, the more her conviction in the new core belief increased.

Case examples

Having provided a theoretical and empirical basis for understanding and working effectively with clients who have complicated emotional and interpersonal difficulties, we conclude this chapter with two examples from our own casework.

'Martina' – an acute inpatient

Martina is a 32-year-old single woman who was admitted to an acute inpatient unit following a recent suicide attempt. Six weeks prior to the attempt, she had been sacked from her job as a sales assistant and was in danger of becoming homeless.

She was referred for CB work due to her 'acting out behaviour' and 'disruptiveness' in the unit, where her treatment plan was based on risk management, nursing observation and treatment for depression.

The staff's experience of Martina

The majority of the staff team believed that Martina was in control of her actions, that she was manipulative and should not be in the unit as she was using up resources that 'should be for the serious mentally ill'. Her problems were described as 'behavioural', and she was seen as merely avoiding getting on with her life by not actively seeking out new employment – the assumption being that work would reduce her distress. She had been using 'cutting as coping' since her early teens and staff evaluated this as Martina was using self-harm and hostility as a 'weapon' against them. Characteristic of the 'splitting' phenomena, a minority of staff, however, believed that Martina was severely depressed and needed more time to reorganise her life.

Martina's experience of the staff

Martina's story was one of spiteful dismissive staff who sought to punish her at any given opportunity. She firmly believed that the staff treated her like a child and never saw any of them for more than a few minutes at a time. She strongly believed that she was being punished for wanting to kill herself and that no one was interested in her problems.

Individual narratives

The primary nurse and Martina agreed to be interviewed on tape by the CB therapist (Mulhern) to talk about their understandings of Martina's problems and reasons for both parties experiencing her admission as unhelpful. They agreed to listen to each others' tapes and, later, meet together with Mulhern to share their views.

Martina's taped account centred on present events being a repetition of previous experiences. Thematic in her story were accounts of abusive relationships. This included sexual abuse at an early age, bullying at school, intimate partner abuse, being sacked and previous experiences of abusive healthcare systems. She was angry at repeatedly asking for help in the face of her perception that no one wanted to listen – 'Staff are paid to help but do nothing.'

The primary nurse's account of Martina's problems – fuelled by the nurse's frustration, anxiety, anger and confusion – centred on Martina's repertoire of 'disruptive' behaviour and did not include any reference to Martina's history of traumatic events and abuse. The bulk of the nurse's account focused on complaints about Martina's poor self-control, bad timing of attempts of self-harm – 'She only does it when we are stretched' – the effect of her actions on staff – 'She is tiring us all out' – and her selfishness – 'She is depriving others of input.'

Shared narratives

Both parties expressed surprise and concern regarding how each other's behaviour was interpreted. They agreed that they shared similar unhelpful emotional responses and that trust and understanding were absent from their relationship.

Over the next few sessions, a shared conceptualisation of Martina's difficulties was developed, integrating a formulation of the invalidating environment. The relationship between the staff team and Martina was an integral component for testing out new and old beliefs. Gradually the relationship improved and Martina's distress reduced.

'Samina' – an outpatient

Samina approached her family doctor for help with a variety of difficulties nearly four years after a significant relationship had broken up. These difficulties included feeling anxious most of the time, episodes of feeling very sad and unmotivated, drinking alcohol excessively, restricting her eating and occasionally resorting to cutting herself.

She grudgingly agreed to a referral being made to a community mental health team. After a few meetings with a community worker, the team become concerned about her risk of self-harm. Samina reacted angrily to suggestions that she was unsafe, accusing the team of being more concerned with their policies than her needs. She expressed a need to come to terms with events from her past and was eventually referred to a CB therapist (Mills).

At the first meeting, Samina found herself feeling extremely anxious and somewhat detached from reality. She remembered very little of what was discussed, but recalled that the therapist had mentioned something about unhelpful thoughts and beliefs contributing to her distress. She thought that she also remembered the therapist saying how she should be able to help herself. She felt heavily criticised after assuming that he had said that her problems were of her own making. Samina found herself ruminating on these thoughts for a couple of days and eventually felt so angry that she decided to phone and complain to the therapist directly.

The therapist acknowledged that to tell someone they were to blame for their own problems would be wrong and he tried to reassure Samina that this was not what he had said. Samina then became more angry, feeling that she had been accused of lying. The therapist suggested that they should discuss the issue in more detail at their next meeting and, although she wanted to avoid the meeting, Samina agreed to that as she felt desperate for help.

At the next meeting, Samina expected the therapist to be defensive and critical towards her, but, to her surprise, he greeted her warmly. This left her feeling quite suspicious of him. He noted that she looked uncomfortable and said that he was sorry the last meeting had been difficult for her. He asked her for feedback about the session and she told him about the thoughts, feelings and memories she had about it.

They explored how she had reached the conclusion that he had said so many upsetting things and discovered how little of the discussion she could remember. They also found that this had happened to her before in other situations. Samina acknowledged that when she felt very anxious, she switched off, that this itself caused her to feel more anxious as it added to her perception of being unsafe. In the next few sessions they worked together to find ways of reducing the impact of this response. These included:

- identifying signs of switching off
- agreeing that the therapist should say her name to help bring her back
- identifying particular topics that made her feel more anxious and developing a plan for discussing these gradually
- having an agreement that the therapist would not knowingly criticise her
- having an agreement that Samina would give ongoing feedback about her anxiety levels and whether or not she felt criticised
- taking home a tape recording of the session so that she could review what was said.

Samina began to trust the therapist more and, consequently, felt less anxious during their meetings. They made a list of things she wanted help with and discussed how these were connected. This involved letting Samina recount her narrative as she saw it and discussing connections between her life experiences, beliefs, feelings and actions. They summarised their understanding after each session by drawing it out, shoulder to shoulder together, on a flip chart, each taking turns to add things as they were discussed. The summary case formulation – shown below – and subsequent discussion were constructed as a result of a number of incidents and include reactions that Samina recognised as ones she had on a regular basis.

Samina's case formulation: discussion

The formulation below illustrates how Samina had learned to protect herself from the devastating effects of criticism, bullying and abuse. She recognised that, in some ways, she had put on a tough exterior, but continued to feel vulnerable around other people, and cutting herself was a way of controlling her emotions when all else failed. This also explained how anxious she felt when people tried to stop her from doing it.

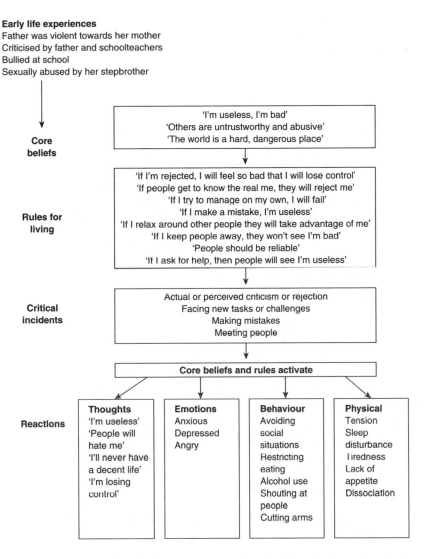

Early life experiences
Father was violent towards her mother
Criticised by father and schoolteachers
Bullied at school
Sexually abused by her stepbrother

Core beliefs

'I'm useless, I'm bad'
'Others are untrustworthy and abusive'
'The world is a hard, dangerous place'

Rules for living

'If I'm rejected, I will feel so bad that I will lose control'
'If people get to know the real me, they will reject me'
'If I try to manage on my own, I will fail'
'If I make a mistake, I'm useless'
'If I relax around other people they will take advantage of me'
'If I keep people away, they won't see I'm bad'
'People should be reliable'
'If I ask for help, then people will see I'm useless'

Critical incidents

Actual or perceived criticism or rejection
Facing new tasks or challenges
Making mistakes
Meeting people

Core beliefs and rules activate

Reactions

Thoughts	Emotions	Behaviour	Physical
'I'm useless'	Anxious	Avoiding social situations	Tension
'People will hate me'	Depressed	Restricting eating	Sleep disturbance
'I'll never have a decent life'	Angry	Alcohol use	Tiredness
'I'm losing control'		Shouting at people	Lack of appetite
		Cutting arms	Dissociation

The formulation also cast light on Samina's high level of anxiety in the first session and she felt that it explained the initial predictions she had made about therapy. She worried that the therapist would not want to work with her when he got to know her and this would leave her with no other source of help. This enabled a focus on Samina's reactions to the therapy and her relationship with the therapist. Both parties acknowledged that entering therapy seemed like a great risk and talked about the fact that Samina would at times feel let down and criticised by the therapist. They agreed to discuss this as and when it occurred, with the understanding that they both had the same goals in mind.

As for many people with such complex difficulties, casework with Samina was long-term and involved continual work to develop greater flexibility in the area of core beliefs. Short- to medium-term goals were identified, which were for Samina to:

- feel more in control of emotions
- ask for help without feeling useless
- accept herself more.

Working on rules for living

Both parties discussed the various ways in which the above goals could be approached, referring to the case formulation to identify how specific beliefs, thoughts, feelings and behaviour interacted around each problem. For instance, Samina's beliefs that emotions could lead to her losing control led to her predicting such loss in specific situations. This, in turn, led to efforts to regain control by cutting herself or using alcohol, although these control methods eventually led to her feeling less stable in life and contributed to her view of herself as being useless and bad.

The core beliefs – 'useless' and 'bad' – lay behind her extreme anxiety and were being confirmed by her reactions to that anxiety. Samina and her therapist settled on a two-pronged approach to worries about losing control.

Behavioural experiments (see Chapter 4) were generated to support an alternative rule that emotions, although uncomfortable, did not signal impending loss of control. New rule development work included reading about dissociation, entering anxiety-provoking situations and reducing her previous maladaptive schema avoidance control strategies, particularly relating to alcohol and cutting.

The second approach was to learn new ways in which to deal with and reduce her anxiety and dissociation. This involved Samina in:

- learning some grounding skills (Kennerly, 2000)
- tackling her sleep difficulties
- learning how to meditate
- learning to ask for help with managing her finances and housing problems.

The last aspect of dealing with anxiety tied in with another phase of therapy in which she tackled her difficulties by asking other people for help. In a similar vein to the above discussion, the approach was to identify a more helpful alternative to her rule 'If I ask for help, then people will see I'm useless.' Her preferred new rule was summarised as 'If I ask the right people for help, they might like to and I will learn to trust them more.'

Working on core beliefs

This work developed from Samina's feeling that she wanted to accept herself more. The relationship between this and her core sense of self, others and the world was discussed. She identified a variety of factors that detracted from her ability to accept herself. These included:

- regularly reflecting on self-critical thoughts
- having very high and unachievable standards for herself
- avoiding others, leading to never having the opportunity to find out what people thought of her unless they became angry about her behaviour
- avoiding challenges.

The therapist introduced the concept of self-prejudice (Padesky, 1994), which helped Samina to identify that, by acting as if she actually was useless and bad, she was contributing to her conviction that this was true.

This discussion became quite heated at some points because Samina began to feel that the therapist was doubting her, which in turn was making her feel useless. They dealt with this by stopping the discussion and focusing on the details of what had just happened. They returned to the case formulation and agreed that her core belief had been activated by the discussion, which, after reviewing their reasons for having it, helped Samina to feel calmer.

This event was significant for Samina in that she had never spoken so openly so soon after feeling abused by someone and she was impressed by how she was able to calm down relatively quickly. This in turn led to her realising that she could have understandably strong beliefs that were unhelpful and sometimes inaccurate.

Tackling the beliefs 'I'm useless, I'm bad' began with identifying a more helpful alternative that Samina felt would contribute to a more balanced view of herself. She decided that 'I'm all right' was an alternative to both.

The continuum method they adopted (Padesky, 1994) included rating her conviction in the new belief, which she placed at 0 per cent. She also identified that she would like to believe it 100 per cent and then worked out a list of characteristics that, in her mind, made a person 'all right'. She found this easier when thinking of a specific person (her favourite television celebrity) whom she considered to be a role model for being 'all right'. The following list of characteristics became the basis for the next discussion:

- relaxed
- confident
- good listener
- organised
- friendly
- independent.

The discussion began with rating Samina (0–100 per cent) on each individual item. Often this would start with Samina rating herself as zero, followed by the therapist helping her to search for any evidence she might have discounted, ignored or distorted. This was especially relevant to the 'organised' and 'independent' items, which she was quite good at, given her rules for living. In the end, her average rating based on these items for being 'all right' was 30 per cent.

Samina and her therapist also discussed what it would be like to meet a person who exhibited all of these characteristics to the 100 per cent level all the time. Samina conjured up an image of an annoyingly independent, overly relaxed person and decided that she did not want to be like that. She rerated her goal to 80 per cent, and, consequently, felt more confident about moving from her present 30 per cent to her goal of 80 per cent.

Later, Samina rerated herself again to 40 per cent after asking her older sister her opinion on the subject. The remainder of the work involved finding ways of either building on her 'all right' characteristics or undertaking increasingly challenging tasks to discover whether or not her view of them was accurate. She kept a record of her work, which, when reading it subsequently, helped her to recover from setbacks when her 'I'm useless, I'm bad' beliefs were activated again.

After six months of this type of work, Samina rated herself as 60 per cent 'all right' and had reduced many of the reactions and habits that she felt were feeding into her sense of being useless and bad.

SUMMARY

- The diagnostic view of borderline personality disorder (BPD) can be understood in the more general context of the psychiatric classification of personality disorder.
- The developmental context of people with complex emotional and relationship difficulties suggests that psychological rather than psychiatric understandings are more helpful to them.
- However, despite such available understandings, BPD and PD more generally continue to function as labels of social exclusion in mental health services.
- In the context of case formulation, schema maintenance, schema avoidance and schema compensation processes help us to understand important features of behavioural, cognitive and mood management among these clients.
- Important features of more effective service provision emerge from a case formulation perspective.
- These include some key CB interventions.

Activities

- Compare the service provided to individuals given the 'borderline' label in your area with the information given in this chapter.
- Follow up at least one book from the further reading list below.
- Talk to staff in your area about their attitudes to this client group.

Further reading

Davidson, K., 2002, *Cognitive Therapy for Personality Disorders: A Guide for Therapists.* **London: Arnold.**
A very useful practical introduction to cognitive therapy in this area, with a good focus on borderline personality disorder.

Morse, S.B., 2002, 'Letting it go: using cognitive therapy to treat borderline personality disorder', in Simos, G. (ed.), *Cognitive Behaviour Therapy: A Guide for the Practising Clinician.* **Hove: Brunner-Routledge.**
A good current and helpful contemporary book with a very useful and detailed section on the role of developmental processes.

Young, J., 1990, *Cognitive Therapy for Personality Disorders: A Schema-focused Approach,* **3rd edn. Sarasota, FL: Professional Resource Exchange.**
This brief, but very detailed, monograph will help the interested reader delve further into issues surrounding early maladaptive schemas and related maintenance, avoidance and compensatory processes.

EIGHT Working with People Who have a Dual Diagnosis

Dave Jones and Ronan Mulhern

Learning objectives

After reading this chapter and completing the activities at the end of it you should be able to:

1 describe the picture of substance misuse in the UK
2 outline what is meant by 'dual diagnosis'
3 describe the problems encountered by dual diagnosis clients
4 describe the relationship between substance misuse and mental health
5 identify the important features of the therapeutic alliance in working with dual diagnosis clients
6 describe the skills needed in the assessment of dual diagnosis clients
7 demonstrate an understanding of the four-stage intervention framework.

Introduction

The use of so-called psychoactive substances is common in British society, and illicit substances, including cannabis, cocaine, ecstasy and amphetamines, are also used by around four million people (Aust et al., 2002). While most people seem to be able to drink or take drugs in moderation, there is a smaller group who encounter problems with their use. The Home Office Drugs Strategy Directorate (2002) estimates that a quarter of a million people in Britain are problem drug users, while Alcohol Concern (2002) suggests that 29 per cent of men and 17 per cent of women drink over the recommended safe limits.

What is a dual diagnosis?

The term 'dual diagnosis' has been applied to a variety of concurrent or coexisting diagnoses. Studies carried out in the UK, USA and Australia in the past 15 years have demonstrated that approximately one third of clients who have a serious mental illness also have a substance misuse problem, with alcohol and cannabis the substances being most commonly misused (Regier et al., 1990; Hall et al., 1999; Wright et al., 2000). It is also suggested that around half of clients in contact with a substance misuse treatment service in the UK have a psychiatric diagnosis, the two most prevalent being depression and personality disorder (Banerjee et al., 2002). For the purposes of this chapter, the term will be understood as applying to someone who encounters problems with their misuse of psychoactive substances as well as having psychotic experiences.

What is the relationship between substance misuse and mental health?

Lehman et al. (1989) suggest the following four subtypes of dual diagnosis:

- primary mental illness with substance misuse
- primary substance misuse with psychiatric consequences
- dual primary diagnosis
- mental illness and substance misuse that have a common aetiological factor, as in the case of post-traumatic stress disorder.

Considering these subtypes can be useful when working towards a case conceptualisation, but clients often suggest other reasons for their misuse of psychoactive substances. Many people enjoy taking drugs or drinking alcohol simply because they like their effects. Clients with mental health problems often try to manage the unwanted effects of prescribed medication – for example, smoking cannabis to deal with the stiffness related to antipsychotic medication. However, although this may be effective in the short term, it may eventually result in more severe psychotic symptoms (Spencer et al., 2002). Someone might also manage their distressing symptoms in the short term by drinking alcohol, but this might lead to unwanted behaviour when intoxicated or the misuse of alcohol becoming a regular coping behaviour.

Substance misuse can provide an easily accessible social network of other people who misuse psychoactive substances, which may seem attractive to someone who has difficulty meeting people.

The reasons for misusing drugs and alcohol may change over time and people can have several reasons at any one time for doing so. For example, some people with mental health problems may drink alcohol to manage the voices that they hear, but also because they like the feelings that alcohol produces (Mueser et al., 1998).

Probably the best way to discover a client's reasons for misusing psychoactive substances is by establishing a good working relationship with them, which should then create an atmosphere of trust in which a comprehensive, accurate assessment can be conducted. Given, too, that the misuse of psychoactive substances can have an adverse impact on the severity of psychiatric symptoms and that they can often themselves be a trigger for substance misuse, it is important to work with both sets of problems at the same time. If no intervention is provided, the two problem areas can form a vicious circle, with one exacerbating the other. If, instead, interventions are provided for both, progress in one area can have a positive impact on the other.

The therapeutic alliance

The attitude that the practitioner displays towards the client is a key ingredient in any therapeutic relationship (see Chapter 2). An empathic, non-judgemental approach to clients who have substance misuse problems is vital. A major threat to the therapeutic alliance is the temptation for practitioners to impose their own beliefs about the rights, wrongs, benefits and costs of substance misuse on their clients. Making use of clinical supervision concerning, this issue is crucial in helping us to become more aware of our own, possibly unhelpful, beliefs and attitudes towards substance misuse (see Chapter 5).

Behaviour change

The transtheoretical model of change (Prochaska, 1999) suggests that behaviour change is a process, with people moving through distinct stages as they change their behaviour and often fluctuating between these stages. This can sometimes prove confusing or frustrating for the practitioner, but does highlight the need to move at the client's pace in order to pre-empt client resistance. Practitioners should be mindful of the following.

- *Client ambivalence*   Most people can see both positive and negative sides to any behaviour that they engage in, whether this is smoking tobacco or turning up to work in the morning. For example, a client who has a dual diagnosis may accept that drinking too much alcohol may be detrimental to their physical health, but may also be unable to see how they will cope with the voices they hear without drinking.
- *Client motivation*   Motivation is a dynamic state that can change rapidly according to the circumstances that the person encounters. It is safe to assume that a person who feels in control of their treatment is likely to feel more motivated to change than someone who feels they are being told what they should be doing.

Assessment

Clients who have a dual diagnosis present in many different contexts, with a wide variety of problems, many of which do not fall neatly into either the mental health or substance misuse diagnoses (APA, 1994). It is therefore vital that an accurate assessment is conducted, so that the nature of the relationship between a client's substance misuse and their mental health can be ascertained. While assessment is usually emphasised at the beginning of a therapeutic relationship and contact with a service, it should also form part of the extended process of developing a working relationship with a client, as worker and client get to know each other. Too much time spent working through bulky assessment documents can lead to the client taking an extremely passive role, which is antithetical to CB collaboration.

Specific skills for assessment

One of the more obvious skills required to conduct an assessment is a working knowledge of drugs and alcohol, such as the typical effects of psychoactive substances and quantities commonly misused. It is beyond the scope of this chapter to provide such information, so the reader is directed towards such sources as Rassool (1998) and Seivewright (2000).

It is vital that the client is allowed to tell their story with the minimum intervention from the practitioner. Many people are unclear as to the actual extent of their substance misuse when they present for help, so it is often useful both to them and to practitioners to build their awareness of the amount that they consume and the contexts in which they consume those substances. Apart from the clinical interview, which would form the basis of the assessment, it can be extremely useful to encourage the client to keep a diary of their drinking and/or drug-taking between treatment sessions in order to examine the pattern of misuse. A simple form such as the one below can be used to collect this type of information.

Day/Time	Location	Situation	Who was I with?	What did I use? How much?	What effect did it have?
Thursday 5 p.m.	Home	Had an argument with my girlfriend on the phone.	On my own.	2 joints of skunk.	Helped me to calm down.

A useful method of examining any link between mental health problems and substance misuse is a timeline analysis – an example of which is given below. The client should be encouraged to describe their mental health history as they would in any other assessment interview, with a timeline being constructed by the client and the therapist. Once this has been done, the client can then describe their history of substance misuse and another timeline can be constructed. When the client feels ready to examine the relationship between the two, the timelines can be compared to see if there may be any link. Let us consider an example of a timeline.

'Robert'

Life events/mental health	Substance misuse
Aged 12 Father leaves home. Mother's substance misuse increases. Violence and neglect increase. Robert feels confused rejected and unloved.	Peer group begins experimenting with solvents. Robert misuses solvents as a means for peer group acceptance and emotional escape.
Aged 12–14 Home situation becomes more volatile. Robert feels rejected, hurt and alone.	Solitary usage increases to daily. Then, finds relief in peer group – is no longer interested in solvent use.
Aged 14 School and child services become involved due to Robert's erratic and problematic behaviour. Feels others are punishing him.	Stops solvent use and commences recreational use of alcohol, cannabis and LSD. Adverse reaction to solvents.
Aged 15–18 Robert goes to live with his father and develops new friendships. Feels accepted and loved. Meets girlfriend and they plan to attend university together.	Cannabis becomes drug of choice. Used in a peer/social situation, 3–4 times per week.
Aged 19 Attends university with girlfriend. Feels pressured, stressed and isolated, becomes questioning and suspicious of girlfriend. Falls behind in college work, becomes down and low in mood. Girlfriend angry at cannabis use.	Increases daily use of cannabis to in excess of 1 oz per week.
Aged 20 girlfriend ends relationship due to Robert's cannabis use. Rejection confirms Robert's view of himself as unlovable, leading to low mood. This may be the early phase of a psychotic disorder.	Cannabis use continues, supplemented with LSD.
Aged 21 Robert begins to hear voices and believes others are trying to harm him. Becomes very distressed, angry, fearful and isolated. Severs contact with father and friends.	Cannabis and LSD use continues with daily alcohol use now at 10 units per day.

Robert's case conceptualisation

The diagram opposite illustrates how, in a vicious circle, Robert's problems are maintained.

A framework for intervention

A useful framework to guide interventions with clients who have a dual diagnosis is the four-stage model devised by Osher and Kofoed (1989), described below. Clients frequently move between stages – someone who has begun to change their substance misuse may experience lapses or setbacks, for example. Equally, clients may well be at different stages of progress with their substance misuse and mental health treatment, highlighting the need to remain flexible with regard to the intervention offered and maintain both a long-term view and a sense of optimism and hope (see Chapter 2).

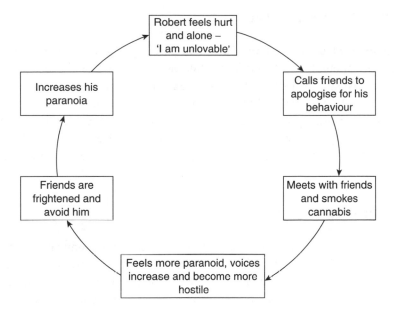

Stage 1: engagement

Traditional models of service engagement fail to fully engage people with substance misuse problems (Wu et al., 2003). The main type of intervention for this stage of the model is, therefore, assertive outreach (see Chapter 11). This more flexible approach takes the range of services offered to the client in their own environment and concentrates on practical assistance, such as helping with any problems that the client may be encountering with housing or benefits.

As has been previously stated, many clients cite their reasons for using psychoactive substances as being either to manage their symptoms or the unwanted side-effects of currently prescribed medication. This presents the practitioner with the opportunity to look at the client's attitudes towards, and use of, their medication. If this is done, some of the reasons for a person's misuse of drugs or alcohol may be resolved. An important principle to bear in mind at this stage is to avoid focusing on the client's substance misuse as a cause of their mental health or life problems. Such a focus is likely to provoke resistance and may well lead to the client disengaging from the intervention. However, even though the practitioner will take care not to link the client's substance misuse with their other problems, this does not imply that they should offer no intervention for the latter. Trying to help clients remain safe while still engaged in their substance misuse should be a priority for workers, so offering clean needles, syringes and other paraphernalia to injectors has been a key intervention in harm-reduction approaches for substance misuse (Derricott et al., 1999). Another option might be to discuss the possibility of smoking cannabis through a water-pipe (also called a 'bong') or inhaling through a vapouriser to minimise the adverse impact of tobacco smoking on the client.

Stage 2: building motivation

This stage is characterised by the client having begun to maintain regular contact with mental health services while not yet being ready to change their substance misuse. It is important not to trigger the client's resistance to change, thus undoing the progress achieved in the engagement stage.

The intervention goals at this stage are to raise the client's awareness of their substance misuse, help them to identify the good and less good aspects of that substance misuse and enhance their motivation to change (see Chapter 2).

Interventions for building motivation

Interventions at this stage include individual and family education about the problem(s) and, because the client may have difficulty in structuring their own time, structured activities, including activity scheduling, may be useful (see Chapter 13). However, perhaps the most crucial intervention at this stage is motivational interviewing.

Motivational interviewing is a style of dialogue aimed at helping the client to resolve their ambivalence towards their substance misuse, thus increasing motivation to change their behaviour (Miller and Rollnick, 2002). The client is assisted in exploring their ambivalence about substance misuse by engaging in a decisional balance exercise, using the matrix below.

What I like about my use	What I don't like about my use
What will be good about change	What won't be so good about change

Using the example of Robert, whose timeline we saw above, the following is an excerpt from the kind of motivational interviewing dialogue that is required to support the process of motivation enhancement.

Practitioner: You say that your substance use has only had beneficial effects on your life. Can I just check out with you again what reasons Anne stated for ending your relationship?

Client: She got angry that we did nothing together other than sit and watch television, rather than do the stuff all her other friends at college were doing. She hated the smell of weed and did not want to come home to the flat at times.

Practitioner: What made her not want to come home?

Client:	I was usually sitting there a bit wasted, not having gone to classes, and when she started to get annoyed and angry at that I would just skin up again and that would drive her crazy. She just would not chill. I think that if she had started smoking it would have been OK.
Practitioner:	How did you feel when she didn't chill and got upset at your cannabis use?
Client:	It just made me want to do it more. I thought at the time she was becoming less keen on me.
Practitioner:	What made you think she was getting less keen?
Client:	She was always telling me to cut down on my smoking and to go to class, to go do this and that with her friends or our old friends. It got to a stage when I thought she was always having a go and didn't care for me any more.
Practitioner:	Looking back now, how would you explain her actions at that time?
Client:	I guess she wanted the best for me and her, but she went about it in the wrong way. She felt that the weed was the cause of all my problems and it was not. I can see I was a bit messed up, but there were a lot of other things.
Practitioner:	OK. From our understanding of events, how did the weed help?
Client:	It chilled me out, relaxed me.
Practitioner:	How did it not help?
Client:	It really upset Anne, I suppose. It certainly stopped me from going to classes I guess and prevented me from going out and doing the whole college thing.
Practitioner:	So it upset Anne and stopped you from going out. How does that fit with the view that the weed has only been beneficial?
Client:	I guess not.

It can often be difficult for the worker to ascertain at what point the client becomes ready to change their behaviour. One way in which to gauge this is by using scaling to assess their readiness (Rollnick et al., 1999). The client is asked at which point on a scale of 1 to 10 (with 1 equalling 'not ready') they feel they would be ready to change. Then, practitioner and client jointly consider strategies and exercises to move them towards that score.

Stage 3: active engagement

At this stage, the client will have made a decision to change their substance misuse and need information on the range of intervention options available, as well as the support to see those changes through. The client's goals need to be individualised and arrived at in a collaborative fashion (see Chapter 3). Frequently, this can be frustrating for the practitioner, as the client's goals may well be different from the goals of the clinical team. For example, the clinical team may see that a client's cannabis smoking has an adverse effect on the frequency or intensity of the voices that they hear or activates some odd, distressing beliefs and so be of the view that they should stop smoking cannabis altogether. The client, on the other hand, may feel comfortable with their cannabis misuse in general, but might accept that, on occasion, they tend to 'overdo' it.

Interventions for active engagement

People tend to experiment with psychoactive substances relatively early in life, with peer group participation being an influential factor in this (Holt, 1993). Conversely, the adverse effects of substance misuse, such as dependency, have a marked effect on the person's intimate social group and society generally. The psychosocial context of unhelpful substance misuse therefore needs to be incorporated into both assessment and interventions. At this stage, these include helping the client change their behaviour by, for example, substituting activities such as work or sport for substance misuse time, and by encouraging them to make changes in their social environment to minimise temptation. In addition, behavioural experiments may be useful in helping clients to challenge and change their rules for living (see Chapter 4).

'Henry'

Henry – a 23-year-old single man, grew up in a series of foster and State care homes. Understandably, he had developed unhelpful core beliefs regarding his self-worth ('I am unlovable'), acceptance and abandonment ('Others will reject me'), and his ability to survive ('The world is a cruel place').

From the age of 16, he became a member of a peer group – referred to as his 'family' – with whom he felt a true sense of belonging, although he was always vigilant for signs of rejection.

Henry experienced three psychotic-type episodes, which resulted in hospitalisation, and placed great value on how his family had stuck by him in the past, but was uncertain why they had done this. The group tended to misuse alcohol and cannabis regularly and this was an integral ritual in the socialisation of the group.

As the years passed, Henry recognised the association between his heavy cannabis misuse, fear of rejection, paranoia and hearing voices. However, for some time, he had been reluctant to address his cannabis use for fear of alienation.

Henry was able to construct his case formulation with his practitioner and could see how smoking cannabis had its benefits but also its drawbacks. He identified the assumption, 'If I do not smoke weed with the family then I will not fit in and they will reject me.' His belief in this assumption was rated as 50 per cent in the session, but rose to 95 per cent when socialising with his peer group.

Due to Henry's fear of rejection and abandonment, it was agreed that a straightforward 'use or don't use' behavioural experiment constituted too great a risk for him. It was decided instead that it would be helpful for the therapist to meet with the family and find out their views on the subject. Henry's prediction was that they would respond in neutral or negative ways.

Over a period of weeks, the family agreed to a meeting where Henry's cannabis misuse would be openly and honestly discussed. The assumption to be tested was identified as, 'If I say that I no longer want to smoke weed then I will not fit in and they will want nothing to do with me any more' and Henry's belief in this prior to the meeting was 85 per cent. This assumption was to be tested by asking individual 'family members' to speak openly and honestly about what their actions would be if Henry was to stop smoking cannabis.

The outcome surprised Henry, in that his friends spoke openly about the fact that they did not like the changes in his behaviour when smoking cannabis and much preferred his company when he was straight. They had wanted to tell him for some time, but were frightened of his feeling rejected. Henry's subsequent belief rating reduced to 20 per cent, with him remaining slightly suspicious of the outcome. His family subsequently committed themselves to taking an active part in Henry's recovery plan. They agreed to:

- meet monthly with him and his worker
- incorporate non-substance-based activities into their social repertoire
- reduce their own frequency of substance misuse
- contact the therapist if they were concerned for Henry's health.

As anticipated, the plan did not work out neatly, with lapses and waning of commitment occurring from time to time. However, what it did achieve was to allow Henry choices in his substance misuse that were not entirely dependent on his fear of abandonment.

Stage 4: relapse prevention

By this stage, the client should no longer experience problems related to their substance misuse. The interventions employed should enable them to anticipate and deal effectively with trigger or high-risk situations, as well as implementing changes in other areas of their life. Prochaska and DiClemente (1986) found that relapse is the most common outcome in the treatment of substance misuse problems. Relapse prevention is a self-control programme that combines behavioural skills training, cognitive interventions and lifestyle change procedures (Wanigaratne et al., 1990).

A useful model of relapse prevention is provided by Marlatt and Gordon (1985). Someone who has managed to change their substance-misusing behaviour will encounter environmental circumstances where they may be tempted to use again. If they are able to resist that temptation, they will feel more confident and be less likely to relapse in the future. If, on the other hand, they feel unable to resist the tempting situation, they will slip up and use, triggering what Marlatt and Gordon call the 'rule violation effect'. This is characterised by feelings of guilt and loss of control, which further increase the likelihood of relapse into substance misuse.

Intervention for relapse prevention

Given the impact that substance misuse can have on clients' mental health, the goals at this stage are to teach them to identify and cope with stress, the symptoms of their psychiatric disorder and the desire to use psychoactive substances to manage the situation. It is also useful for the client to learn that a slip need not lead to a complete relapse into substance misuse. In bringing this chapter to a close, returning to Robert, the following dialogue serves to illustrate a relapse prevention discussion and the importance of helping clients to identify trigger situations and ways to handle or avoid them.

Practitioner: OK then Robert, from what we have discussed so far, can you tell me the times when you are tempted to smoke cannabis?

Robert: Well, there's the times when I feel down, when I feel no one likes me. I could go and see some of my mates and smoke a few joints. That sometimes used to cheer me up.

Practitioner: So feeling down or unhappy is a tempting time for you. Are there any other situations where you feel tempted?

Robert: Yeah, seeing my mates can be tempting, too. Then there are the times when I feel stressed or angry – like the time when I had a row with my girlfriend on the phone. I had a couple of joints and that calmed me down.

Practitioner: So, in addition to feeling down, feeling angry or stressed is a tricky time, too. Are there any other times when you're tempted?

Robert: Yeah, I guess I want to smoke more when I am bored as well, 'cause it helps me think of new things and makes time pass.

Practitioner: Right, so boredom is a trigger for you as well. Are there any other times when you feel tempted to have a joint?

Robert: Maybe, but that's all I can think of at the moment.

Practitioner: OK, so we've identified feeling down, feeling angry and feeling bored as times when you want to smoke. Now let's look at when you are tempted to drink. What sorts of things make you feel you need beer?

Robert: Well, I guess the worst time is when I hear those voices telling me other people are after me. That's really scary and the beer helped me ignore the voices and feel a bit safer.

Practitioner: OK, so your voices are a trigger for drinking. Are there any other situations that make you want to drink?

Robert: Well, yeah, sometimes when I had a couple of spliffs, maybe three or four, I started to get a bit edgy and think that someone might be coming for me. A few cans of beer helped take the edge off a bit.

Practitioner: So sometimes you needed the beer to help you deal with the effects of too much cannabis.

Robert: Yeah, so sometimes smoking is a temptation to drink.

Practitioner: So how have you dealt with the temptation?

Robert: Well, I have tried to stay away from my mates who I smoke with. I didn't think that was going to be easy, but when I get lonely or bored, I go to see Pete instead. Pete doesn't drink.

SUMMARY

- The picture of substance misuse in the UK includes a subset of people with problems relating to substance misuse.
- 'Dual diagnosis' in this chapter refers to people who encounter problems with their use of psychoactive substances as well as having psychotic experiences.
- Dual diagnosis clients encounter specific problems, including offending behaviour and difficulty in engaging with services.
- It is important to consider the relationship between dual diagnosis and mental health on an individual basis by means of careful assessment and case formulation.
- This, in turn, highlights important features of both the therapeutic alliance and assessment in helping dual diagnosis clients.
- A useful framework for helping these clients is the four stages of engagement, building motivation, active engagement and relapse prevention.

Activities

- Rate your own knowledge about the following substances and treatments employed:

  - alcohol
  - cannabis
  - heroin
  - amphetamines
  - cocaine, LSD.

- What will it take to improve your knowledge?
- Talk to clients who have a dual diagnosis. Which interpersonal interventions have they found helpful or unhelpful and for what reasons?
- Talk to friends or colleagues about their own attempts to change health-related behaviour change.

Further reading

Graham, H.L., Copello, A., Birchwood, M.J. and Mueser, K.T. (eds), 2002, *Substance Misuse in Psychosis: Approaches to Treatment and Service Delivery*. Chichester: John Wiley.
An up-to-date and in-depth comprehensive overview of dual diagnosis.

Miller, W.R., and Rollnick, S., 2002, *Motivational Interviewing: Preparing People to Change Addictive Behaviour* 2nd edition. New York: The Guilford Press.

This book is an excellent, in-depth guide to using motivational interviewing and contains a very useful introduction to Prochaska and DiClemente's transtheoretical model of change.

Rassool, G.H. (ed.), 2002, *Dual Diagnosis: Substance Misuse and Psychiatric Disorders*. Oxford: Blackwell.
A comprehensive overview of the area that is a useful sourcebook for practitioners.

NINE Working with People Who are Violent in Mental Health Settings and Relationships

Ian Dyer and Ronan Mulhern

Learning objectives

After reading this chapter and completing the activities at the end of it you should be able to:

1 identify the potential triggers to violence in mental health settings
2 describe the fundamentals of good practice for practitioners in relation to minimising and responding to violence and aggression
3 describe the environmental contributors to violence and aggression in inpatient settings
4 identify the importance of practitioners' own belief systems in relation to violence
5 identify the importance of considering the organisational rules and beliefs of staff in conceptualising inpatient violence
6 be able to outline the determinants and consequences model of anger
7 describe the key points of assessment and intervention emerging from this model
8 identify the significance of, and key issues emerging from, intimate partner violence for practitioners.

Introduction

Practitioners may be faced with different forms of aggression during their working lives as a direct result of the problems, frustrations and limitations of those in their care and their designated responsibility in given clinical situations. The issue of violence within the mental health setting is one of increasing concern for practitioners (Trenoweth, 2003), making awareness of the potential triggers for violence essential. It would be impractical to attempt to cover all of those within this chapter, but the following selected areas illustrate how violence may be triggered by the ways in which people can interpret events.

Fear, humiliation and frustration

Triggers for violence often relate to the experience of fear, humiliation or frustration among service users, who neither know what is happening to them nor what the future holds for them. Fear may also be driven by false beliefs and hallucinations – particularly command hallucinations (see Chapter 10) – or increased levels of anxiety. Humiliation may also trigger aggression and violence, including not being able to make decisions for oneself or experiencing a lack of choice and loss of control over one's life. Frustration relating to the perception of loss of life skills and being unable to learn or achieve or loss of independence can also result in violence or aggression.

Try the following exercise.

Imaginal exercise

Imagine a scenario in which you hear voices that others don't hear. You are frightened and go to see your doctor who suggests that you should see a specialist – a psychiatrist.

After being questioned by the psychiatrist for a considerable time about you, your past, family, voices and a number of other very personal areas of your life, it is suggested that you should go into hospital and you agree to this.

You arrive and the environment is not what you expect a hospital to be like. You have to check in all your property with a nurse and items that you have always had with you are removed and placed in safekeeping. You have to share your environment with people you have never met before and whose behaviour reflects the fact that they too need to be in hospital. Some of your fellow residents are very quiet and avoid any eye-contact or intervention, some are boisterous and over friendly and others are aggressive. You are then invited to take some medication that you previously agreed to. However, the content of that discussion has been forgotten by you, in large part due to the experience of your new environment. You are asked not to leave the ward without first asking a member of staff. Someone 'checks' on you at regular intervals, and still you keep hearing the voices.

How might you feel, think and behave if you were that client? The above scenario is not an uncommon experience for a number of people coming to psychiatric inpatient services for the first time.

Fundamentals of good practice

You, the practitioner, are possibly the single most important factor in minimising the risk of anger or aggression escalating to violence. The ways in which you respond will have been shaped by your past experiences, training and level of flexibility within your clinical practice. Before going on to explore crucial aspects of your own individual belief system, it is important to identify some fundamental points of good practice:

Rules	Components of rules
Be self-aware	Acknowledge your own levels of stress and anxiety. It is not a weakness to be frightened when faced with threat. Know your client and be aware of any distractors or de-escalation techniques that may be of benefit. It may be useful to let the client know how you are feeling and offer ways to tackle the problem that involve less stress for both of you.
Give the potentially violent person personal space	We all have our own comfort zones when interacting with others. These become even more important during times of anger. While interacting with someone who is aroused, the useful rule of thumb is to stand at arm's length or, perhaps more appropriately, at leg's length. This will stop the invasion of personal space and allow you the opportunity to move away from an aggressive limb. There may be times when the aggressor intrudes into your personal space. It would be a mistake to think that you should stand your ground. Be prepared to back away.
Be at the same level or slightly lower than the potentially violent person	Looking down at someone who is angry could be interpreted as threatening. If you feel it is safe to do so, lower your height to reduce any perception of you being a threat. This may be safely done by sitting on the corner edge of a table.
Don't make sudden movements	Any sudden movement may be interpreted as aggressive. Ensure that gestures are overt and not open to misinterpretation.
Manage others in the environment	Having other people in the environment may increase the level of arousal. If and when possible, encourage other patients or bystanders to remove themselves. Other members of staff may need managing. It is not always the case that the most senior or experienced member of the team is the person dealing with the hostility, in which case, you, as the person involved, need to give prompts to your colleagues. If they should arrive at a time that you feel the situation is coming under control let them know, a statement such as, 'Hi, I think things are sorting themselves out – we will be with you shortly', conveys to them not to come charging in. There is nothing more frustrating for a member of staff than to have almost defused a situation only for the 'cavalry' to come charging in and escalate the problem. Alternatively, a statement such as 'We have a difficult situation here, perhaps you can help', will convey to them your relief that they have arrived and invite them to either take over or assist.
Personalise yourself and emphasise cooperation	Allowing the patient to see you as a person, not just part of the system, will encourage responsibility taking for their actions. By emphasising cooperation, you are demonstrating your willingness to work with the patient.
Talk in a clear voice and do not try to speak louder than the angry person	It may feel natural to lower your voice when being confronted by someone who is angry and potentially violent. However, the consequence may be that they do not hear you clearly and either misinterpret what you are saying or become more frustrated. Speaking louder will appear aggressive and threatening. The tone of your voice is important, too. The same statement can be said in a number of different ways. A simple statement such as, 'I'm not in a position to be able to agree to that' can be said negatively, in a condescending or hostile manner, or positively, in a friendly or considerate way.
Keep your body language as non-threatening as possible	The use of open gestures, keeping your hands within sight and palms open will demonstrate that you have nothing to hide. Never have your hands in your pockets or behind your back as this may be interpreted as you not caring or being uninterested or, worse still, that you are concealing something from them.

(Continued)

(Continued)

Rules	Components of rules
Offer solutions if you can, but don't make unrealistic promises	There is a saying 'Don't make a mountain out of a molehill.' This is worth remembering during times of threat or hostility. For someone who is anxious, frightened or feeling humiliated, a small issue may trigger a large response. Attempt to find out what the trigger was. It may be due to missing a phone call, wanting to get out of the environment and having to wait for staff or any similar, easy-to-rectify problem. If the problem can be resolved, resolve it. Don't feel that because someone's behaviour is unacceptable their request is also. When the situation is resolved, there will be ample time to reflect, with the patient, on how they dealt with their frustration and joint care planning, therapeutic intervention and training can be implemented. It is as important not to make unrealistic promises – this will only cause problems at a later stage.
Don't argue	You may be totally in the right and the cause of the hostility may be completely unjustified, but don't argue. Arguing leads to raised voices on both sides. Individuals who are trying to put across their point of view lose the skill of active listening. I am sure we can all recall times that we have engaged in arguments in our personal lives. By the end of the altercation it is often difficult to remember what the initial issue was.
Leave if you can or if you have to	If the hostility has reached a stage where it appears violence is unavoidable and there are no contingency plans and/or recourses to restrain the aggressor, attempt to safely leave the environment. You may suggest that you are going to contact someone who has the authority to make a decision relating to the client's request or you may say that you need to use the toilet or get a glass of water. Whatever the reason, it is best, if possible, to give a rationale for leaving the environment. Being aware that the possibility of having to leave the environment may occur, it is always best to position yourself in such a way that you can gain access to the exit so as not to have to pass too closely to the patient. Similarly, and depending on the room layout, try not to block the client's access to the exit. Often extreme hostility ends in displaced aggression towards inanimate objects, such as a door. It is better to allow the client the opportunity to storm off, slamming the door, than it is to give them the impression that they have to get through you first. If you identify the need to escape, be prepared to play for time. Use diversion tactics or distractions to allow you the opportunity to get away.
Let others know that there is a problem	If you are alone and others are not aware of the situation, you may need to call for help. This may be done by using an alarm system, either static or personal, or by calling out. The principle is much the same as discovering a fire in that the person making the discovery needs to raise the alarm prior to tackling it, if it is safe to do so.
If you find yourself in extreme danger	If you find yourself in a situation that you perceive to be one of extreme danger, then you may have to say or promise anything to get yourself out of that situation. It is far better, as a last resort, to get out and later discuss, truthfully, with the aggressor why you haven't delivered than to be seriously injured.

Violence within inpatient settings

Environmental factors

British acute inpatient environments have been repeatedly described as being overcrowded, frightening, unstimulating and isolating (DoH, 1998). Therefore, when working with potential violence, it is of paramount importance to include environmental factors in our clinical conceptualisations. It has been suggested by Benson et al. (2003) that practitioners have a tendency to engage in discourses of blame rather than developing a more collaborative, accurate and helpful understanding of events. There is an increasing recognition that admitting vulnerable people to such environments can add to, rather than help, with their problems. For example, evidence is emerging that people have been traumatised by admission to inpatient settings (Frame and Morrison, 2001; Morrison, 2003).

Practitioners' beliefs about themselves

Previous chapters have emphasised the crucial role belief systems play within the CB approach and the literature has a strong focus on how to help people whose belief systems are unhelpful or damaging to themselves and others. However, equally, it is as important to recognise the ways in which practitioners' beliefs and attributional styles contribute to both the incidence of, and inappropriate responses to, violence (McNeil et al., 2003; see also Chapter 4).

Unhelpful underlying assumptions	More flexible alternatives
'I should take control.'	'How do I enter negotiations?'
'I must never run away.'	'I need to avoid confrontation that could make the situation worse.'
'I must never admit/show fear.'	'Fear is a normal response in these situations – it's not only me who is afraid.'
'I should never back down to threats.'	'This is not personal. How do I find out what the person's problems are?'
'Only men can deal with aggression and violence.'	'Male (macho) behaviour can make some problems worse. It is the skills of the individual, not their gender, that matters.'
'Because I'm the practitioner, I should know best.'	'It's OK not to know.'
'If I feel fear, then I'm useless.'	'I can accept and use this fear in a productive way.'

By recognising and challenging their own underlying assumptions, introducing more flexibility in this cognitive domain and managing violent incidents differently, practitioners will broaden their repertoire of approaches and reduce the frequency of placing themselves in potentially no-win situations. It is important to note that there is a vast difference between defusing a potentially violent situation and giving in to unreasonable demands. It is also far better to be able to discuss and negotiate issues when the situation has calmed down and it is safe to do so than to be in a hospital bed saying, 'At least I stuck to my guns.'

Incorporating the organisation into case formulation

Although services are continually evolving and developing more flexible ways of helping people in psychological crisis, there is still at present a need for admission to acute care and the challenge for staff is to turn this from a negative experience into an opportunity to engage the client and minimise their distress. The following case example presents a combined organisational and client-centred case formulation to illustrate the importance of factoring in the more or less explicit organisational rules and assumptions at play about inpatient violence.

'Mark'

Mark is a 28-year-old single man who has an 8-year history of hearing disturbing voices and having strongly held beliefs that he is at the centre of a conspiracy. He has had six admissions to an acute mental health unit, which have usually been against his wishes.

Mark tends to alleviate the distress caused by his psychosis by misusing a variety of psychoactive substances (see Chapter 8).

Since his first admission there have been at least six recorded 'serious' assaults. These mainly occurred during the first five days of his admission and the clinical team, since his first admission, has labelled Mark as violent. The management of all admissions subsequent to his first was based on the prediction that he would continue to be violent.

In the community, Mark was working with a CB psychotherapist (Mulhern), examining ways in which to reduce his distress. One of the issues that was predominant in sessions was his traumatic accounts of hospitalisation, which manifested in the form of intrusive thoughts and images.

Prior to any further admissions, the therapist worked with the staff and Mark on their predictions of fear of violence should he be admitted. Based on this, we developed the case formulation shown below.

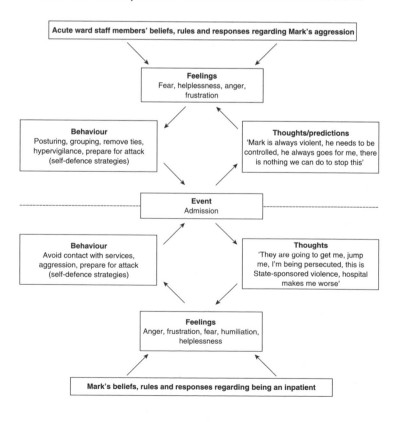

Although Mark had had frequent contact with the inpatient unit, the staff knew very little about the attributions he made about being an inpatient, which, in turn, led to his violent behaviour. Finding it very difficult to understand or empathise with him, they tended instead to protect themselves by labelling and avoiding him, thus negating the possibility of achieving some form of psychological intimacy with him. By sharing accounts of victimisation, fear and helplessness, they were able to appreciate the factors that contributed to Mark being the person he was. The ability to recognise and empathise with each other helped in reducing the barriers to engagement. Mark and the majority of the inpatient team agreed to view any further possible admission(s) as a behavioural experiment, as follows.

Prediction to be tested: Mark will be angry at his admission, but will not become violent

Possible problems	Strategies to overcome these problems	Outcome of the experiment
Mark will be admitted out of hours or when significant team members are absent.	Mark's therapist will liaise with Mark to be admitted during office hours.	No one was assaulted by Mark during the admission.
Mark will no longer remember the plan due to intoxication.	If intoxicated, Mark will not be admitted directly to hospital.	Mark remained in hospital for much shorter than usual.
Staff will develop an anxiety-based hostile/defensive response to Mark's behaviour.	Female staff members willing to undertake the admission are identified.	Mark is slightly less suspicious of inpatient team.
Someone will provoke Mark or be provoked by him, resulting in a violent altercation.	Other staff members will be in areas adjacent to the admission suite, though not in direct sight.	Ongoing.
	De-escalation interventions will be employed to help Mark cope with his anger.	
	Hospital managers are aware of, and supportive towards, the plan.	
	Therapist will review admission process with Mark and principal carers on a regular basis.	

There was no violence in the course of Mark's last admission (which was also six weeks shorter then previous admissions) and Mark's belief that he was being persecuted by staff had reduced by 15 per cent. As described in Chapter 4, such beliefs are unlikely to be altered by a single experiment using the CB approach. They do, however, give us experiential evidence of the possibilities for change and choice in the services we provide.

Anger management training

Almost everybody, at some stage, will experience feeling angry, but, more often than not, this does not result in violence. However, those people who do become violent may well benefit from learning techniques to help them control their anger and, subsequently, reduce the likelihood of behaving violently (Lewis, 2002; Lindsay et al., 2003). Equally, those who experience regular and/or high levels of anger rarely resulting in violence are likely to be aware that anger impinges on areas of their life, such as relationships and physical health (Williams et al., 2002), and they can too benefit from anger management training.

Anger can be functional, enabling the individual to show assertiveness and mobilise resources when faced with threat. However, when linked with aggression, it can be a very dysfunctional emotion, causing many difficulties within personal relationships and for society (Dyer, 2000). CB approaches to anger management are beginning to demonstrate effective outcomes for a number of client groups, including outpatients with mental health problems (Dyer, 2000; Tang, 2001), military personnel (Linkh and Sonnek, 2003) and men with intellectual disabilities convicted of assault (Lindsay et al., 2003).

Novaco (1994), one of the leading researchers in this field, made explicit the relationship between environmental triggers, cognitions, physical arousal, emotion (anger) and behaviour. His model, adapted and illustrated below, can be used as an assessment and psycho-educational tool, as well as a basis for case formulation. It identifies anger triggers within the environment that, in turn, result in physical, cognitive and behavioural responses. It recognises that angry thoughts may fuel physical arousal or vice versa. The behavioural reaction in turn impacts on the environment, on the client's physical arousal and, ultimately, on the intensity and duration of their anger.

'David'

David is a 31-year-old man who lives with his partner and young child and works as a car mechanic for a small company.

For a number of years he has become increasingly aware that his levels of anger have increased. The frequency and duration of his bouts of anger have also become more problematic.

A recent episode of anger occurred when David had agreed to take his partner and child to the cinema after work. He was due to leave work at 5.30 p.m., but was delayed by having to complete a piece of work. On his way home, he was further delayed by roadworks. David started to feel tense and was hitting the steering wheel. He experienced automatic thoughts, such as 'She will blame me for being late', 'It's not my fault', 'I won't take any shit.' When David arrived home, he got out of the car, slamming the door. He entered the house, again slamming the door, and, prior to any interaction between David, his partner or his son, he shouted, 'Don't start, I'm not in the mood for your nagging.'

This case can be formulated using Novaco's determinants and consequences model, as follows.

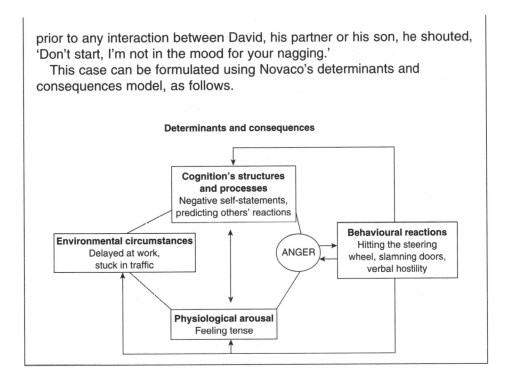

Determinants and consequences

Assessing anger

In helping people with anger problems following Novaco, the focus of the intervention is based mainly in the here and now, rather than the past. It is important to identify the dysfunctional thoughts and behaviour associated with provocation (or perceived provocation) and introduce new coping mechanisms. Anger management can be offered either on a one-to-one basis or as group sessions (Dyer, 2000). Prior to the intervention, the practitioner needs to assess the frequency, intensity, duration and onset of the problem, as well as identifying thoughts, physiological arousal and behavioural responses to perceived provocation.

Part of this assessment can be aided by the use of the Novaco anger scale (NAS) (Novaco, 1994). Part A is a self-assessment questionnaire covering thinking, physical arousal and behavioural domains. Part B contains 25 self-report questions covering perception of provocation in the categories of disrespect, unfairness, frustration, annoying traits and irritations.

Subsequent Interventions for anger

Depending on the outcome of the assessment and the presenting problem, the length and number of sessions may vary – there are no hard and fast rules in this regard. Individual practitioners often have preferences for particular interventions or the intervention may be driven by the ratings gained from the assessment. For example, someone scoring highly in the cognitive domain of the NAS part A may benefit from an intervention geared to helping them explore the validity of their beliefs (see Chapter 4). Equally, someone whose scores are higher in the physical arousal domain may benefit more from exploring methods of physical relaxation (see Leahy and Holland, 2000).

When working with people with anger problems using the anger determinants and consequences model, awareness of environmental circumstances can be raised by means of a self-monitoring diary aimed at provocation identification (see below for an example). Clients are asked to identify and record the date and time that they feel increased levels of anger and the situation they are in. They are then required to rate the level of anger and subjective level of control on a numerical scale. By becoming more aware of differing levels of anger and frustration, and the build-up of anger, the client can commence the introduction of healthy coping techniques.

Anger diary

By keeping a running account of the anger experiences in your life, you will become educated about your own anger patterns. This is an important part of treatment. In keeping this diary you should record each anger incident by describing what happened in one or two sentences. After writing down what happened, rate the amount of anger that you experienced by using the following scale:

total control	much control	moderate control	slight control	no control
0	2	4	6	8
no anger	slight anger	frustration	very angry	violently angry

Then use the same scale to rate how well you handled the situation – that is, to rate the degree to which you were able to manage your anger.

Date and time	Rate anger	Rate ability to manage	Describe incident

---

In David's case, his unhelpful anger-related thoughts included 'She will blame me for being late', 'It's not my fault' and 'I won't take any shit.' Once the practitioner (Mulhern) and David had identified these thoughts, the following discussion ensued.

Practitioner: What do you see as being your problem?
David: Anger – it's happening more and more and getting out of control, it's affecting my relationship.
Practitioner: How does your anger affect you?
David: When I'm under pressure, I feel myself getting wound up and everything pisses me off.
Practitioner: You say you feel wound up. Describe to me how that feels?

David:	I get tense, my head throbs and I start clenching my fists.
Practitioner:	What sorts of things go through your mind when you are this tense?
David:	I always seem to get it into my head that someone has or will have a go.
Practitioner:	When was the last time this happened?
David:	With the wife today. I had a job I couldn't leave and the traffic was awful so I was going to be late. I couldn't say no to my boss.
Practitioner:	It sounds as if you were in a dilemma – completing a piece of work or leaving on time.
David:	It was out of my control, but she wouldn't understand that.
Practitioner:	What opportunity did she have to understand?
David:	There was no point. I know what she thinks.
Practitioner:	What does she think?
David:	She would think I was deliberately avoiding taking them to the cinema.
Practitioner:	Were you?
David:	No, she knows I was looking forward to it.
Practitioner:	So, although she may have been upset at your being late, it is unlikely that she would have thought you were deliberately avoiding taking them to the cinema.

Intimate partner violence and mental health

Concepts of violence in mental health literature often tend to be of a forensic nature rather than the stuff of routine clinical practice. However, there are forms of violence that, although perhaps less newsworthy, occur frequently within society, are extremely damaging physically, psychologically and inter-generationally (Coker et al., 2002) and have serious implications for mental health service provision.

Within mental health settings, it is not unusual to encounter people who have or are currently experiencing violence in the context of interpersonal relationships. Although the psychological and physical needs of victims are being increasingly recognised and addressed, while not always routinely screened for by health care services (McNutt et al., 2002), less attention is paid to the perpetrators of intimate partner violence.

Using a CB approach to work with someone who is a perpetrator of intimate partner violence

Let us now look at an example of an individual who has been violent towards his wife and the kinds of factors that are involved.

'Martin'

Martin is a 30-year-old married man with a couple of children, aged 2 and 4. He was referred to the mental health services by his GP for treatment of a six-month major depressive episode.

On initial assessment the critical incident appeared to be that, in his eyes, he had been 'stitched up at work' and 'passed over for promotion again', even though he could and believed that he 'did the job a lot better than the others'.

During the assessment phase, Martin talked about his history in a matter-of-fact and contained way. When asked about the emotional impact of these events, he would shrug and give monosyllabic responses. Talking about his present familial situation or how he felt at being passed over for promotion would lead to Martin being defensive and avoid answering questions. On these occasions he would warn me (Mulhern) not to ask questions about his family. The emotional temperature of the sessions would rise and the atmosphere would be tense.

Practitioner:	How are you feeling at the moment Martin?
Martin:	OK.
Practitioner:	What happens when I start to ask about these events and situations?
Martin:	Nothing.
Practitioner:	You say nothing, and perhaps I'm wrong here, but you seem to get a bit uptight.
Martin:	No I fucking don't you arsehole. Why does everyone have to wind me up?
Practitioner:	What's going through your mind at the moment?
Martin:	I want to teach you a lesson ... but I won't. It's that sometimes people just seem to be criticising me for no reason. I can't answer your questions, so you think I'm stupid. Well I'm not, OK? You are like everyone else.
Practitioner:	I'm sorry if you see it that way, but what I am trying to do is figure out what the problem is and how we can work together to resolve it. I certainly did not intend to imply that you were stupid.
Martin:	OK. I'm sorry. I know you are trying to help.
Practitioner:	What do you think was happening there?
Martin:	I get a bit sensitive to folk at times and I, you know ...
Practitioner:	A bit sensitive and?
Martin:	I want to teach them a lesson.
Practitioner:	What sort of situations?
Martin:	A bit at work, but mainly at home.

Over the next few sessions, a picture of intermittent intimate partner violence emerged. Being passed over for promotion the first time tended to result in an assault–remorse cycle. Prior to the initial incident at work, there had been no previous incidents of domestic violence. He had striven very hard not to be like his father and treat his loved ones as he had once wanted to be treated. The following case formulation illustrates Martin's depression-related assault.

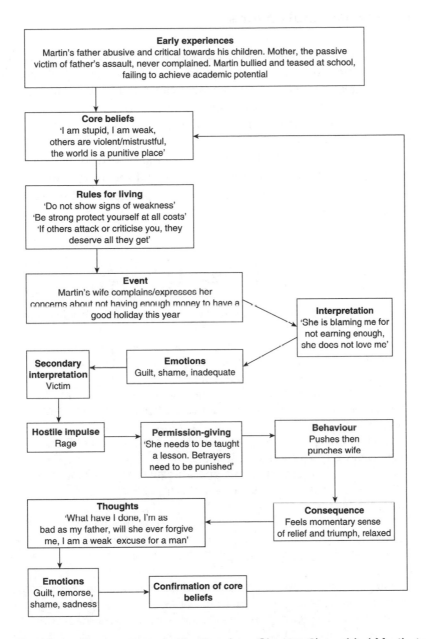

The above linear conceptualisation (see Chapter 2) enabled Martin to understand the way that his behaviour interacted with his mood and thoughts. He agreed that, although the problem was essentially *his*, he needed to involve his spouse in preventing its recurrence.

The therapeutic intervention involved Martin addressing his sense of victimhood without avoiding his emotions. He was able to target unhelpful automatic thoughts in situations and label unhelpful information-processing errors (see Chapter 4). Over time, he managed to effect and maintain change by developing more flexible rules for living that, in turn, resulted in his mood lifting and a cessation of domestic violence.

Broader service implications

Unfortunately, not all people who are perpetrators of domestic violence are as insightful or willing to engage in therapy as Martin. Some incidents are characterised by escalating levels of violence that can result in homicide (Fox and Zawitz, 1999). It is therefore important that practitioners ensure therapeutic interventions are conducted in an environment that is safe for the victim, worker, client and society.

Finally, prior to engaging in therapy it is important to ascertain the extent to which the level of risk of violence may escalate and secure the consent of all relevant stakeholders, including the service user's partner, children, social services, police and legal services.

SUMMARY

- There are clear potential triggers to violence in mental health settings that practitioners need to be aware of.
- Practitioners should also familiarise themselves with, and engage in the fundamentals of, good practice in relation to minimising and responding to violence and aggression.
- Environmental contributors to violence and aggression in inpatient settings are often inadequately considered in a culture of stereotyping and blaming individuals.
- More attention needs to be paid to the importance of practitioners' own belief systems in relation to violence.
- It is important that organisations and practitioners pay more attention to the role of organisational rules and staff beliefs in conceptualising inpatient violence.
- The determinants and consequences model of anger provides a good framework for CB interventions for anger management and there are key points of assessment and intervention emerging from this model.
- Intimate partner violence is an area that has hitherto been eclipsed by more forensic discourses of violence, but is increasingly emerging as a serious concern for both mental health services and practitioners.

Activities

- Reflect on a clinical setting and assess the environment in relation to its potential to reduce the possibility of violent incidents.
- Recall a time when you have been angry and see if it fits within Novaco's determinants and consequences model of anger.

- Reflect on a situation when a patient has been threatening, angry or aggressive. Could that event be explained by the use of Novaco's determinants and consequences model of anger? If so, did the environmental factors (including staff and others) have the effect of decreasing or increasing the behavioural response?

Further reading

Blumenthal, S., and Lavender, T., 2000, *Violence and Mental Disorder: A Critical Aid to the Assessment and Management of Risk.* London: Jessica Kingsley.
A useful guide for practitioners in risk management.

Davies, W., 2000, *Overcoming Anger and Irritability: A Self-help Guide Using CB Techniques.* London: Constable Robinson.
A very good self-help manual appropriate for men and women.

Heery, G., 2001, *Preventing Violence in Relationships: A Programme for Men Who Feel They Have a Problem with Their Use of Controlling Violent Behaviour.* London: Jessica Kingsley.
A very useful programme approach to the group management of domestic violence.

TEN Working with People in Forensic settings

Paul Rogers and Joe Curran

Learning objectives

After reading this chapter and completing the activities at the end of it you should be able to:

1 describe generally the role for CB approaches with forensic clients
2 outline the specific CB skills required
3 describe the ways in which forensic clients may suffer from post-traumatic stress disorder
4 define 'command hallucinations'
5 describe the relationship between risk assessment, compliance with command hallucinations and the role of CB interventions.

Introduction

The English *National Service Framework for Mental Health* (DoH, 1999a) has emphasised the need to prioritise the provision of CB interventions as the central evidence-based, non-pharmacological approach for mental health problems. This has been implemented to some extent within forensic services and a number of medium secure units in Britain currently employ CB psychotherapists, with all three English special hospitals (Broadmoor, Rampton and Ashworth Hospitals) having at one time or another employed one. However, CB interventions in forensic settings continue to be the exception rather than the rule worldwide (Newell and Gournay, 1994; Rogers, 1997a, b; Sullivan and Rogers, 1997; Rogers et al., 2002; Kitchiner, 1999). This chapter aims to demonstrate that forensic service managers and workers internationally should take notice of the therapeutic opportunities offered by the CB approach.

Forensic settings

Forensic settings in Britain are defined as any area where a person may come into contact with the criminal justice system. They include high-, medium- and low-security hospitals, police stations, courts, prisons and probation hostels. This chapter focuses on inpatients in secure hospital environments. Staff in these settings are required to balance the concepts of risk (such as violence to staff), security and containment with care and therapeutic interventions. The culture and leadership within such organisations often determines how well this balance is maintained. For example, where the organisational culture places a great emphasis on security, therapeutic interventions are threatened by bureaucratic red tape, including excessive checking and lack of organisational support. Alternatively, where the organisational culture places a greater emphasis on therapeutic interventions, these are frequently requested and held in high esteem. Given the above, implementing CB approaches in the former kinds of organisations takes time, patience, good communication and an awareness of cultural factors that may influence whether or not an intervention is likely to be successful (see Chapters 5 and 16 for related discussion).

Forensic clients and their problems

Clients are detained in forensic units against their will, due to their having offended or their propensity for offending and the fact that they have a mental health problem. Invariably, when working in such environments, there are two factors that require consideration: the mental health problem and the actual or potential offending behaviour. These provide the following potential scenarios for interventions:

- intervention for offending only – sexual offending, for example
- intervention for disorder only – false beliefs, for example
- intervention for both – such as false belief-driven violence.

CB approaches in such settings are predominantly geared towards the last option, where it is considered that either the offending behaviour harms the individual's mental health or is associated with their offending.

Specific CB skills required

An understanding and working experience of a wide range of CB interventions is required, given the range of clients' problems. Furthermore, experience in formal methods and procedures of risk assessment are desirable. Although, on the whole, many clients will be referred for a clinical problem, it is important that the practitioner is aware of formal, standardised measures of risk and their administration. The HCR-20 (HCR standing for historical, clinical and risk variables) (Webster et al., 1995), for example, is a broad violence risk assessment tool that identifies potential risk indicators for previous, current and future risk (such as previous violence, early maladjustment and insight into mental health problems).

Additionally, an ability to communicate effectively is essential as forensic services depend on this in assessing and managing risks. At first, the need to communicate important points of the assessment and/or intervention may seem tedious and can at times feel intrusive. However, when working with forensic clients, it is important that all members of the clinical team are given information about clients as it is often the case that no one member of the team will have a full picture of them over the full day and week.

Practitioners should also have an ability to remain objective, logical and evidence-based. Sometimes, a client may challenge the beliefs and values of practitioners by the very nature of their offence, (as perpetrators of sexual assault/abuse, for example). Because of this, it is important that workers are able to access clinical supervision and support and able and willing to utilise such resources (see Chapter 5).

As stressed throughout this book, by far the most important skill is collaboration – a concept fundamental to the CB approach. Generally, in adult outpatient settings, practitioners are working with clients who recognise that they have a problem and have some motivation to change. This may not always be the case in forensic settings, where some clients will not discuss their main problems or are ambivalent about therapeutic interventions.

Sometimes, as in false beliefs, this can be as a result of the disorder and the consequent experiences of the client. Equally, it may be an effect of previous interventions – in itself a crucial area of assessment – having been experienced by the client as unhelpful (see Chapter 3). Occasionally, for example, clients may have disclosed things that were then communicated to the clinical team, resulting in a subsequent change of risk status. For example, a patient who informs a practitioner that they are having violent thoughts about certain people may find that their observation levels are increased or even that they are moved to a more secure ward. However, despite the above problems, collaboration is paramount within forensic settings and requires the practitioner to 'work *with*, as opposed to work *against*, people' (Rogers and Vidgen, 2000).

Finally, it is important to work on the client's main problems. Sometimes clinical teams will wrongly define a client's problems. For example, one was referred for a needle phobia as he refused his injections of antipsychotic medication. On assessment, however, it wasn't the needle the client was afraid of, but the side-effects of the medication. In such cases, it is helpful to reformulate the problem. Additionally, and understandably, some clients may test out the practitioner's ability. This can be done by first offering the worker a real, but rather minor, problem and, dependent on the outcome, the client may or may not then disclose a greater problem, while each step of the way assessing the practitioner's ability to cope and assist them.

Post-traumatic stress disorder (PTSD)

PTSD arises from events involving actual or threatened death or serious injury or a threat to the physical integrity of self or others (APA, 1994), during which the sufferer felt intense fear, helplessness or horror. Meichenbaum (1994) has suggested the following classification system for trauma:

- natural disasters – floods, storms, earthquakes and tremors, avalanches
- accidental disasters – plane, train, car, coach
- man-made disasters – bombings, rape, assaults, robbery.

Traumatised individuals develop three clusters of symptom experiences that must be present a month after the traumatic event for a diagnosis of PTSD to be given (APA, 1994):

- *re-experiencing* – having nightmares and intrusive, and unwanted thoughts about the trauma
- *increased arousal* – panic, anxiety and increased jumpiness
- *avoidance* of things that remind the client of their trauma.

It is increasingly being recognised that PTSD is a problem for many patients in forensic settings. Freyne and O'Connor (1992) reported on six prisoners who observed a cellmate's death in prison. Three developed full PTSD and the other three developed some PTSD symptoms. In a separate case, they report how one prisoner developed PTSD after an assault by other prisoners, leading to his attempted suicide. They go on to advise that, due to the high risk of suicidal thoughts and PTSD in this study, all prisoners should be screened for PTSD after witnessing attempted suicide.

Huckle (1995) reported on 22 male rape survivors who had been referred to a forensic psychiatric service over a 6-month period (representing 12.5 per cent of male referrals). Of these 22 subjects, 9 (41 per cent) had a diagnosis of PTSD. Thus, rape-induced PTSD accounted for approximately 6 per cent of all male referrals. Rogers (1997b) described the psychological consequences of male rape in a single case where the client had unwanted and intrusive memories coming to mind, seven times a day and lasting up to an hour each time, when he felt like he was being raped again.

Another interesting area is where PTSD occurs as a consequence of the traumatic effect of killing. To date, research into this has primarily focused on combat veterans or police officers, with little attention being given to mentally disordered offenders. Kruppa et al. (1995) studied the prevalence of PTSD in a sample of 44 inpatients diagnosed as psychopathic who were detained in a British high-security hospital. Of these, 7 (16 per cent) met criteria for a lifetime diagnosis of PTSD related to their index offence. Hambridge (1990) described three cases of grief in perpetrators of homicide. One case – of a 28-year-old man who had strangled his wife – fulfilled the diagnostic criteria for PTSD.

If, as is suggested, PTSD can develop after killing another person, then what are the implications for therapeutic interventions? Rogers et al. (2002) reported on the case of a woman who developed PTSD as a consequence of killing her employer with a knife. The patient had 16 CB sessions and improved on all measures of PTSD and depression symptomatology at 30-month follow-up.

'Michael'

Michael was a 16-year-old male, arrested for attempted murder. He had no previous convictions and no history of mental illness.

Michael's assessing psychiatrist concluded, and reported to the court, that the assault was driven by the client's PTSD.

Michael lived in an inner-city area that had significant drug problems. Two weeks before the attempted murder, three known drug dealers had attacked Michael's mother in her home. Michael awoke in the middle of the night on hearing the front door being kicked in. He ran downstairs and witnessed his mother being attacked. He was then chased upstairs by one of the men, who carried a blood-filled syringe. Michael jumped out of the bedroom window and ran for help. His mother sustained minor physical injuries and the two men were later arrested.

Unfortunately, when news broke of their arrest in the local community, a gang of teenagers began verbally abusing the family and sitting outside their home all day and night. The police were repeatedly called, but, although they would move on, the youths would return soon after.

One day, they began to kick down the door. Michael recounted having a flashback (an intrusive thought or image about the original trauma that produces anxiety similar to that experienced during the trauma) to the previous attack on his mother. As he ran downstairs, he picked up a metal bar and repeatedly attacked the gang, causing significant head injuries to one of them. The judge accepted a defence of diminished responsibility following medical testimony and Michael was released on bail with a condition that he receive outpatient CB help.

On assessment, Michael appeared to be an intelligent, engaging, but shy, muscular young man, highly motivated to engage with the intervention. He had many goals in life, which his problems were stopping him achieving, and he seemed mature for his years. He had been housebound for five months since his arrest and his family had continued to be abused. He reported, confirmed by the police, that three months earlier, following an evening at the gym, he had been followed home by three youths carrying knives. He was convinced that they would have stabbed him had they caught him. He knew them all by name – two having previously been his friends.

Because of the conflict between Michael and his family and known drug dealers in the area, the local police had arranged for a steel door to replace the front door and an emergency alarm was placed in the house that linked directly to the police station.

Michael had heard, through a cousin, that there was a 'notice' out for him to be 'cut up', as, by now, he had been involved in the prosecution of two local drug dealers and put three people in hospital. As a consequence, he rarely slept, keeping vigil from his bedroom at night.

He had a range of makeshift weapons next to every window and door in the house and never left it alone. The only respite he received was when his uncle came in his van twice a week and took him several miles into the countryside where he would exercise by riding his bike for four hours.

An explicit definition of Michael's problem was collaboratively developed and agreed with him:

> Panic and flashbacks when reminded of the attack on my mum, causing me to avoid leaving the house, frequently checking the doors and windows, leading to low mood, lack of independence and anger.

Michael's case formulation

A three systems model was used to draw up the case formulation of Michael's problem (see Chapter 2).

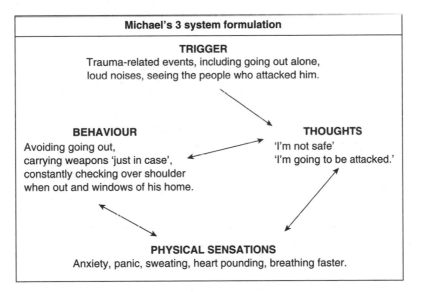

Although Michael clearly met the diagnostic criteria for PTSD (APA, 1994), his case was complicated. The central dilemma in the intervention was that, although a CB intervention was justified, how could it be carried out in circumstances where Michael could be killed if he left the house? In addition, if the 'safety' weapons were removed and the house was attacked again, what could this mean for Michael and his family?

The formulation in such a case is difficult. Here, it proved impossible to determine which experiences were associated with PTSD (such as 'hypervigilance' – regularly looking or checking for signs of danger – increased startle response, avoidance of going out and intrusive thoughts of the original attack) and which were normal responses to the levels of threat that he and his family were being subjected to. Furthermore, and as worrying, was the question of what might happen to Michael if he were exposed to a circumstance that resulted in him having to defend himself and attack another person? Thus, the issues of the risk to him and the risk of him harming other people could not be ignored.

Consequently, following open and honest discussion between Michael and his therapist, it was jointly decided that CB work could only take place once he (and his family) were removed from the situation. Only then could the true extent of his PTSD be assessed. This was a major task as relocation of families in such circumstances can be difficult to organise. Nonetheless, following a number of multi-agency meetings taking four months, it was achieved. These meetings involved the probation service, the local psychiatric service, forensic psychiatric service, social services and housing department and were usually attended by senior managers of these services and senior police officers.

It was agreed that, in the best interests of the family and the local community, the family would be relocated and their address kept secret. Michael often became frustrated at the lack of progress during the period leading up to this outcome, but, at the same time, reported that he was very pleased with his therapist as he could see that he was actively doing something to resolve his difficulties. This strengthened their collaboration and the therapeutic alliance, which was valuable later on in the course of the intervention. During the period of relocation, the role of the therapist was to offer support to Michael and his family and problem-solving (Hawton and Kirk, 1989) regarding potential eventualities – what to do if the house was attacked, for example. Interestingly, according to his self-report, the effect of moving the family significantly reduced Michael's PTSD symptoms, by at least 50 per cent.

Case reassessment

On reassessment following the family's relocation, Michael reported being able to leave his house regularly during daylight hours, though only while carrying a knife. He still had the following problems:

- trouble getting off to sleep
- nightmares about the attack on his mother and the attack on himself
- nightmares about the attack that he carried out
- being hypervigilant when out of the house
- startle response to people running behind him, fast cars, people shouting or similar loud noises
- panic whenever he saw groups of youths
- flashbacks throughout the day involving images of his mother being attacked.

Michael's CB intervention

Michael took part in 12 sessions of exposure (Leahy and Holland, 2000) to real-life, day-to-day situations that triggered off his fear, including leaving his house. However, the priority at this stage was to stop him carrying weapons. This was achieved by problem-solving what to do if he were attacked and Michael decided to join a self-defence class at a local college.

Within six weeks, Micheal was confidently leaving the house without a weapon and stated that he no longer felt the need for one. At the same time, imaginal exposure to both traumas (his mother being attacked and his attack on the youths) was facilitated with a very good reduction in anxiety, nightmares and intrusive thoughts. 'Imaginal exposure' involves assisting the client to recount their memories of the trauma, including their thoughts and feelings at the time, and this is audiotaped. Clients are then encouraged to listen to the audiotape daily. Although this usually results in short-term distress, it greatly reduces with repeated exposure over time (Falsetti, 1997).

Still adhering to the exposure rationale, the next stage of the intervention was designed to reduce Michael's hypervigilance. An audiotape was made that had intermittent noises on it. These included shouting, loud noises, crashing windows, banging doors, fast cars and footsteps. Michael was encouraged to listen to this on his way to college and back every day and resist the urge to look back and scan his environment. He soon got used to this and gradually, over three weeks, his checking behaviour stopped.

Evaluation showed that Michael no longer met the criteria for PTSD and his scores on the psychological questionnaires all supported this. Michael was discharged and followed up at one-, three- and six-month intervals. At each follow-up session, Michael reported that he had maintained all the gains he had made during the intervention.

Command hallucinations

The CB approach offers many opportunities for individuals experiencing command hallucinations within forensic environments. Hellerstein et al. (1987: 219) defined command hallucinations as auditory hallucinations that:

> Order particular acts, often violent or destructive ones ... [and] ... instruct a patient to act in a certain manner – ranging from making a gesture or grimace to committing suicidal or homicidal acts.

The experience of command hallucinations is clearly a concern in forensic settings, given that people may respond to hallucinatory instructions to commit violent acts and Rogers et al. (1990) found that 38 per cent of all patients in a secure hospital experienced command hallucinations. However, only recently have the true risks of command hallucinations been quantified (Rogers et al., 2002). Specifically, an examination of the research literature shows that:

- there is no relationship between unspecified content command hallucinations (non-dangerous content commands such as 'Make a cup of tea') and risk

- there is evidence for a relationship between violent content command hallucinations ('Hit him, hit him') and violence for patients during the three-month period preceding admission when individuals are able to act freely and therefore behave violently
- there is a relationship between self-harm command hallucinations ('Cut yourself') and self-harm behaviour in inpatient settings.

Command hallucination *content* therefore appears to be a specific factor in determining risk. However, this alone is not sufficient for understanding the risk as not all clients do what command hallucinations tell them to do. At present, it is unknown exactly what factors predict which patients will do what the commands tell them and which will not. Nonetheless, when a person *does* comply with command hallucinations, the risks are enormous.

Numerous case reports have described people acting on a dangerous command – sexual offending (Pam and Rivera, 1995), violence to others (Good, 1997), self-amputation of a limb (Hall et al., 1981), self-amputation of the penis (Hall et al., 1981), swallowing objects (Karp et al., 1991), self-mutilation of the eyes (Field and Waldfogel, 1995), self-inflicted lacerations (Rowan and Malone, 1997) and suicide (Zisook et al., 1995).

'James'

James was a man in his late thirties, detained in a secure hospital.

James' early family history was characterised by numerous violent attacks by his natural father, who had received treatment for alcoholism. His parents divorced when James was nine and his mother remarried a year later. James described a relatively stable family environment thereafter.

James first came into contact with the police at the age of 14, for minor stealing offences. In his mid-twenties, James and 5 other people robbed a 93-year-old lady. During the robbery, she sustained a broken arm, a black eye, was tied to the bed and had £500-worth of goods stolen from her. James, the lookout during this offence, maintained that he did not know the others would be violent.

James received a two-year prison sentence, while the others received between five and eight years. At the time there was a public outcry, as the victim later died in hospital from cardiac failure and a stroke. Consequently, other prisoners had targeted the group for punishment beatings.

James asked for, and was granted, 'rule 43' (self-imposed isolation in prison) and it was at this time that he first began hearing a single male voice telling him that he should kill himself. Thereafter, for the following 12 years, James had a significant history of psychiatric contact (including numerous inpatient admissions), due to the voice telling him to self-harm and attempt suicide, which he had complied with or tried to comply with on many occasions. During this time, James occasionally reported that the voice told him to hurt others, which he occasionally acted on.

James was admitted to the secure hospital after he had stabbed his stepfather three times with a knife while his stepfather was asleep. After the attack, he immediately reported the attack to the police and ambulance services and said that the voice 'told him to do it'. James was drinking heavily at the time of his offence, which he said quietened the voice. Additionally, he was using amphetamines and heroin on a daily basis.

On assessment, James was very motivated to obtain help and expressed remorse for his actions. He reported hearing a voice from a number of objects (television, stereo, fan, the taps), calling him abusive names and telling him to 'hit', 'attack' or 'kill'. On average, he reported that they occurred twice a day and lasted for an hour, with the volume of the voice varying from a whisper to shouting. However, on the day of the attack, the voice had been continuous all day and at a loud volume.

Although the voice never identified itself by name, James was totally convinced that it belonged to the son of the old lady whose assault he had been involved in, the purpose of it was to torment him for his part in the robbery and it would not stop until he killed himself. The voice had not left him alone since the offence and frequently told him to kill himself. James believed that the voice was extremely powerful, could predict the future and as powerful as the devil but not as powerful as God.

James reported that the only way he was able to stop or 'turn off' the voice was by drinking great amounts of alcohol and/or taking illicit drugs (see Chapter 8). He reported that some commands were obeyed all the time ('drink tea', 'eat food', 'smoke', 'go to the toilet', 'have a bath', 'listen to the radio', watch TV').

On the day of the offence, the voice told James that his stepfather was the devil, whom he should kill, which would, in turn, free him from the torment of the voice.

On assessment, measurement consisted of the following:

- problem and target measurement (see Chapter 3)
- strength of belief ratings (SoB; Chadwick and Birchwood, 1994). This is a self-report measure of percentage conviction in identified beliefs. Items are rated by the client on a 0–100 per cent point scale.

James' case formulation

James' risk was clearly attributable to his command hallucinations, which, in turn, were significant in determining risk. He was detained under an enforced hospital treatment order. A successful intervention for his command hallucinations would be likely to reduce his risk status. Alternatively, should this not be possible, then an intervention to reduce his compliance with the command hallucinations would be warranted. Additionally, his misuse of disinhibiting substances needed to be addressed.

In understanding James' command hallucinations, it is important to remember that they began after he was found guilty of aiding the robbery of the old lady's home and being 'targeted' within prison perpetuated this guilt. Chadwick et al. (1996) have developed a very useful clinical aid when working with such cases – that of persecution or punishment or 'poor me/bad me'. People with 'poor me' beliefs assume a victim position and usually do not engage with the voices, which they perceive to be undeserved and unwarranted. People with 'bad me' beliefs, however, feel that their voices are deserved and perceive themselves to be bad and have done bad things and so are more likely to respond to the instructions of their voices. James felt very guilty about the offence regarding the old lady and believed that he deserved to be punished. As such, it was James' beliefs about the voice (origin, intent, deservedness) that fuelled it and contributed to his risk, guilt, alcohol misuse and drug taking. This is illustrated in his case formulation.

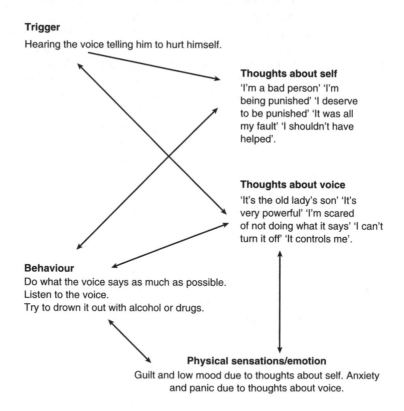

Trigger
Hearing the voice telling him to hurt himself.

Thoughts about self
'I'm a bad person' 'I'm being punished' 'I deserve to be punished' 'It was all my fault' 'I shouldn't have helped'.

Thoughts about voice
'It's the old lady's son' 'It's very powerful' 'I'm scared of not doing what it says' 'I can't turn it off' 'It controls me'.

Behaviour
Do what the voice says as much as possible.
Listen to the voice.
Try to drown it out with alcohol or drugs.

Physical sensations/emotion
Guilt and low mood due to thoughts about self. Anxiety and panic due to thoughts about voice.

James' CB intervention

The CB intervention used to help James consisted of, first, developing a collaborative relationship, then helping James to self-monitor his voice, challenge his beliefs about it and engage in behavioural experiments (see Chapter 4).

James' beliefs about the power of the voice were the focus of therapy. The following beliefs James identified on assessment were as follows (the original strength of each belief (SoB) is given in parenthesis after it).

- the voice is so powerful it can communicate to everyone (SoB 95 per cent)
- the voice belongs to the lady's son (SoB 100 per cent)
- the voice controls everything that I do (SoB 100 per cent)
- the voice is so powerful because I cannot control it (SoB 100 per cent)

The last belief listed above was the first worked on and James was taught coping strategy enhancement (CSE; Yusopoff and Tarrier, 2000). CSE is a technique that helps people to learn strategies for coping with voices by using distraction – loud music, physical activity and so on. This involves, first, trying to bring on the voice. James was initially very reluctant to try this as he had never previously been able to turn it off. This was the first and only time that the therapeutic alliance was challenged as he was being asked to place significant trust in his therapist and do something that he feared. However, with encouragement and support, he agreed to try. The main strategy used to bring on the voice was to ask James to think of the robbery of the old lady and her death, thereby inducing guilt. Within seconds, James' voice began and he recounted what it said in session: 'evil', 'weak', 'her', 'kill you', 'run bastard', 'kill them', 'kill', 'die', 'kill, die'.

James was asked to try and stop the voice, but didn't know how to. He became frightened and said that the voice was 'very strong'. James was asked what he would ordinarily do if his voice was this bad and he replied, 'Get drunk and drown it out.' Instead, James was encouraged to try out a range of different coping strategies. He found the most useful were listening to loud music on his headphones, engaging in conversation about things he found interesting (such as horse racing) and going to the gym. This behavioural experiment was agreed as daily homework.

After two weeks, James reported that he was able to turn the voices on and off at will, which, naturally, weakened his belief that he could not control the voice. Furthermore, this had a strong effect on the therapeutic alliance (see Chapter 2) as James had placed his trust in the therapist despite his fears. This allowed both parties to strengthen the relationship, which served to benefit later work.

The results of this first experiment encouraged James to fully engage with the therapeutic aims and he became noticeably more confident in discussing the voice, its meaning and other possible experiments. Thus, an experiment was agreed to test out his belief that the voice was heard by others. Previously, James had rarely discussed his voice and had always assumed that other people could also hear it. The experiment consisted of James randomly picking 12 members of the nursing staff and asking them if they could hear the voice. He also asked friends and family when they visited. As all people said they didn't hear it, the strength of this belief reduced to 0 per cent – and he started to independently question the power of the voice and how he had previously viewed it.

After this, James' belief as to the meaning of the voice and why it was punishing him was examined by discussing his own guilt about the offence. He rated this as 100 per cent and said, 'If I had stopped them going in, then it wouldn't have happened.' James stated that he had, in fact, tried to dissuade the men from going into the house, but, with hindsight, felt that he should have tried to physically stop them. He also stated he shouldn't have taken the money and could have phoned the police afterwards.

This belief was examined by asking James to reconsider his options at the time and not with hindsight and also to apportion percentage responsibility to all involved. Three sessions later, his belief of 100 per cent responsibility reduced to 20 per cent. He reported that he was frightened of the men who attacked the lady and it wasn't his idea. He disclosed that he had managed to dissuade those involved from the robbery on one previous occasion. Further, he reported that he thought the house was empty, had no idea what they did while he was outside keeping watch and didn't accept any of the goods they stole.

A written record was made of these responses and James was encouraged to keep this record and to take it out whenever the voice started and he felt strong guilt about his actions. As time went by, James reported that the punishing content of the voice was changing and it was less likely to command him to self-harm or try to kill himself. Consequently, his belief about the origin of the voice changed. He still thought that it could be the old lady's son, but was less certain and rated his belief in this as 40 per cent.

The third belief – that the voice controlled everything that James did – was challenged during one session after he automatically and innocently scratched his arm. He was asked why he did this and said that his arm was itchy. This was used to then generate doubt that the voice controlled all his actions all the time.

A behavioural experiment was set up whereby James recorded whether everyday tasks over two weeks were completed because he wanted to do them or because the voice told him and made him. These tasks included walking, smoking, talking, going to the toilet and other day-to-day activities.

At the following session, James had recorded that, in the vast majority of cases, the tasks had been self-generated and, after he thought about the task, the voice would then tell him to do it. On the occasions when the voice told him to do something and he hadn't thought about this beforehand, he reported that he only did the task if he wanted to. Thereafter, James was asked to record all tasks that the voice made him do, against his will, over a one-week period. The result was none. James' strength of belief ratings significantly improved with no endorsements of previously held beliefs.

Following this, James received general psycho-education about psychosis and how other people report similar experiences. Kingdon and Turkington (1991) argued that cognitive techniques can help clients construe false beliefs in non-psychotic terms by examining their beliefs in a collaborative non-confrontational manner and offering alternative explanations (see Chapter 6). James found the information that he had been given to read about psychosis very helpful and became confident that his experiences were a psychological disorder made worse by guilt rather than him being persecuted by malevolent forces. The client's clinical team corroborated these improvements.

James' voice, while still present, no longer holds the same fear as previously. At the end of the intervention, James described feeling more in control and able to turn the voice on and off at will.

Emerging issues

Previous clinical intervention outcome research for people with command hallucinations has excluded patients who have acted on commands to seriously injure themselves or others. James' case offers further support for the CB interventions first proposed by Chadwick and Birchwood (1994) and suggests that such an intervention may be of benefit to those clients who have a history of doing what the commands tell them, even when they are severe commands.

The current available risk literature strongly suggests that analysis of risk should be confined to 'static' factors, such as a person's history of offending, and, on the whole, this has benefits for understanding the relative risk that a person poses. However, such models of risk do not allow for individual identification of factors, which either inhibit or increase risk. Therefore, a more detailed analysis, involving the identification and appraisal of other factors, is required, including cognitive factors (Beck-Sander and Clark, 1998).

If beliefs about voices affect compliance with CB interventions, then undoubtedly this presents many possible opportunities. In relation to command hallucinations, risk assessment could be improved by identifying those clients who are at risk of complying with command hallucinations and those who are not. This will allow services to better determine which clients are in need of the scant resources available to forensic services. Furthermore, and of equal importance, by identifying those likely to comply, we will also be able to more accurately determine which clients are safe to be discharged back into the community. The ability to identify which beliefs affect compliance leads to the possibility of CB interventions being employed in an attempt to alter them.

SUMMARY

- Despite a clearly emerging, evidence-based role for CB approaches with forensic clients, such interventions are the exception rather than the rule, worldwide.
- There are clear general and specific skills required in order to use CB interventions with forensic clients.
- Forensic clients may suffer from post-traumatic stress disorder in several distinct ways, illustrated in the case formulation and intervention for 'Michael'.
- Command hallucinations represent another area where the CB approach can be of great benefit, illustrated in the case formulation and intervention for 'James'.
- The relationship between risk assessment and compliance with command hallucinations, gives a clear and exciting future role for CB interventions.

Activities

- Michael's case demonstrates one of the core assessment issues that can never be overlooked in forensic settings – specifically, the effects that an intervention will have and the potential consequences of such effects. Discuss this with a colleague who has read this chapter.
- Discuss the advantages and limitations of applying the intervention described in James' case to similar clients.

Further reading

Chadwick, P., Birchwood, M., and Trower, P., 1996, *Cognitive Therapy for Hallucinations, Delusions, Voices and Paranoia*. Chichester: John Wiley.
Written by respected authors who have been working actively in this area to establish both principles of theory and practice, this book gives very good descriptions of how to make a cognitive assessment of both hallucinations and delusions, which measures to use and the latest methods of intervention. This book formed the basis for the second case study in this chapter.

Foa, E., Keane, T., and Friedman, M., 2000, *Effective Treatments for PTSD*. New York: Guilford Press.
This comprehensive book from the leading authorities on psychological trauma provides best practice guidelines for the treatment of PTSD. It was developed under the auspices of the PTSD Treatment Guidelines Task Force of the International Society for Traumatic Stress Studies. The book is a well-used reference book and source of advice, and greatly assisted in the intervention provided for the first case in this chapter.

ELEVEN Working with People in Assertive Outreach

Jem Mills, Alec Grant,
Ronan Mulhern and Nigel Short

Learning objectives

After reading this chapter and completing the activities at the end of it you should be able to:

1 identify the key aspects of assertive outreach
2 identify the people most likely to benefit from an assertive outreach approach
3 discuss the relationship between assertive outreach and social control
4 identify how the CB approach fits with the recovery concept
5 generate CB formulations of resistance
6 identify how the CB approach might be incorporated into assertive outreach work.

Introduction

Assertive outreach is the British version of an intensive, community-based mental health service first developed in North America in the 1970s. Although assertive outreach has varied in its development internationally, research evidence indicates a number of shared core components (DoH, 2001b):

- a self-contained team responsible for providing the full range of interventions
- a single responsible medical officer who is an active member of the team
- treatment provided on a long-term basis with an emphasis on continuity of care
- the majority of services delivered in the community
- emphasis on maintaining contact with service users and building relationships
- care coordination provided by the assertive outreach team
- small caseload – no more than 12 service users per member of staff.

The approach is aimed at people for whom traditional services have proved unpalatable. This could apply to many in the population, but the Department of Health (2001b) describes a common profile. This includes people with a severe and persistent mental disorder (such as psychosis), a history of high use of inpatient or intensive home-based care, and those who have difficulty in maintaining lasting and consenting contact with services and have multiple and complicated needs.

People with this profile commonly experience a variety of practical and social difficulties (Hemming et al., 1999) such as poor general health, low income and unemployment. In addition, such people are likely to be homeless or in unstable accommodation, with few social contacts and experiencing difficulties with shopping, budgeting and personal hygiene.

The potential outcomes of the assertive outreach approach have been identified as (DoH, 2001b):

- improved engagement with services
- reduced hospital admissions
- reduced length of stay in hospital
- increased stability in the lives of service users and their carers/family
- improved social functioning
- cost-effectiveness.

Assertive outreach as social control?

The term 'assertive outreach' first became prominent in British government literature with the publication of the White Paper 'Modernising Mental Health Services' (DoH, 1998). The central message – that services would become more 'safe, sound and supportive' – followed a wave of policy development concerned with public safety. This notably occurred at the same time as a small number of high-profile incidents in which carers or professionals were killed by people experiencing mental illness (Ryan, 1999). The underlying implication was that the rapid refocusing of mental health services from residential to community-based care had failed to provide adequate monitoring of those people at risk of harming others and this had led to an increase in violence by people experiencing mental health problems. However, it has since been strenuously argued that the community care of people experiencing mental distress has contributed nothing to the general rise in violence in British society and over-reporting is to blame for this misconception (Hemming et al., 1999).

Despite this, Morrall (2000) argues that public fear of people with severe emotional and psychological difficulties is not just a product of overzealous media reporting, but also stems from mental health professionals' reluctance to acknowledge the social control aspects of their roles. He argues that the increasingly controlling nature of mental health services is a consequence of society's failure to address this negative public perception. Interestingly, professional resistance to the social control aspects of assertive outreach is not explicit in mainstream mental health literature.

Confusion about the function of assertive outreach

... there has been considerable debate about, and resistance to, the prescription of the model, and this has served to confuse local service developers and hamper their attempts to implement the service effectively.

(Davidson and Lowe, 2001: 2)

Ryan (1999) shows that at the outset the message 'safe, sound and supportive' (DoH, 1998) contains inherent contradictions that serve to confuse those seeking to develop assertive outreach services. Despite the clear link to a social control agenda, the term 'safe' is applied to the public, mental health service users and their carers. As Ryan (1999: 4) rightly asks, 'whose safety actually comes first? Where are services to place priorities?'

Right from the very beginning it seems as if assertive outreach has been influenced by the need to address a variety of organisational and public health issues, not just the needs of those most affected by mental distress. These apparently contradictory influences are arguably difficult to contain within the everyday practice of assertive outreach workers. The result can be conflict among the professionals involved in its delivery, which has its own deleterious consequences (Mills, 2003). A sad consequence of this is the tendency for professionals to blame themselves for not being able to contain these conflicting influences. Professionals can view themselves as deviant when they choose to prioritise client need over the needs of the organisation (Mills, 2003). Dealing with these conflicting influences, along with the reluctance towards acknowledging the social control aspects of the work, may be a factor in the rise of a more client-focused model of care within assertive outreach – namely the recovery model.

What is recovery?

Recovery is the process by which people start to live their lives more fully after experiencing catastrophic events, such as serious illness, accidents, bereavement, financial devastation or personal attacks. The concept is more commonly associated with managing physical disabilities and illnesses, moving beyond the idea of cure to living with suffering or reduced abilities.

Anthony (1993) describes the inclusive nature of the concept, given that all human beings will experience some catastrophic event in their lifetimes. The event will never be forgotten – it becomes part of the person as they find a way to move on. The process is an individual one, although commonalities are shared.

The concept of recovering from mental illness varies among people, particularly between practitioners and their clients. Meddings and Perkins (2002) found that people with mental health problems were more likely to associate recovery with having more money, a job and somewhere nice to live. Practitioners from a range of disciplines tended to give higher priority to accessing help and daily living activities as signs of recovery. Although both groups identified symptom reduction as important, improved mental well-being is often only a first step in the process within a recovery model:

> People with mental illness may have to recover from the stigma they have incorporated into their very being; from the iatrogenic effects of treatment settings; from the lack of recent opportunities for self-determination; from the negative side-effects of unemployment; and from crushed dreams.
>
> Anthony, 1993: 15

It is difficult to describe a process of recovery, given the individual nature of people's experiences. However, Townsend et al. (2000) identify a number of principles (described below) that can guide the application of a recovery model to mental health and, in particular, to the incorporation of the CB approach within assertive outreach work.

Recovery, compassion and CB case formulation

The principles of the recovery model arguably have much to offer the development of the CB approach. For instance, the problem-focused nature of CB work can leave people feeling as if all their worst points have suddenly been placed before them or that their current distress is related to deeply ingrained inadequacies (James, 2001). This is not so within a strengths/assets model, which seeks to build on the helpful aspects of the person's reactions to their difficult circumstances. One way in which to incorporate these ideas into a CB approach is to develop the notion of a 'compassionate case formulation'. This attempts to highlight the adaptive nature of the compensatory strategies that the person has developed as a result of their life experiences. It suggests reducing the use of these strategies in less helpful contexts, but building them up in the helpful ones. One example is the tendency to 'people please' that those with low self-esteem often develop (Fennell, 1997). This strategy is usually adopted in childhood as a way of avoiding rejection or some kind of abuse. In adult circumstances, it can have a range of more or less helpful consequences, including:

- being able to easily put one's own needs second to those requiring care
- being extremely helpful to others
- not letting people down
- being very diplomatic
- not being able to say no
- not looking after oneself properly
- coming across as disingenuous.

The compassionate case formulation would lead the person and the practitioner to understand that the people-pleasing strategy was once very useful, if not vital. It also sees it as a potentially useful way of operating that is sometimes overused or used to the person's own detriment. In this way, the person is left with the less daunting prospect of modifying how they apply a natural tendency rather than righting a lifelong problem.

The 12 guiding principles of the recovery concept (Townsend et al., 2000) are listed below, alongside aspects of the CB approach that either fit well or have the potential to be developed.

Recovery model principles	Corresponding aspects of the CB approach
The consumer directs the recovery process, so consumer input is essential throughout the process.	The collaborative and educational nature of the approach seeks to enable the person to apply CB theory and strategies independently – in essence becoming their own therapist.
The mental health system must be aware of its tendency to enable and encourage consumer dependency.	The approach fosters independence and encourages attention to relapse prevention by means of self-knowledge/management. There are times when limited periods of dependence on the practitioner are a useful part of the process and these are discussed explicitly (Beck et al., 1990; Young, 1990; Leahy, 2001).
Consumers are able to recover more quickly when their: • hope is encouraged, enhanced, and/or maintained • life roles with respect to work and meaningful activities are defined • spirituality is considered • culture is understood • education needs as well as those of their family/significant others are identified • socialisation needs are identified.	The linking of CB work to explicit goals defined with the person help to foster hope and make it directly relevant to their life circumstances. However, the CB approach has a tendency to individualise problems and concentrate on internal psychological mechanisms. For instance, there is great scope for developing the cultural and gender sensitivity of CB work (see also Chapter 15).
Individual differences are considered and valued across their lifespan.	An individualised, compassionate case formulation approach can incorporate these aspects, but is less apparent with more technique-focused styles of CB work (see Epilogue).
Recovery from mental illness is most effective when a holistic approach is considered. In order to reflect current best practice, there is a need to merge all intervention models, including medical, psychological, social and recovery.	CB psychotherapy is often presented as having great potential for integrating other approaches. For instance, the application of CB methods for people hearing voices draws heavily on vulnerability stress models (Kingdon and Turkington, 1994), which have the capacity to draw together a bio-psychosocial approach.
Practitioners' initial emphasis on hope and the ability to develop trusting relationships influences the consumer's recovery.	This principle is fundamental to any psychotherapeutic approach (see Chapter 2).
Practitioners operate from a strengths/assets model.	The CB approach has a problem focus, which can have negative consequences. These can possibly be addressed by developing the notion of a compassionate case formulation (see above).

(Continued)

(Continued)

Recovery model principles	Corresponding aspects of the CB approach
Practitioners and consumers collaboratively develop a recovery management plan. This plan focuses on the interventions that will facilitate recovery and the resources that will support the recovery process.	The problem-solving nature of CB work, alongside attention to environmental factors impeding recovery, can work well with this principle.
Family involvement may enhance the recovery process. The consumer defines their family unit.	Mainstream CB work is not usually associated with family involvement. There is a tradition of including significant others as co-therapists, but attention to wider family dynamics and the potential for drawing on family resources is often neglected.
Mental health services are most effective when delivery is within the context of the consumer's community.	Traditionally, like other psychological interventions, the CB approach has been applied within healthcare settings. However, there are examples of using telephone and Internet contact (Burgess and Chalder 2001; Kenardy et al., 2003). Adapting CB methods to suit the client's own environment is something that an assertive outreach approach can bring to CB work.
Community involvement as defined by the consumer is important to the recovery process.	The CB approach has hitherto paid very little attention to community aspects of a person's recovery. This presents another development opportunity for the approach.

Engagement and resistance

People in all walks of life resist healthcare services for a variety of reasons. For instance, it is quite common for people to stop taking medication such as antibiotics when they start to feel better. Fear and avoidance of dental treatment is commonplace and people often ignore physical symptoms of illness, hoping that they will right themselves. These types of resistance obviously occur with mental health problems as well, but are complicated by three major factors:

- mental health treatment can be compulsory
- there is great stigma associated with mental health problems
- mental health services can be invalidating, abusive and traumatising (Johnstone, 2000).

People targeted by assertive outreach teams have been described as:

> ... a small number of people with severe mental health problems with complex needs who have difficulty engaging with services and often require repeat admission to hospital.
>
> DoH, 2001b: 26

This description demonstrates a problematic, one-sided view of the issue of engagement. Conceiving people's resistance to mental health services in this way plays down the possibility that previous contact with services may have:

- failed to meet people's needs
- been invalidating
- been experienced as abusive or unsafe
- constituted a traumatic incident, leading to enduring psychological and emotional consequences.

Moving beyond the view that people mainly resist mental health services because of a lack of insight into their illness can lead to more flexible and creative approaches to building collaborative relationships. The CB approach has two particularly valuable sources of flexibility and creativity applicable to the issue of engagement. These are structured assessment and models of resistance.

Structured assessment

A process of structured, comprehensive assessment can be very useful in developing an in-depth understanding of issues surrounding resistance to services. In particular, the service engagement scale (Tait et al., 2002) highlights the following 14 aspects of client difficulty with engagement, grouped under 4 headings:

- **availability**

  1 the client seems to make it difficult to arrange appointments
  2 when a visit is arranged, the client is available*
  3 the client seems to avoid making appointments

- **collaboration**

  4 if you offer advice, does the client usually resist it?
  5 the client takes an active part in the setting of goals or treatment plans*
  6 the client actively participates in managing their illness*

- **seeking help**

  7 the client seeks help when assistance is needed*
  8 the client finds it difficult to ask for help
  9 the client seeks help to prevent a crisis*
  10 the client does not actively seek help

- **treatment adherence**

  11 the client agrees to take prescribed medication*
  12 the client is clear about what medications they are taking and why*
  13 the client refuses to cooperate with treatment
  14 the client has difficulty in adhering to the prescribed medication.

The items are rated 0 (not at all or rarely) 1 (sometimes), 2 (often), 3 (most of the time).The items with asterisks are reverse scored.

Although the service engagement scale necessarily focuses on client behaviour as an observable measure, the authors emphasise that 'there are often valid reasons

Dimensions of resistance	How this dimension might be triggered	Clinical example
Validation	Dominance of medical model prioritises focus on symptoms of illness and taking medication. This can invalidate the person's individual perspective of distress.	'Sally' avoids appointments with her psychiatrist because she finds him unwilling to engage in discussion about her spiritual crises. She refuses to take medication as it interferes with her ability to hear God's commands. The mental health services describe this journey to enlightenment as an illness.
Emotional schemas	All mental health services include a process of assessment of the person's distress.	'Adrian' believes that, if he talks about his difficulties, he will be overwhelmed by his emotions. He thinks that if he starts to feel emotional, he might lose control of himself and hurt someone. He avoids any depth of discussion about his distressing experiences by referring to his problems as a pain in his head.
Self-consistency	Mental health services highlight the need for change.	'Bijal' has just about coped with her problems by never throwing anything away. It feels as if this way of coping is part of who she is as a person. She feels that if she changes now she will be giving up a big part of herself.
Schematic resistance	Mental health services offer help.	Because 'Dave' believes that he is evil, he also believes he does not deserve to be helped. He tries to make sure that he is out when his practitioner calls.
Victim resistance	Mental health services encourage people to take responsibility for their problems.	'Izzy' believes that her difficulties stem from her relationship with her family. Her family say that Izzy is to blame for her troubles. She thinks that accepting help for her problems is giving in to this view. She becomes angry when practitioners suggest change.
Moral resistance	Mental health services encourage change and a focus on various factors that trigger distress.	'Cyril' believes that his voices are a punishment for a series of things he did in his childhood. Although he knows that medication helps, he also believes that he deserves this punishment and so regularly stops taking it.
Risk-aversion	Mental health services encourage independence.	'Marie' believes that she will always need help. When she feels unsupported, she has thoughts about suicide. She worries that if she improves, she will be discharged from the service and end up killing herself. She tries to underplay her progress and ensure that she always has a problem she needs help with.
Self-handicapping	Mental health services encourage people's involvement in their care.	'Danny' believes that he is a failure and anything he tries will go wrong. He believes that if he tries to change, he will fail and people will see how useless he is. He finds ways in which to avoid the changes to his lifestyle suggested by his practitioner.

for client withdrawal from services or non-acceptance of services' (Tait et al., 2002: 92). Once an individualised and specific profile of a person's behaviour towards services is understood, a more in-depth understanding of the factors at play can be achieved by considering the reasons behind this resistance.

Leahy's (2001) model of resistance to therapy formulates a range of interactions between the therapist or therapy process and clients' beliefs about themselves or their difficulties. He presents eight dimensions of resistance, related to both client and therapist beliefs and behaviour. This model – outlined in the dimensions of resistance table above – can arguably be mapped on to the process of engagement with mental health services.

Applying these principles within a recovery model encourages collaborative reflection on the relationship between people and mental health services. The first steps in addressing resistance involve acknowledging the process and accepting the person's need for validation. It is helpful to acknowledge that services need to make changes as much as those using them. When trying to help a person understand their avoidance of services, the perspective outlined here poses questions such as the following.

- What have previous contacts with mental health services been like for this person?
- What implicit messages have been given about their experiences and themselves?
- What needs does the person have and how well have these been met in the past?
- What skills can this person develop in order to get more from services?
- What feelings and thoughts does this person have about the process of change?

Previous negative experiences of mental health services or current emotional distress can affect a person's expectations (see Chapter 3). Once a person has explored their resistance and understood it more fully, they may well choose to test out some of their ideas tentatively by engaging in small pieces of work. The practitioner can also be careful to work within the confines of the person's resistance and encourage discussion about the costs and benefits of alternative strategies before attempting to engage the person in change-focused work. This approach was central to the way 'Jane' was helped to participate more fully in her care.

'Jane' – using CB principles to understand and foster collaboration

Jane became involved with an assertive outreach team after six years of contact with mental health services. She had originally contacted her family doctor for help with a number of anxiety problems and what she described as anorexia. She saw a series of therapists for behaviour therapy, then CB therapy and finally counselling. Each of these approaches sought to help her with one aspect or another of her list of difficulties including:

- fear of vomiting
- fear of going out alone
- obsessional cleaning rituals
- trying to maintain a healthy low weight
- an abusive relationship with her husband
- regular overdose attempts.

She managed to keep these problems from getting worse with the help of a community nurse and a day hospital team until two years later when her husband died.

Although he had been quite abusive towards her, the circumstances of his death left her feeling extremely guilty. She was admitted to a psychiatric unit after developing voices and visions of her husband and others urging her to harm herself. The following two years saw these problems persist and led to her being regularly readmitted to the same unit.

Jane found it quite easy to engage with the assertive outreach team and soon found that she was quite emotionally dependent on them. This led to practitioners finding it hard to reconcile their attempts to help Jane towards independence with her wish to have more contact with the team. One aspect of Jane's recovery process where this played out was in her care plan review meetings. Clinicians felt that, despite their best efforts, Jane was resisting meaningful involvement in the process. She would appear nervous, not venture any opinions and agree with anything proposed.

A CB approach to this issue began with an engagement process that started with social trips with a practitioner to a local coffee house and took place over six meetings, leading to a period of focus on the problem as it emerged in the relationship with the practitioner. The next ten meetings, mostly in Jane's house, aided the engagement process. This process aimed to develop trust and empathy and drew on the notion of a compassionate case formulation.

The therapist gently acknowledged that getting to know him seemed very difficult for Jane and asked if they could explore this further. Jane agreed, with the condition that she could stop the process if it became too upsetting. Following the methods described in Chapters 2 and 3, they began a process of assessment and formulation. Each step in the process was shared with Jane as reactions to current events were related to previous experiences and underlying beliefs. In the end, she was independently identifying some of the connections and underlying worries described below.

Jane's compassionate case formulation

Jane grew up in a State-run care home after her parents found caring for her too difficult. They both had significant emotional problems of their own. Despite feeling unable to cope with caring for Jane, her mother also insisted that she should not be adopted by another family. This made it difficult for Jane to settle in temporary foster care and, as a result, she spent the majority of her life in the children's home. She was a withdrawn child and was targeted by a member of staff who sexually abused her. She found that the only time she got any feeling of being cared for was when she was physically ill and had to be nursed.

During her time in the children's home, she found that keeping her true feelings and needs to herself reduced the chances of feeling rejected and abandoned when they were not acknowledged or met. However, she found that her emotions became unbearable at times, leading to her cutting herself as a way of controlling them. She also regularly complained of physical health problems, although not so regularly as to arouse suspicion. Jane grew up believing that her needs were not important and, consequently, fell into a series of relationships with men who abused her physically, emotionally and psychologically. She learned that keeping feelings to herself in her relationships protected her from psychological abuse from others. She also found as an adult that if she disclosed her experiences to friends, they would later use the information against her if they fell out. Jane developed a number of beliefs and corresponding strategies from these experiences that were activated during care plan review meetings, as shown in the table below.

Belief	Resistance strategy	Reactions in care plan review meetings
'If I got too anxious I'll lose control and cut myself.'	Avoid or escape from anxiety-provoking situations.	Doing whatever she could to make the meeting as short as possible.
'I can only be cared for if I have problems.'	Always maintaining need for care.	Thinking, 'If I get over my problems I'll be discharged and I won't cope. Avoid talking about any progress being made. Focus on remaining problems.'
'If I'm abandoned I will not survive.'	Avoid rejection by others by people pleasing, hiding true feelings.	Agree to anything suggested by clinicians. Avoid talking about distress regarding independence.

The care team acknowledged Jane's worries first of all, then discussed with her how understandable this reaction was, given her life experiences and consequent beliefs. They also discussed the costs and benefits of her avoidance in this situation. Jane decided to look at ways of addressing her fears about the meetings.

Drawing on the recovery model and the shared formulation of Jane's difficulties with review meetings, the following aims were agreed:

- to acknowledge how difficult reviewing progress is for Jane
- to find ways in which to reduce Jane's anxiety in meetings
- for Jane to feel that she will not be abandoned by the assertive outreach team
- for Jane to feel more in control of decisions about her care.

The care review process was adapted to meet these aims in discussion with Jane. She chose the venue and the practitioners she felt most comfortable about having at the review. The next session, therefore, took place over a picnic in a park close to her home.

Jane was encouraged to give ongoing feedback about the process as it went on and the staff responded to this by adjusting the pace and depth of questions. The first issue discussed was Jane's worry about being abandoned by the team. This was discussed as being quite understandable, given her life experiences, including her previous contact with mental health services. Jane spoke openly about her fears of discussing positive progress and outlined some steps that might reassure her. These included:

- requesting a letter from the service manager explaining the circumstances in which people were discharged from the assertive outreach service and how clients are involved in the process
- having long-term, sequential goals that would help her to see progress as less threatening
- speaking to another client who had had similar fears and later negotiated discharge successfully
- hearing how some clients of the assertive outreach service were more independent than her but still had involvement with the team.

Jane found that, as her anxiety reduced, she was less likely to agree to absolutely anything suggested and more likely to discuss her needs. She was able to bring up a need that the team had not identified and became involved in a plan to meet it.

In the end, both Jane and the assertive outreach workers felt that she was much more directive in the meeting and she felt able to build on this experience of being more open.

CB interventions and techniques in assertive outreach – what works for whom?

As discussed earlier in this book, CB methods have been adapted during the last few decades to address the needs of people for whom medication has always been the mainstay of treatment. Problems include:

- low motivation and energy
- hearing voices
- strange, worrying beliefs
- problems forming and maintaining relationships
- problems with substance misuse
- consequences of childhood trauma
- problems with managing emotions

- rapid shifts in mood
- long-term depression.

These problems are often associated with psychiatric diagnoses of schizophrenia, bipolar disorder, chronic depression and personality disorder.

The publication of the *National Service Framework for Mental Health* (DoH, 1999a) and the creation of the National Institute for Clinical Excellence can be seen as signposts directing a process of policy change for psychiatric care in Britain, mirrored throughout Europe and North America. This prioritises the needs of people experiencing serious mental illness over those with so-called 'common' mental health problems (such as anxiety-based problems and eating disorders).

The National Institute for Clinical Excellence in Britain and the American Psychological Association task force have collated research findings on the efficacy of interventions, citing the randomised controlled trial (RCT) as the gold standard for research methods. In this way, interventions tested for efficacy by RCT are privileged over others (see also Chapter 15). It is not surprising, then, that the CB approach features heavily in policy documents.

The British Mental Health Implementation Guide identifies CB therapy as a key component of the assertive outreach approach and states that 'a range of techniques should be available within the team and used appropriately' (DoH, 2001b: 31). There is no more detail about which techniques are meant or what constitutes 'appropriate use'. What follows here, therefore, is an attempt to explore these issues and offer some ideas about how the CB approach might be further adapted within the context of assertive outreach work.

CB principles, approaches and techniques

A regular criticism of the CB approach is its tendency to view people, and the distress they experience, with medical model-like reductionism. In some respects this criticism is justified, as there is a strong movement within the CB literature arguing for specific 'single strand' 'treatments' for disorders that are derived from the identification of underlying psychological mechanisms (Richards and Lovell, 2000a). However, others – including the four main authors of this book – advocate complicated or multistrand interventions, drawing on in-depth case formulations (see also Epilogue). On a positive note, this tension allows for a spectrum of ideas and techniques to emerge that can be put into practice in a variety of ways.

CB practice available within an assertive outreach approach could be described as within a continuum between broad underpinning principles and in-depth psychotherapy. At the broad principle end of this continuum one might find:

- commitment to collaborative working
- developing more structure in care plans
- developing individual and standardised assessment and evaluation of difficulties.

The example given earlier of how Jane was helped demonstrates this level of work. Further along the contimuum one might find specific techniques that might be made available to a wide range of clients and professionals, such as:

- tests of control over voices
- problem-solving techniques
- engagement strategies, such as addressing beliefs and the meaning of delusions by means of detailed assessment
- coping strategies.

At the other end of the continuum one might find a therapist or student therapist working under supervision to provide more long-term, in-depth help to people, as is the case in the following example.

'Vicky'

When Vicky was first approached by assertive outreach workers she was very dismissive of their claims that they were able to offer her help. Her attitude to her difficulties was that they would be a lot better if mental health services just left her alone. She was avidly trying to negotiate her discharge from hospital after a compulsory admission that she felt she had not needed. She had agreed to take medication, but the care team on the ward felt sure that she was doing this to speed up her discharge and, once out of hospital, she would stop taking it. Vicky refused to discuss this with anyone, especially her psychiatrist, saying that nobody trusted her to do things her way. When asked about her way of doing things, she answered, 'Living independently, working, and having nothing to do with mental health services.' Unfortunately for Vicky, she had tried this three times in two years and ended up in hospital after each attempt.

During a previous admission, Vicky had expressed a need for counselling about some things that had happened to her at school. Although she had recently declared that she was not ready for counselling, it was decided that the CB therapist from the team (Mills) should get to know her in case she changed her mind. The therapist had been visiting her on the ward for a number of weeks, introducing himself and offering to help her with small tasks, such as contacting her family and getting items from the local shop when staff were too busy to escort her. One day, Vicky angrily told him that if he wanted to help he should 'tell that stupid doctor to let me out of hospital'. The therapist acknowledged how frustrated she felt and asked her to tell him more about it. She began by telling him about how she saw her needs very differently to the mental health services staff. She was able to describe how important it was for her to do things independently. Together they began to understand where this drive had originated and acknowledge how demoralising it was having contact with mental health services.

Vicky's story and compassionate case formulation

When Vicky was young, her mother developed a serious physical illness and had to be cared for by her father. She described her father as a very kind man who found coping with his wife's illness very difficult, especially when Vicky's older brother left home. Vicky was often told to look after herself and she tried her best to do this. Her parents' friends always remarked on how good she was to be helping her father in this way.

After a few years, Vicky's mother was somewhat fitter, although still unable to return to work. With her father having a little more time and her mother feeling better, Vicky hoped to do more things as a family. Her requests were nearly always refused and, in protest, she would stop trying to be helpful around the house. Her father suddenly left her and her mother without warning, setting up home with a friend of her mother's.

Life was very difficult for Vicky after this. Her father had little contact with her and her mother was very focused on balancing her regular bouts of ill health with providing for herself and Vicky. Her brother had little contact with the family after he left home. Vicky's school work suffered and she was later bullied for being quiet in class. She tried to tell her mother and a teacher about the bullying, but it continued.

In the end, Vicky left school early with no qualifications and got a job in a local shop. She did well in the shop, despite her shyness, and was given more and more responsibility by the owner. However, in the end, Vicky felt that she was being put upon as she was working long hours for little pay and the one time she had mentioned it to her mother she was advised to keep her complaints to herself.

After a year of relentless work, Vicky was exhausted and probably experiencing depression. However, she carried on, despite her lack of sleep and poor appetite. She became quite low and began to develop a strong feeling that something was seriously wrong. One day, while she was working in the back of the shop, she had a feeling that the other shop staff were against her in some way. She stopped working and listened to their muffled voices from behind the door. Vicky thought that she heard one of the women say, 'She's no use at all' and instantly worried that they might report her poor progress and she might lose her job. She also worried that, if she lost this job, she would have no chance of finding another.

Vicky worked even harder and kept looking out for signs that her colleagues were displeased. A vicious cycle emerged whereby Vicky worked harder and harder, but found her ability to work compromised by the effects of trying so hard. Vicky's first admission to hospital was compulsory after her work colleagues found her crying and she became aggressive towards them.

After two days in hospital, Vicky felt rested and demanded to be discharged so that she could get back to work. She tried to explain to the hospital staff that her future at the shop was in jeopardy. However, when this was investigated, the shop owner denied it, saying he was happy to have Vicky back as soon as she was well. This made Vicky even more suspicious, but she kept her feelings to herself and was discharged a week later.

The following two years saw a repeat of this cycle as Vicky worked hard to keep her job but became very low and suspicious of her colleagues. Eventually she did lose her job and ended up convinced that there had been a conspiracy behind this involving the shop owner and members of the mental health service. She was desperate to find a new job and the longer she left it the more she worried about being unemployable.

Vicky and the therapist agreed that she had a natural talent for hard work, which she had developed in childhood. The difficulty was that her view of herself as a person was heavily dependent on her ability to work. Vicky acknowledged that having contact with mental health services made her worry about her employment prospects.

Following discussion of these issues, Vicky identified a number of areas that could help her find and maintain work in future:

- increase confidence
- learn to recognise a tendency to overwork
- identify acceptable levels of work
- learn to say 'No' and ask for help.

New rules for living and core beliefs

The CB approach to these areas included planning and undertaking a test of the belief 'If I show people my weaknesses they'll reject me.' This belief was being activated whenever Vicky considered asking for help, leading her to feel anxious and, ultimately, avoid getting help.

Vicky and the therapist followed a process described in Chapter 4, which led to two tests. First, they undertook a survey of people's attitudes to requests for help. They found that, of the 12 people they canvassed, only 1 thought that it showed weakness. Vicky found this very useful, particularly because it was her brother who endorsed her belief and he had become depressed following a period of overwork.

The second test involved Vicky actually telling someone that she needed help. Vicky had always avoided collecting any State benefit monies and she had a complicated claim to make if she wanted any financial assistance. She predicted that, if she asked for the benefit, it would be refused and she also expected professionals to look down on her if she asked for help with the application process.

Vicky's new, more helpful, rule was, 'I have every right to ask for help, most people will offer help if they can, some people think asking for help is weak but that's their problem.' Vicky tested this new rule repeatedly by asking for help in different situations. On some occasions people refused, which at first made her feel very distressed. She was able to ask for help dealing with this, which led to the second major piece of work.

Vicky decided to tackle her confidence. This involved working on her core belief, 'I'm no good.' Work started by reviewing the compassionate case formulation to explain how she had grown up believing this. She identified an alternative belief about herself, 'I'm OK', which she believed 10 per cent since being able to ask for help (Padesky, 1994). She then identified her definition of 'I'm OK' as having eight characteristics:

- positive outlook
- ability to share feelings with others
- ability to say 'No'
- kind to others
- good listener
- ambitious
- ability to work hard
- trustworthy.

Classically, Vicky had first identified the characteristics that she felt she *didn't* have. However, while discussing and rating the characteristics individually on a scale of 0–100 per cent, Vicky found that she habitually underrated herself on all of them. Overall, her individual ratings averaged out at 45 per cent OK. Vicky and her therapist planned ways in which to gain more experience of these characteristics, which initially led to a five point plan:

- share feelings with a few people
- have individual assertiveness lessons from the team's occupational therapist
- carry on saying 'No' and asking for help
- undertake a back-to-work course and look for a job involving helping others
- keep a record of times when 'OK' characteristics are demonstrated.

Vicky found herself gradually more and more able to negotiate aspects of her care, including medication, especially as she became more open with the professionals involved. She continues to receive help from the assertive outreach service and has plans to undertake a local college course in herbal medicine.

SUMMARY

- People often have very good reasons for avoiding mental health services.
- Mental health policy surrounding assertive outreach is subject to a variety of potentially conflicting influences.
- Social control aspects of assertive outreach should be discussed more openly than is usually the case.
- The recovery model is a useful perspective for developing assertive outreach and CBT practice.
- Routine assessment of engagement and formulation of resistance can be helpful.
- CB approaches can be helpful to people who are offered an assertive outreach approach, but the research evidence is small and still developing.
- CB practice can be included in assertive outreach work in a variety of ways.

Activities

- When presented with a service delivery problem, consider the wider influences, such as organisational factors and conflicting policy advice.
- Identify and acknowledge dilemmas in practice between caring and social control aspects of assertive outreach work.
- Develop a compassionate case formulation – including patterns of resistance – collaboratively with a client and plan work on this basis.

Further reading

Johnstone, L., 2000, *Users and Abusers of Psychiatry: A Critical Look at Psychiatric Practice*. London: Routledge.
A critical perspective on everyday mental health practice, which should help the reader to gain more of an insight into why users often lose confidence in the mainstream psychiatric system.

Kingdon, D., and Turkington, D., 2002, *The Case Study Guide to Cognitive Behaviour Therapy of Psychosis*. Chichester: John Wiley.
An excellent, in-depth description of CB approaches to helping people with psychosis.

TWELVE Working with People Who have Psychological Problems because of a Physical Illness

Neil Kitchiner and Nigel Short

Learning objectives

After reading this chapter and completing the activities at the end of it you should be able to:

1 demonstrate some understanding of the background and evidence base of the CB approach for medical difficulties
2 describe the role of the psychiatric liaison services in this context
3 describe the main features of the argument for the contribution of the CB approach to this
4 outline the main CB skills required
5 demonstrate an understanding of some of the dilemmas in the area of referral and some strategies for dealing with this
6 make links between the clinical information given in the two case studies with other key parts of this book.

Introduction

There has been an expansion of 'liaison psychiatry' departments in British general hospitals in recent years. The aim of this expansion is to allow mental health professionals to make their skills and knowledge readily available to general medical personnel in order to achieve a comprehensive physical and psychological service, based on the following rationale.

Roberts (2002a) argued that separate services for mental and physical distress are unhelpful, while Engel (1980) suggested that the biomedical model – which focused only on illness and physical cause and effect – did not adequately meet the needs of patients. Engel advocated a bio-psychosocial model, to include patients' experiences, behaviour and social setting. This was supported by Mayou et al. (1995), who argued that the causes of physical complaints having a clear psychological component are multiple and interactive, involving physical, psychological and social factors.

The case formulation approach (see Chapter 2) constitutes an ideal response to these issues, offering mental health practitioners opportunities to work in a structured and logical way with physically ill individuals suffering psychological distress.

The evidence base for the CB approach in medical difficulties

There is an emerging evidence base supporting the use of the CB approach in a variety of medical difficulties, including renal medicine (Phipps and Turkington, 2001), deliberate self-harm (Evans et al., 1999), rheumatoid arthritis (Sharpe et al., 2001), facially disfigured people (Newell and Marks, 2000), irritable bowel syndrome (Keefer and Blanchard, 2001), hypochondriasis (Clark et al., 1998), non-insulin-dependent diabetes mellitus (Henry et al., 1997; Lustman et al., 1998), chronic lower or back pain (Johansson et al., 1998; Morley et al., 1999), cancer (Edelman and Kidman, 2000) and dizziness (Andersson and Yardley, 1998).

The role of the liaison psychiatry service

The Royal College of Physicians and The Royal College of Psychiatrists (1995, 2003) produced guidelines on the 'Psychological care of medical patients' within UK general hospitals. Within these, it is argued that, on the basis of the available evidence, liaison psychiatry services should target the following groups of individuals.

- *Those with organic disease and an associated psychiatric disorder* 'Adjustment disorders' occur in about a quarter of medical patients, with a prevalence of anxiety and depressive disorders at levels of 12–15 per cent. This is twice as high as in the general population and can reach 25–35 per cent in particular groups of patients.
- *Those with cerebral complications of organic disease* Delirium is detected in 10 per cent of acute admissions while 25–35 per cent of elderly medical inpatients have dementia.
- *Those with physical symptoms that are not due to organic disease* Between 25 and 50 per cent of all new medical outpatients experience physical symptoms that cannot be explained on the basis of organic disease, and up to half of such patients have underlying anxiety or depression. These individuals are termed as suffering from somatoform disorders. Within this group there will be a proportion of individuals with chronic multiple unexplained symptoms. Both groups are expensive, due to the costs incurred for tests to eliminate organic disease and multiple hospital admissions.
- *Those requiring medical assessment for treatment following deliberate self-harm (DSH)* Approximately 150,000 DSH admissions occur annually

in England and Wales. In addition, many DSH patients are seen in accident and emergency departments, but not admitted.

- *Those with sexual or relationship problems and eating disorders* These problems are often not detected because patients are reluctant to disclose their difficulties. Sexual problems may be straightforward to remedy and if an eating disorder occurs with a physical illness, such as diabetes, specialised inpatient treatment may be recommended.

These guidelines highlight the enormous psychological distress experienced within the population and the potential work for psychologically trained practitioners working within medical settings. They also illustrate the need to employ trained mental health professionals within liaison psychiatry departments. For example, there is a clear need for liaison nurses in A&E units for individuals who deliberately self-harm (Whitehead and Royles, 2002; Eastwick and Grant, 2004), oncology units (Roberts, 2002b), HIV and AIDS clinics (Wright and Lavery, 2002), cardiac rehabilitation units (Fisher and Tunmore, 2002), gastrointestinal clinics (Leibbrand and Hiller, 2002; Moorey and Greer, 2002) and liaison outpatient clinics (Short and Kitchiner, 2003).

Is there provision of CB within liaison psychiatry?

Despite the Royal College's guidelines, many general hospitals and primary care trusts within the UK National Health Service do not have dedicated CB services for patients with chronic medical problems (Barker, 2002). This may, in part, be influenced by the lack of suitable trained and accredited CB practitioners within the UK (Gournay, 2000). Of those currently practising, many are likely to be based in established liaison psychiatry departments (Short and Kitchiner, 2003) or clinical psychology services. These practitioners are also likely to have defined sessional commitments, usually to discrete populations such as those with chronic fatigue (Deale and Chalder, 2002) or facial disfigurement (Newell, 2002).

Bloch and Kissane (2000) argue for more psychotherapy to be applied in medical settings, but discuss major stumbling blocks to this occurring. The first of these is the lack of quality randomised controlled trials (RCTs) within psychotherapies that would add new knowledge to evidence-based medicine (see Chapter 15). The authors also highlight resource allocation issues, where government bureaucracies may shy away from provision of resources for patients who do not justify the spurious label of severe mental illness. Hiller et al. (1997) highlight that people with multiple somatic complaints not only present formidable management problems, but also have severe functional impairments that possibly outweigh those of patients with so-called severe mental illnesses, such as schizophrenia.

It would seem evident from the literature discussed above that there is a wide range of CB interventions readily available to the psychologically minded practitioner. The challenge is to translate the evidence base to the client in a way that is likely to have the greatest impact.

How can mental health practitioners best apply CB knowledge and skills?

White (2001) suggested the following:

- CB assessment and interventions for clients with psychological problems and disorders associated with chronic medical problems
- CB-orientated advice to staff on the medical management of clients' problems – for example, where there may be an interaction between emotional and physical factors
- consultancy and supervision for staff in basic psychosocial assessments according to a CB model of psychological functioning – for example, providing specialist nurses with information on ways in which to elicit automatic thoughts during a nursing assessment
- teaching and training for staff about CB models and interventions – such as the provision of a workshop on how to prepare patients for referral to a CB practitioner
- ongoing research of CB factors in chronic medical problems, including the effectiveness of the approach and the interface between clients, staff and hospital systems.

I (Kitchiner) would add from my own experience that it is not unusual for CB practitioners to be invited to provide lectures, workshops, supervision and educational forums or training programmes to many disciplines, including nursing, psychiatry, occupational therapy and physiotherapy. These involve disseminating knowledge about the approach in order to help others understand the psychological management of medical difficulties with associated psychological distress.

These events can also help colleagues to reconsider their choice of non-evidence-based, therefore redundant and inappropriate, psychological interventions. For example, imagine that someone experiences unwanted thoughts about cancer eating away at their body after successful oncology treatment. Unfortunately, some mental health and non-mental health practitioners continue to recommend to patients that they should wear an elastic band on their wrist and flick the band against their skin when they experience an intrusive thought (Short et al., 2004). This type of intervention, although originally intended as a useful control technique (Rachman and De Silva, 1978), tends to result in an increase in intrusive thoughts and a sense of helplessness and failure in the individual (Salkovskis and Campbell, 1994).

The need for creativity in improving CB provision

It is known from research that there is, and will continue to be, a shortage of trained CB practitioners in Britain (Gournay, 2000). National Health Service providers have therefore to become more inventive in funding this highly sought after workforce. Short and Kitchiner (2003) argue that organisations may have to be particularly creative and inventive in their bids to secure financial arrangements to employ trained CB practitioners – particularly within medical settings.

Short and Kitchiner (2003) report on a unique partnership arrangement between a local NHS department of liaison psychiatry and the South Wales Fire Service, which was instrumental in securing a trained CB practitioner within the University Hospital of Wales (UHW) in Cardiff. The impact a single practitioner can have within the first 12 months of setting up a CB outpatient service within a university teaching hospital is described. A total of 44 referrals were received. These came from the Consultant Liaison Psychiatrist, his team of junior doctors, with some direct referrals from general practitioners and departments in the UHW. The diagnoses, when broken down into the diagnostic criteria described by the American Psychiatric Association (APA, 1994), were categorised as shown in the graph of referral patterns below.

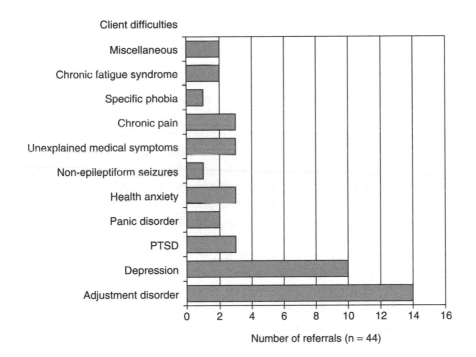

These individual referrals expand on the range described in the Royal Colleges of Physicians and Psychiatrists' guidelines above. This, in part, may be due to the success of the CB approach being tested and expanded to offer help to individuals with a broad range of mental health difficulties associated with medical illness.

All individuals referred were offered an initial screening interview. If their psychological difficulty was suitable for the approach – if there was available evidence for its efficacy – an intervention would then be offered. This either involved individual work on the part of the CB practitioner, individual work on the part of a health professional with training in the approach under supervision, a six-week CB stress control course (White, 2000) or various forms of guided reading. Two of the individuals referred will be discussed briefly in the case studies below, with particular reference to the CB skills used.

CB skills required

At a general level, there is evidence to suggest that CB practitioners are equipped to transfer core skills learned in training and from experience of working with the more traditional anxiety and depressive disorders in order to help individuals suffering psychological distress associated with chronic medical conditions (Sheffield Hallam University, 1997). More specifically, a therapeutic alliance needs to be established at the outset, by means of the process of engaging the patient in a collaborative manner (see Chapter 2). For example, 'I have an hour set aside for this meeting – is that all right with you?', 'What would you like to discuss today?' Throughout the session, the practitioner makes brief, regular summaries of the client's account, to check on understanding, and feedback is sought by the practitioner at the end of the session on anything that may have upset or offended the client (see Chapter 3).

I then try to develop and share an initial case formulation from the assessment material, which will be discussed in subsequent sessions and amended until a mutual agreement is reached (see Chapter 2). The case formulation then helps guide the appropriate cognitive and behavioural interventions in an effort to reduce psychological distress and help the individual to reach their agreed goals by the end of the intervention. Well-delivered CB interventions are both educational and supportive, with the aim of minimising emotional distress. The aim is to move clients towards re-evaluating their distressing, disturbing feelings and thoughts in order to help them gain mastery over their difficulties.

In my experience, people who are referred for a psychological assessment are often surprised as they have invested much time and energy in seeking a medical answer to their physical problems, only to be referred to the psychiatric/psychological department. They may present with a mixture of negative emotions – denial or anger, for example. It is not unusual for people to say, 'Why have they sent me to see you? I'm not mad' and/or 'They think it's all in my head and that I'm putting this on.'

Developing a therapeutic alliance with someone with these understandable thoughts presents the CB practitioner with a major therapeutic challenge. It is important to tread very carefully in those first few minutes of an initial session and put the individual at ease with basic pleasantries, setting the scene with details such as the time allowed for interview and that there will be an opportunity to ask questions before the assessment is conducted. The referral letter can often be a good starting point and basis for review. Tests and examinations from the medical setting and their results can be used to reinforce the non-organic illness view often seen in somatoform disorders, such as irritable bowel disease, chronic fatigue syndrome and chronic back pain (Raine et al., 2002).

At the end of the session, the practitioner should be able to offer the client a basic explanation of their formulation and treatment options. It is often helpful to explain in some detail, with diagrams where possible, how such psychological interventions may moderate clients' emotional distress. If, after some discussion, the client is still very resistant, then it is probably better to agree that an intervention may not be helpful at this time, but give them the option that they can be seen again in the future. From my experience, there is little to be gained by dragging individuals through therapy kicking and screaming if they are unable to entertain the idea that their difficulties may be influenced by many psychological and social factors (see also Chapter 2).

Overcoming cognitive distortions

Often patients will experience cognitive distortions in how they view themselves, their environment and their future. Cancer patients who are concerned about the recurrence of the disease may have unhelpful automatic thoughts that they are in some way to blame for their illness – 'It's because I am a bad person' or 'I'm unfit' or 'There's no point in carrying on as it will only come back and kill me next time.'

Cognitive distortions can also affect the patient–physician relationship and reduce adherence to treatment recommendations. As beliefs play an important role in adjustment to illness and, ultimately, coping, CB therapy techniques can be usefully applied in these situations. Monitoring for cognitive distortions, challenging unhelpful thinking styles and substituting more useful conceptualisations and beliefs with a rational response are all helpful strategies (see also Chapter 4 and Yates and Bowers, 2000).

Flexibility

From my experience of working with these groups, there is a need for the practitioner to be flexible – perhaps more so than in traditional CB outpatient departments. This is in part due to the often chronic nature of the disease process – as is the case for those living with HIV or cancer. This can lead to longer-lasting therapeutic relationships, where patients may dip in and out of therapy depending on the course of the illness over time. At different stages in the development of the disease – from acute to chronic to terminal – these 'milestones' all bring different problems for the individual to cope with.

It may be appropriate for the practitioner to refer the individual on for further psychological therapy or supportive counselling once the goals set for CB interventions have been achieved.

Use of the Internet

Morton (2002) reports on the new breed of 'Internet-empowered patients' or 'e-patients' who use the Internet seeking credible information about their health. Morton reports that nearly all patients (92 per cent) in his study found the information they were looking for, 88 per cent said that the information they found improved the way they took care of their health and 81 per cent said that they learned something new about their health as a result their Internet search.

With this in mind, the challenge for health providers will be to make our evidenced-based information readily available on the Internet for the growing number of e-patients to download and implement, which in some cases may result in saving a referral to their physician, who then refers them for psychological therapy.

I have found the Internet and e-mail to be helpful tools in the long-term management of some patients, either to allow the therapeutic relationship to be maintained while the individual is awaiting therapy or, in some cases, where the medical illness has resulted in a temporary halt to therapy due to hospitalisation for further tests and operations.

Internet and e-mail use also allows the patient the freedom to contact their therapist at any time and for the busy therapist to respond when convenient to them (see the National Institute for Clinical Excellence (NICE) website at www.nice.org.uk for a review of the computer-assisted CB intervention debate).

Group CB interventions

Group interventions may be aimed at symptom reduction in people with medically unexplained problems or focus on the specific needs of patients with a particular illness – for example, AIDS, cancer or who have suffered a heart attack. Research has also suggested that such groups – which may also include health education, coping skills enhancement and stress management as well as psychological support – can lead to better coping with the illness and an enhanced sense of well-being. In some cases, working in groups was found to be more effective than similar interventions offered individually (Fawzy et al., 1996).

Researchers have found using CB interventions with groups to be extremely useful for individuals with a common medical diagnosis or helping people to manage unwanted stress. There is little doubt from the literature that group therapy for the medically ill enhances their quality of life and there is even some suggestion that it can increase the quantity of life, too. For example, Spiegel et al. (1989) conducted a prospective randomised trial (see Chapter 16) of group therapy for women with metastatic (multisite cancer) breast cancer. The intervention lasted one year and consisted of weekly supportive groups with training in self-hypnosis. The authors revisited the data five years after finishing the study and were surprised to find a survival advantage in the group that had been involved in the intervention – the groups' members lived an average of 18 months longer than did the members of the control group.

Gore-Felton and Spiegel (2000) speculate that patients in such groups listen to health advice and make helpful behavioural changes, such as better adherence to medication, diet, exercise, sleep and hygiene. These subjects can be discussed within group settings. The authors suggest that several components are important for the optimal utilisation of supportive expressive techniques in the context of illness. These include:

- social support that comes from the common bond of illness
- emotional expression
- reduced isolation and improved coping
- detoxifying death, by examining the threat of death in a straightforward manner, which is not possible or encouraged in other settings
- reordering life's priorities, so as to take realistic control of aspects of life that can still be influenced and relinquish those that cannot be
- enhancing communication with physicians and encouraging patients to participate more actively in their treatment
- teaching CB techniques for control of such symptoms as anxiety, anticipatory nausea and pain
- enhancing family support.

Family involvement

The importance of involving family and carers in the therapeutic relationship and interventions cannot be underestimated. This can help alleviate family distress and enhance the level of support available to the patient as the burden of care often falls on family members, who may make great sacrifices to support their loved one. Family members should also be encouraged to attend stress-control courses as a matter of routine as they often suffer from stress-related problems themselves, which can be controlled by their attending educational CB groups (White, 2000).

Another advantage of having family or partners attend group courses is that it allows the patient to be easily transported to the venue. Also, experienced CB practitioners know just how difficult it can be to care for someone who is psychologically distressed. Thus, the advantage of having the 'significant other' there is that two can be helped for the price of one, as it were, as well as encouraging mutual support and shared understanding.

The social benefits of meeting new people should not be understated and can bring ample opportunities for the individual to practise techniques that they have learned – for example, exposure for the individual who has become socially phobic following facial disfigurement due to burns (Newell and Marks, 2000).

The referral process

The need for referral guidelines

Referrals made directly to CB practitioners from non-mental health colleagues are often inappropriate. In response to this problem, it is necessary to utilise clear referral guidelines, which are described below. These are easy to understand and are intended to help colleagues to consider who may benefit from CB interventions.

White (2001) provided useful tips for the overwhelmed CB practitioner to actively help clients to 'opt in' for therapy. He devised a first appointment letter, which provided details of the nature of the referral process and invited individuals to 'opt-in' for their appointment. The system is based on the assumption that individuals who have no intention of attending can indicate this and/or practitioners can reallocate appointments when people fail to respond to an 'opt in' referral letter. The letter can also outline what will happen when they attend the CB screening assessment (see also Short and Kitchiner, 2003).

In some cases, particularly when the individual's disorder is already known, it may be helpful to send out an information leaflet on the patient's particular problem with examples of how therapy may be helpful. At the time of writing, the British Association for Behavioural and Cognitive Psychotherapies (BABCP) has devised 16 specific leaflets that can be downloaded from its website at www.babcp.com without charge or can be ordered in bulk for a reasonable fee.

The Department of Liaison Psychiatry at UHW, Cardiff, routinely writes to individuals and invites them to contact the CB practitioner by telephone to arrange a mutually convenient appointment. The telephone conversation enables initial concerns about the intervention to be briefly discussed – for example, 'How long will the meeting take?', 'Can I bring my partner or a friend?', 'What can psychological therapy do for me?' It is also an opportunity to discuss any difficulties that may impede attendance, such as childcare arrangements.

Individuals are routinely sent a set of core clinical self-report measures, including the Beck depression inventory (Beck, 1996), fear questionnaire (Marks and Mathews, 1979) and life adjustment scale (Marks, 1986) and, where there is a traumatic incident resulting in referral, the Davidson trauma scale (Davidson, 1996). These supplement and assist in the initial screening interview. Suitable case-specific measures are then used to achieve a baseline picture of the client's difficulties prior to beginning the intervention (see Chapter 3). Individuals deemed suitable and interested in the approach may then have to be placed on a waiting list.

Prioritising referrals

Deciding who should be offered help can often present the practitioner with a moral dilemma. For example, consider a client who is experiencing an adjustment difficulty, such as having been diagnosed with cancer, and is experiencing anxiety and depression. Compare this with someone who has mild panic disorder.

Who should be seen first? White (2001) gives the following useful categorisation for prioritising treatment.

- *High priority*

  – Clients with seriously incapacitating symptoms of depression or anxiety who have poor levels of social support and infrequent access to healthcare services.
  – Clients with significant psychological problems where there is evidence of deteriorating physical health status and/or in need of palliative care.

- *Medium priority*

  – Clients with clinically significant symptoms who have not responded completely to other therapies – for example, medication, nursing interventions.
  – Clients with access to ongoing support for their problems – for example, a client who has contact with a community psychiatric nurse for supportive counselling and medication review.

- *Low priority*

  – Clients with one or two circumscribed psychological problems that do not interfere with their everyday psychological functioning and who have a range of adequate coping strategies or access to coping strategies.
  – Clients who have had previous CB interventions, whose referrals are to address residual issues in the form of booster or relapse management issues.

It is helpful, when developing referral criteria, to discuss the contents with appropriate clinical managers and referring clinicians. Screening systems that allow for suitable flexibility are encouraged. This then takes into account how clients' problems may deteriorate after screening, requiring a change in priority status as a result. At the UHW, patients are prioritised depending on severity of symptoms, where possible, and people with less complicated problems are referred to junior psychiatrists or experienced mental health nurses with specific training and ongoing supervision in CB interventions (Short and Kitchiner, 2003). Interventions are then monitored by means of weekly group clinical supervision (see Chapter 5).

CB self-help guided reading

It may be useful to provide the client with information to take away in the form of homework – for example, reading the appropriate BABCP leaflet – while awaiting the intervention. Clients are also often encouraged to either borrow or purchase various self-help books. This strategy has two advantages: it may help the client to develop self-directed work and can also complement subsequent interventions. Useful books, which are routinely recommended, include *Overcoming Depression* (Williams, 2001), *Living with Fear* (Marks, 1978), *Understanding Your Reactions to Trauma* (Herbert, 1995). It can also be very helpful to encourage local librarians to stock various CB self-help books, which clients then can borrow.

Two illustrative case studies

In rounding this chapter off, two case studies from a liaison psychiatry caseload follow to illustrate how CB interventions can be delivered to alleviate emotional distress. I should stress that case-specific and standardised measures (see Chapter 3) are routinely used. However, to avoid repetition, a detailed and illustrative tabular representation of this is given for the second case study only.

'Rose'

Rose is a 26-year-old single woman with multiple sclerosis (MS) who has a past psychiatric history of panic disorder. She was referred by the department of neurology to the liaison psychiatrist, for management of her panic attacks and depression. The liaison psychiatrist listed her problems as being:

- a subjective failure to accept her diagnosis of MS
- a six-month history of worsening low mood, poor self-esteem, ideas of hopelessness, low energy levels and disturbed sleep
- increasing frequency of panic attacks (three to four per week), which were spontaneous in nature and involved a fear of fainting, derealisation and breathing difficulties, leading to increasing social isolation
- increased alcohol intake, to a level of 60 units per week.

Rose had a past psychiatric history with the above problems, which emerged after her diagnosis of MS in 1998. She required the use of crutches most of the time and suffered from early bilateral cataracts and frequent migraine headaches. She lived five doors from her parents and received regular support from them. She also cared for two daughters, aged three and eight, and had recently ended a two-year relationship.

The liaison psychiatrist who referred her to me felt that there was a low risk of suicide and could detect no evidence of psychosis.

Initial CB assessment

The main problems for Rose were daily panic attacks with agoraphobia. She avoided leaving her home alone for fear of passing out, resulting in social embarrassment. She reported periods of low mood and crying, with markedly reduced activities and a range of automatic negative thoughts, including 'Why do I have to have MS?', and feelings of hopelessness.

Rose was anxious and tearful at interview when describing her symptoms. She reported a range of biological symptoms, including poor appetite and weight loss. Rose described her view of herself as 'lonely and depressed with no pleasure' in her life, her world as 'shit' with no goals and her future as 'a steady decline into disability and being wheelchair-bound' due to MS.

Rose was self-motivated enough to engage in fortnightly CB work as an outpatient, encouraged to purchase *Overcoming Depression* (Williams, 2001) and provided with a treatment manual on panic disorder and agoraphobia (Andrews et al., 1994). She was placed on the waiting list for four weeks.

COGNITIVE CONCEPTUALISATION DIAGRAM

Patient's name: Rose *Date:* January 2002

Diagnosis (APA 1994): Axis I: Panic disorder with agoraphobia

Axis III: Multiple sclerosis

Relevant childhood data
Born into large family with limited financial status in a deprived area.
Father misused alcohol regularly and was unemployed for long periods.
Emotionally deprived due to above.

Core belief(s)
'I am vulnerable.'
'I am unimportant.'

Conditional assumptions/beliefs/rules
'If I am good, then I may get noticed.'
'If I do not fit in, then I will be forgotten.'

Compensatory strategy(ies)
Easily led by peer group in experimenting with alcohol and illicit substances.

Situation 1	*Situation 2*	*Situation 3*
Children misbehaving.	Had a panic attack on the bus with kids.	Unable to walk properly due to MS.
Automatic thought 'I can't cope with my life.'	*Automatic thought* 'I will faint in front of others.'	*Automatic thought* 'Why me?' (MS)
Meaning of AT 'I am worthless.'	*Meaning of AT* 'I'm vulnerable.'	*Meaning of AT* 'I am damaged.'
Emotion Lonely, sad, hopeless.	*Emotion* Anxiety/fearful.	*Emotion* Hopeless and depressed.
Behaviour Cut arms, crying, call mother to help out.	*Behaviour* Stay home and drink alcohol.	*Behaviour* Lie on settee, crying.

Intervention

Following assessment, from which developed the case formulation below, all sessions adhered to the following common, CB session structure:

- orientation to session – how long we have
- mood check of patient – 'How are you feeling today?'
- collaborative agenda set
- review of homework or significant events
- specific CB intervention in session – such as psycho-education, imaginal exposure, cognitive disputation
- regular summaries throughout to check on her/my understanding
- homework agreed and set – diary keeping, behavioural experiments and so on
- feedback on session – anything not understood, for example.

Session 1

Rose spoke about recent events, reporting cutting her arm superficially as a result of stressors. These included her children playing up, feelings of loneliness and inability to leave her home alone due to agoraphobia. She had attended a local MS support group, which had helped her see her feelings as normal in the circumstances. She had also read material supplied on agoraphobia, which she rated as helpful.

During the session, clinical measures were made of her list of problems. Rose's misuse of alcohol to self-medicate was reviewed and she was encouraged to reduce her intake over the next week. Also, breathing retraining (described as 'breathing relaxation' by Leahy and Holland, 2000) was taught in the session, to help Rose control her panic attacks. This was agreed as homework, to be recorded in a diary, which was supplied.

Session 2

Rose reported two panic attacks in the past two weeks. She continued to misuse alcohol, caffeine, diazepam and had avoided going on a school trip with her child due to fear.

Rose's recent panic attacks were used to socialise her to Wells' (1997) description of Clarke and Salkovskis' cognitive model for panic and behavioural experiments were discussed. These included stopping herself from practising her safety behaviour and avoidances (see Chapter 14) in order to test her unhelpful belief – 'I'm going to die' – when she experienced palpitations. The following between-session homework was agreed:

- to continue breathing retraining four times daily
- reduce alcohol, caffeine and diazepam intakes
- complete her panic diary.

Session 3

Rose had started exposure (see Leahy and Holland, 2000) to travelling on buses between sessions. She had reduced her alcohol, caffeine and diazepam intakes and reported an improvement in her mood. Her panic diary revealed two panic attacks. This information was discussed in the context of Wells' (1997) model.

Rose's misinterpretation of the likelihood of palpitations leading to fainting/collapsing were challenged by brief psycho-education – that is, that fear increases blood pressure, making it impossible for her to faint/collapse.

Rose was encouraged to record rational responses on a blank postcard and use these to challenge unhelpful beliefs. Her attempts at breathing retraining were reviewed and she was encouraged to do this at the first sign of panic.

The homework agreed was to:

- continue with breathing retraining
- read a section on re-evaluating the unhelpful thoughts in the CB manual supplied.

Session 4
Rose reported success in controlling her panic symptoms using breathing retraining and cue cards. She had continued exposure to leaving her home and public transport and had started collecting her children from school again. She had attended a second meeting of the MS support group, which she found very positive and supportive. Her alcohol and caffeine intake was now within normal limits. She was praised for safety behaviour and avoidances.

Rose reported an increase in mood and self-confidence. Her clinical measures were completed, demonstrating a 78 per cent improvement in her problem and target ratings. With her agreement, Rose was discharged from active CB work and made a follow-up appointment in a month's time.

Session 5
At the follow-up appointment, Rose reported that she had continued to manage her anxiety using CB strategies and had no panic attacks to report. She declined any further follow-up appointments and felt confident in her ability to cope with any symptoms of anxiety.

'Debbie'

Debbie, a 38-year-old married woman, was referred to the department of liaison psychiatry by a consultant in rheumatology for a psychiatric assessment following a traumatic operation on her neck. She was diagnosed with an adjustment disorder (APA, 1994) to the operation two years ago and referred to me for CB help.

At our first session, Debbie described her main problems as being those of:

- daily intrusive memories, accompanied by anxious feelings, of the operation on her neck that she perceived as traumatic because of the thought that she could have been left paralysed
- nightmares about the operation
- anger at medical staff prior to her operation for not taking her symptoms seriously

- avoiding the ward where the operation took place, her consultant rheumatologist, television medical programmes, newspapers and discussing the symptoms and feelings with her family.

Debbie was offered outpatient CB work, including imaginal exposure for the intrusive symptoms and anger.

COGNITIVE CONCEPTUALISATION DIAGRAM

Patient's name: Debbie   *Date:* February 2002

Diagnosis (APA, 1994):   *Axis I:* Adjustment disorder and Post-traumatic stress disorder symptoms
Axis III: Rheumatoid arthritis

Relevant childhood data Diagnosed with rheumatoid arthritis at 16 years and underwent several investigations and operations.
Core belief(s) 'I am fragile.' 'I am different.'
Conditional Assumptions/Beliefs/Rules 'I must be careful then no harm will come to me.' 'I must avoid dangerous situations.' 'I must be independent or else I am not normal.'
Compensatory Strategy(ies) Attempt all activities that are safe and not likely to cause harm. Strive to be seen as normal despite obvious disability.

Situation 1 'Doctors did not listen to me when in pain.'	Situation 2 Post in vivo exposure.	Situation 3 Friends invited her to party.
Automatic thought 'I am not happy now, I have changed.'	*Automatic thought* 'I nearly gave up on fighting to be normal.'	*Automatic thought* 'Others only feel sorry for me.'
Meaning of AT 'I am unimportant.'	*Meaning of AT* 'I am fragile.'	*Meaning of AT* 'I am damaged.'
Emotion Angry, scared.	*Emotion* Angry, scared.	*Emotion* Sad and hopeless.
Behaviour Avoid hospital appointments where possible.	*Behaviour* Withdraw from family, reduce socialising.	*Behaviour* Went to bed alone and avoided others for two days.

Session 1
Debbie reported a slight improvement in her sleep and mood since assessment, experiencing intrusive memories of the operation 30 per cent of her waking day.

Clinical measures were completed and returned (see page 180). In the session, problem and target measures were agreed and baseline measures recorded. A model of post-traumatic stress disorder and the imaginal exposure method were described (Richards and Lovell, 2000b).

Automatic thoughts that were elicited included, 'I'm not happy any more' and 'They [doctors] had not listened to me.'

The following homework was agreed:

- read *Understanding Your Reactions to Trauma* (Herbert, 1995)
- read and comment on her case formulation.

Session 2
Debbie had read the booklet by Herbert and reported feeling better after reading other people's accounts, in that she could see her experiences were understandable. She had also read the above case formulation and agreed on its accuracy.

Debbie described having slept better, although she experienced early morning wakening. She had attended an outpatient appointment with the rheumatologist and described feeling very anxious, angry and tearful while there. Debbie wanted the doctor who assessed her and decided not to admit her to apologise that he had been wrong.

Debbie was encouraged to describe in the first person, present tense, her traumatic memory in detail. This part of the session was audiotaped to allow for in vivo exposure to traumatic memories (see Richards and Lovell, 2000b).

The following homework was agreed:

- to listen to the tape of exposure daily until she experienced a 50 per cent reduction in anxiety
- to record this in her homework diary
- to draft a letter to the doctor and explain why she was still angry two years on.

Session 3
Debbie reported feeling very anxious for a couple of hours after the last CB session. She had commenced daily imaginal exposure using the audiotape from the previous session and reported a lifting in her general mood, saying 'My brain feels brighter', and that she was socialising more.

Debbie had drafted a letter to the doctor at the hospital, describing in detail why she remained angry. Problem-solving (Hawton and Kirk, 1989) options were reviewed regarding what to do with the letter.

A second audiotape was made of 'hot spots' – that is, parts of the story that evoke a rise in distress (Richards and Lovell, 2000b).

The following homework was agreed:

- exposure to the new tape until a 50 per cent reduction in anxiety was achieved
- to review problem-solving options and decide by the next session whether or not to send the letter to the doctor or access the hospital complaints system.

Session 4

After the last session of imaginal exposure, Debbie complained of an increase in insomnia, fear and distress for one week and so she had avoided listening to her audiotape. She was still unsure of what she wanted to do with the letter of complaint.

In the second week between sessions, Debbie had started daily imaginal exposure to the audiotape for approximately one hour until her anxiety level reduced by 50 per cent. She had felt much improved, experiencing less hopelessness (see Chapters 2 and 14), and these positive feelings generalised to other past traumas, including the failure of infertility treatment, the death of her father and past operations on her neck.

We spent time discussing options for making a complaint and Debbie decided to access the hospital complaints procedure. Also, imaginal exposure was encouraged to the remaining trauma hot spots of her operation.

The following homework was agreed:

- to continue with exposure using the audiotape until there is a 50 per cent reduction in anxiety
- to record any nightmares or intrusions.

Session 5

Debbie had sent the letter to the complaints manager and copied it to the doctor she was angry with.

Debbie reported feeling upset after our last session, due to thoughts that emerged during our discussion, including, 'I'm just carrying on with life for others.' She had challenged this belief using the dysfunctional thought record (DTR; see Chapter 4 and Greenberger and Padesky, 1995) and substituted it with 'I'm getting there now for me.' She reported no further nightmares.

The hospital complaints procedure allowed for an opportunity to have a face-to-face meeting to discuss her concerns. We reviewed the pros and cons for this option in session and agreed that it might constitute a useful behavioural experiment (see Chapter 4). Imaginal exposure was suspended due to no reported nightmares or other 're-experiencing symptoms' (APA, 1994).

The following homework was agreed:

- to ring the hospital complaints department and arrange a meeting.

Session 6

Debbie was expecting a letter from the hospital complaints department following its investigation.

Debbie reported that her mood was much brighter, with a reduction in anger and anxiety. Clinical measures were repeated due to the absence of any symptoms. An improvement of 53 per cent was noted for problem and target ratings.

Discharge arrangements were discussed and Debbie agreed to come for a follow-up appointment a month later.

Homework was agreed:

- to increase socialising and other pleasurable activities.

Session 7

At the follow-up appointment, Debbie showed a letter she had received that morning from the hospital complaints department, which had informed her that there was no case to answer against the doctor. She was very unhappy with this outcome and decided to arrange to meet the complaints manager.

Clinical measures were repeated and an improvement of 80 per cent on problem and target ratings was noted. Attending a CB stress control course ('Stresspac', White, 2000) was discussed and arranged to help with any future setbacks and develop a relapse prevention plan. A follow-up appointment was arranged for three months' time.

Session 8

Debbie had met with the consultant rheumatologist and the complaints department. She had described to them the breakdown in her care and thoughts and feelings that resulted, of being let down by the hospital, and had been encouraged to hear that it was changing its practice by setting up an emergency response team and employing a clinical nurse specialist. She had been invited to attend focus groups as a user of its services in the future. Debbie felt like a weight had been lifted following this meeting and was not experiencing any of the problems that had brought her to me.

The following homework was agreed:

- to complete and return her clinical measures
- to read the Stresspac psycho-educational literature before the stress control course started the following week

Debbie's clinical measures, received by post, noted a 100 per cent improvement in relation to the problem and targets. Debbie's progress – as measured by standardised and case-specific (problem and target) ratings – is set out below.

Debbie attended each of the six sessions of the stress control course, which she found useful in gaining CBT control techniques.

Problems and targets measurements (total) (Marks, 1986)

Problems and targets	Pre-intervention	Post-intervention	1MFU*	3MFU
	45	21	9	0

Fear questionnaire measurements (Marks and Matthews, 1979)

Fear Questionnaire	Pre-intervention	Post-intervention	1MFU	3MFU
Total phobia	26	17	8	5
General anxiety	14	1	0	2
Main phobia	3	1	0	0

Life and social adjustment scale measurements (Marks, 1986)

LSAS	Pre-intervention	Post-intervention	1MFU	3MFU
Home	2	0	0	0
Work	0	0	0	0
Private leisure	2	0	0	0
Social leisure	2	2	0	0
Relationships	2	1	0	0

Beck depression inventory II (Beck, 1996)

BDI II	Pre-intervention	Post-intervention	1MFU	3MFU
	10	0	0	1

Davidson trauma scale (Davidson, 1996)

DTS	Pre-intervention	Post-intervention	1MFU	3MFU
	65	8	6	3

*MFU stands for month follow-up

SUMMARY

- The background and evidence base of the CB approach for medical difficulties affords many opportunities for practitioners using case formulation-driven interventions.
- The practice context of this, in Britain, is in liaison psychiatry.
- The CB skills required can be adapted from training and experience of working with the common mental health problems, although there are specific skills issues that need to be considered – including the need to work flexibly.
- CB practitioners working in this area will need to grapple with key dilemmas concerning the referral process – strategies for dealing with these are available.
- Links are made between the clinical information given in the two case studies and other parts of this book.

Activities

- Investigate the extent and provision of liaison services, or geographical equivalent, in your area.
- Check out whether or not CB provision is on offer.
- If the approach is undeveloped, copy this chapter for service managers to read and comment on.

Further reading

White, J., 2000, *Treating Anxiety and Stress: A Group Psycho-educational Approach using Brief CBT*. Chichester: John Wiley.
This excellent book summarises White's research on his group approach and offers the CB worker session plans for delivering the stress control course over six weeks.

Regel, S., and Roberts, D, 2002, *Mental Health Liaison: A Handbook for Nurses and Health Professionals*. London: Baillière Tindall and the Royal College of Nursing, Harcourt.
A useful text written and aimed at liaison psychiatry workers. Many of the authors are BABCP accredited CB psychotherapists and offer excellent examples of the approach in different medical settings.

White, C.A., 2001, *Cognitive Behaviour Therapy for Chronic Medical Problems: A Guide to Assessment and Treatment in Practice*. Chichester: John Wiley.
A good introduction to CB within liaison psychiatry settings, with useful chapters on CB for various diseases, such as cancer.

THIRTEEN   Working with People Who are
            Depressed

*Ronan Mulhern, Nigel Short,
Alec Grant and Jem Mills*

Learning objectives

After reading this chapter and completing the activities at the end of it you
should be able to:

1 identify the significance of depression as a worldwide health problem
2 identify the strengths and limitations of a classification of depression
3 outline CB explanations of depression
4 describe the relationship between unhelpful thinking, emotion and
   behaviour in depression
5 describe key issues concerning the initial contact with a person
   suffering from depression
6 outline the significance of the therapeutic alliance in helping a person
   with depression
7 understand the importance of careful assessment in helping a person
   with depression, including assessment of underlying psychological
   vulnerability, and measures used
8 describe the significance of client homework in helping someone with
   depression
9 understand the importance of assessing the client's activity levels
10 describe the principles and strategies of task analysis, graded task
   assignment and activity scheduling
11 outline the importance of matching an intervention to the client's environment and monitoring interventions.

Introduction

Estimates of the frequency rate of clinical depression vary, but tend to range
between 3 and 16 per cent of the total population, and the diagnosis is more
likely to be made for women (Andrade et al., 2003). The World Health
Organisation predicts that clinical depression will become the disorder accounting

for the highest burden of ill health in developed countries by the year 2020 (WHO, 2001).

Depression is something that is expected to fall within the range of normal human experience, for example after bereavement. In some respects it is something that most of us will have some direct or indirect experience of and this can inform our understanding and help direct our clinical practice. Theoretically, we know that it is highly unlikely that we will go through life without having experienced some form of low mood due to actual or perceived loss, yet it is something that most of us will try very stringently to avoid experiencing. We therefore tend to classify depression as an unwanted or abnormal experience.

Classification issues

Depression can be classified in a number of different ways depending on the frequency and severity of its features. Traditionally, it has been categorised as a collection of subtypes of disorder, or syndrome. In this context, depression can occur on its own or in conjunction with or as the result of other forms of physical, mental or psychological disorders.

By accepting that it is a universal term open to differing interpretations, it is helpful for practitioners and researchers to employ specific terms of reference to communicate shared meanings effectively. The following must be present before a diagnosis of specific depressive disorders can be made (APA, 2000):

- depressed mood most of the day, nearly every day
- markedly diminished interest or pleasure in all or almost all activities
- significant weight loss or gain or decrease in appetite
- insomnia or hypersomnia
- psychomotor agitation or retardation
- fatigue or loss of energy nearly every day
- feelings of worthlessness or excessive/inappropriate guilt
- diminished ability to concentrate or think or indecisiveness
- recurrent thoughts of death, suicidal ideation, suicidal intent or suicidal attempt.

These 'symptoms' of depression can occur in a one-off episode (a major depressive episode), can recur more than once (a major depressive disorder) or be less severe but more persistent (dysthymia). Major depression includes a number of predominant features, such as melancholia or psychosis. In order to meet this classification these features must occur in the absence of other disorders, such as bipolar disorder, and should not be the result of a physical illness or be substance induced. There are limitations to this form of symptom classification, in that the links between individual experiences and environmental and psychosocial stressors – important elements in the development of depression – are not made explicit (APA, 2000).

Finally, although from a diagnostic perspective there are clear subtypes or clusters, from the perspective of clinical practice the meaning of these symptoms for clients can vary greatly, with no presentation being identical to the next. The people at our clinics or wards tend to have very personal narratives and interpretations of their depression experience and, in contrast to homogenising effects of diagnostic classifications, the clients we meet tend to be remarkable because of their differences. All of the above highlight the crucial role of case formulation in helping depressed individuals (see Chapter 2).

Cognitive accounts of depression

Key research, and clinical work on depression by Beck and his collaborators triggered the early theoretical development of cognitive therapy (Beck et al., 1979; Rachman, 1997), resulting in the CB approach becoming the psychotherapeutic intervention of choice for depression.

Beck developed an understanding of depression that, at the time, must have been viewed as radical, if not indeed revolutionary. As well as developing a psychological model for understanding depression that matched clients' experiences, he pioneered a way of working with each client in partnership (Beck, 1983).

Beck's theory of depression centres on a 'diathesis-stress' model. Stated simply, the proposition is that early life experiences make some individuals vulnerable to depression, which can be activated later in life by stressful events. In keeping with the cognitive model generally (see Chapter 2), this suggests that our early experiences are major factors in how we view ourselves, others and the world.

Formative early experiences lead to the development of unhelpful core beliefs. These, in turn, influence the development of subsequent compensatory assumptions or rules that function to prevent the activation of these core beliefs. If, for example, someone who grew up in a family environment where warmth, love and approval were absent, they may grow up with the core belief that they are unlovable. Over the years, they may attempt to gain love by applying rules aimed at eliciting favourable responses from others – for example, 'If I put the needs of others first, then they will love me.' It is important to emphasise that these processes are usually outside the attention of the person experiencing them and can remain dormant until activated by an external event (Beck et al., 1979).

Sociotropic and autonomous styles

Beck initially emphasised the role of uniquely individual latent unhelpful core beliefs and assumptions in the development of depression. However, his position subsequently shifted to a broader understanding of cognitive processes that reflected personality styles, suggesting that 'sociotropy' and 'autonomy' were possible predisposing factors (Beck, 1983). This view suggests that someone with a predominantly sociotropic personality style will have a greater need to be accepted by or have approval from others, placing their self-worth and individual needs after those of others. In contrast, autonomous personality types tend to place a greater value on independence, achievement of personal goals and being able to act without the need of others.

Of course, people tend not to be always trustworthy or reliable, so someone whose worth depends on the responses of others may be vulnerable to threats to their personal integrity. A sociotropic style will leave individuals vulnerable to depression when interpersonal relationships are threatened or lost. In contrast, people who are highly autonomous tend to derive their self-worth from achievements, such as education or employment. Autonomous individuals can thus have an increased vulnerability to depression as a result of failure in attainment, social isolation or environmental stressors, such as unemployment.

Unhelpful thinking

Vulnerability factors are activated by acute or chronic environmental stressors and, when activated, the way in which we view ourselves, our world and our future can radically change. Depression taints the way in which we process information and sufferers tend to have a bias towards the kinds of negative interpretations of interpersonal events described in Chapter 4. For example, someone with an unlovability schema, as mentioned above, may not answer a telephone call as they fear the possibility of a disapproving caller. Because of this prediction, their sense of isolation is increased, levels of activity reduced and they will have automatic thoughts regarding their unlovability, such as 'I should have answered the phone', 'They hate me' and 'I can't let them see me this way.'

Such unhelpful automatic thinking, (see Chapter 2), plays a significant role in the maintenance of depression, rather than causing it. However, in the context of depression, its significance changes as a result of low mood and related – often greatly reduced – behaviour (see Segal et al., 2001). In depression, negative automatic thoughts can be so habitual that they are taken for granted as being true. By identifying and challenging them and, subsequently, attaining a more balanced/realistic interpretation of such thoughts, people are able to reduce their levels of distress.

Does it work?

CB interventions for depression have been subject to intensive scientific testing for over 30 years. In randomised clinical control trials, they have been found to be as effective as antidepressant medication and other forms of therapy (Blackburn and Moorehead, 2000) and result in the reduction of recurring episodes (Teasdale et al., 2002). The approach can help individuals understand the development and maintenance of their depression, provide relatively quick relief from the distressing experiences associated with it and enable them to develop a proactive approach to managing their problems in the future. In terms of evidence-based practice (see also Chapter 15), as an empowering and cost-effective form of therapy, it constitutes a frontline intervention for depression (Cascalenda et al., 2002), with proven utility across the spectrum of mild to moderate levels of depression through to its more enduring forms (Scott et al., 2003).

Initial contact

Clients who tend to present to mental health practitioners have usually had depressive symptoms for some time (Segal et al., 2001). In the majority of cases the initial diagnosis will be made by a family practitioner and the client may already have received either medication and/or counselling (Sharp and Lipsky, 2002). The detection rates for depression in primary care can be relatively low, with clients having already tried to cope with or overcome their symptoms by themselves. It is important to remember from Chapters 2 and 4 that strategies such as avoidance of activity are personal attempts at coping and not maladaptive behaviours. For some people, for example, with high autonomy traits, the act of seeking help can be a confirmation of personal failure.

Within this context, our initial contacts must be marked with a high degree of non-judgemental sensitivity (see also Chapter 3). Our primary aim is to understand how the person is experiencing depression, as opposed to developing a checklist mentality to gathering information. The subjective experience of depression can make the assessment process problematic, as difficulty with concentration and memory and disruptive and distressing feelings, such as hopelessness, can inhibit both the client and the therapist. For this reason, it is important to fully explain the structure of the initial session(s) and explain that depressive experiences occuring during the session are both expected to occur during the assessment process and useful for it.

Let us now look at an example to illustrate these points. This and all the subsequent examples of cases given in this chapter are drawn from the clinical work of Mulhern.

'Dave'

Dave, a 38-year-old solicitor, was referred for CB help for depression. When asked how he felt about meeting a therapist and what he wanted to get out of our initial meeting, Dave became quite dejected, stating that 'it was the last straw.' What he meant was that needing to see me confirmed both that he had failed in his attempts to have control over his symptoms and his view of himself as a failure. He had never been able to talk to others about his emotions and felt threatened and disempowered in this situation.

Dave did not like the feeling of others being in control or revealing his emotional vulnerability. When asked how best to proceed, he said 'How am I supposed to know? You are the therapist.' At this juncture, rather than proceed with the assessment task of finding out about features of his depression, we formulated what it was like for him to feel vulnerable and not in control. By means of a collaborative, problem-solving approach and being able to agree that Dave had control over the pace and content of his self-disclosure, Dave felt abler to commit to the assessment process.

At the end of this initial session, I sought feedback on what Dave found most helpful. His reply was that what helped most was being listened to and feeling involved and empowered.

Although we had not addressed Dave's depression directly, we had examined a depressive process that would have inhibited engagement. When asked how he would have responded to my asking about his depressive experiences, he said that 'due to feeling frightened and not in control, I'm fairly sure I would have stormed out.' This emphasises the fact that there can be differing agendas for client and practitioner at initial assessment, especially as many service users will have had negative experiences of mental health care. In order to develop a good therapeutic alliance, therefore, it is essential that the contextual meaning for the client of the initial contact event is explored in an open, honest and collaborative manner (see Chapter 2).

The therapeutic alliance and depression

As practitioners, we are generally trained to believe that we are capable of developing the core sensitivities or building blocks essential in establishing good working relationships with those we seek to help. However, therapeutic alliances with depressed clients are not always formed as readily as we would like to think. Developing such a relationship with someone who is depressed involves attention to a number of factors.

We may bring our own assumptions and expectations of what the intervention should be about and what the client's role in the process 'should be'. Texts on mental health care interventions often betray the agenda that 'If only clients could see their problems the way we do, then they would be much more equipped to manage their distressing experiences more effectively.' Instead, in order to gain an empathic understanding of the person's experiences we need to work to see the world through their eyes.

Assessment

The main principles for the assessment of depression are similar to those outlined in Chapter 3. The assessment process can be viewed in four separate domains – namely context, content, process and outcome. As practitioners, we need to understand that the assessment process can be frightening, shameful and invalidating for some of the people we see. We must work to provide a therapeutic assessment environment within which people will feel able to let us into their inner world so we can begin to understand the uniquely personal content of someone's disclosure.

The information that clients give us can also have great interpersonal significance. We therefore have to listen very carefully to what is being said and what is not being said and the 'emotional temperature' of disclosures (Safran, 1998). In essence, we are not merely looking for historical or clinical facts, but also the personal, interpersonal and emotional meanings of what we hear.

Equally, we need to gain information on how the problem exists, how it is maintained and what the vulnerability factors are that have led to someone's individual experience of depression. We need to establish whether the principle problem is in fact depression, as it is not uncommon for people with other mental health problems or major environmental stressors, such as being a victim of domestic violence (see Chapter 9), to present as depressed.

The initial step in determining what someone's problems are is to ask them what they see as being their present difficulties. People can respond in a number of ways. It is not unusual to hear clients define their problems in terms of a diagnosis or feel overwhelmed and define their lives as the problem. When we are looking to clarify someone's difficulties, it is important to gather as much detailed information as possible. The example below illustrates the importance of helping someone to focus on the detail rather than the global experience of depression.

'Billy'

Therapist: What do you see as being the problem?

Billy: I'm depressed.

Therapist: When you say 'depressed' what do you mean by being depressed?

Billy: My life is a mess.

Therapist: That sounds overwhelming. In what ways has this affected your day-to-day life?

Billy: I can't go to work, I no longer see my friends and I can't be bothered to do anything.

Therapist: How do you feel when you are no longer doing these things?

Billy: I feel depressed.

Therapist: Can you give me a recent example of when you felt this way?

Billy: This morning.

Therapist: What was happening this morning?

Billy: The alarm went off, I was lying in bed and I just couldn't get up, I felt so tired.

Therapist: OK, so you are lying in bed, the alarm is going off and you feel unable to get up, what sorts of things were going through your mind?

Billy: I should be at work, but I know I can't face it. I'm lazy and I'm going to end up getting fired.

Therapist: How did you feel when all these things were going through your mind?

Billy: I felt angry with myself and useless – I wanted to scream.

Therapist: I've got an image of you lying in bed, the alarm has just gone off, you are physically tired, you have these unhelpful thoughts going through your head, like 'I should be at work' and having all these unpleasant feelings. What did you do?

Billy: I pulled the duvet over my head and tried to block the world out.

Therapist: When you did that, what happened next?

Billy: I couldn't stop thinking about how I should be getting up and getting on with things.

Therapist: What types of thoughts or images went through your mind then?

Billy: I could just see me standing in front of my boss, who was very angry and sacking me.

Therapist: That seems a scary image to have. How did you feel?

Billy: I felt frightened.

Therapist: Can I check this out with you? If we look at this morning, what happens is that the alarm goes off, you feel tired and stay in bed. When this happens you think that you are lazy and should be at work and will possibly be fired. When these thoughts go through your head, you feel angry and frightened. When you feel this way you try to shut the world out by staying in bed, but the thoughts and feelings return. When you say 'depressed' is this the type of experience you are describing?

Billy: Yes.

This vignette shows how, by asking for a recent example, the client is able to give a detailed account of their experience of depression rather than a global description. The questions asked were used to not only understand the person's experience, but also to link the physical, emotional, cognitive and behavioural domains that are involved in maintaining the problem (see Greenberger and Padesky, 1995 and Chapter 2). This model helps clients and clinicians to understand depression in a much clearer and subsequently manageable format. The various domains help to identify and position physical responses, such as insomnia and lethargy, and make links to unhelpful thoughts, unpleasant emotions and unhelpful behavioural coping strategies.

'Mary'

Mary is a 52-year-old widow who has lived alone for the last 20 years. She described her life as changing following a number of operations. These medical procedures were mainly exploratory, but resulted in Mary being physically incapacitated for a three-month period. During this time, she was unable to look after herself and found that relying on others made her feel sad, guilty, helpless and no longer in control of her day-to-day life. Once she was able to get back on her feet, she became aware of episodes of tearfulness, tiredness and a general feeling of uselessness.

In terms of helping her to understand her difficulties, the critical point of her series of operations was discussed as a major factor in her changes in mood. The model was explained by using a specific incident that had occurred that morning. The events and words used were the client's actual experience and were drawn out in diagrammatical form to assist Mary in the objectification and understanding of her responses. The case formulation diagram below represents how Mary, in a depressed mode, reacted to losing her house keys that morning.

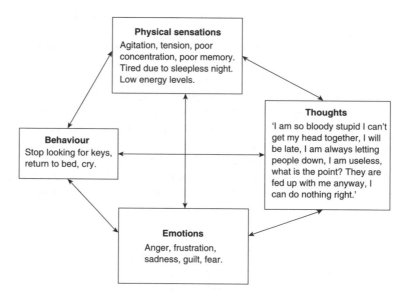

Contrast this with how she would have responded to losing her keys prior to her operations

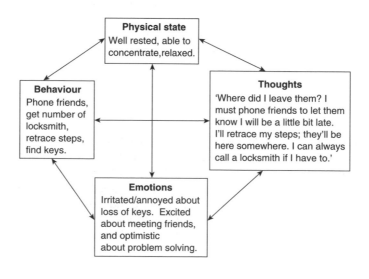

Mary was able to recognise that, since the operations, the way in which she responded to, and thought about, events had changed and she could make the connection between her unhelpful thinking, distressing emotions and returning to bed. By contrasting her depressive response with her more usual one, Mary was able to identify her thoughts and interpretations of events as key factors in the maintenance of her low mood.

This last example illustrates how helping the client to understand the rationale for the CB approach involves a process of gathering the relevant information, being able to understand where it fits into someone's experience and then presenting this understanding in a way that the client can easily relate to.

Having established a picture of what maintains the depression, it is then helpful to examine the precipitating and predisposing factors. When did the problem start? What was happening around this time? What underlying vulnerability factors led to its occurrence? Precipitating factors can vary from person to person. Also, it is not these incidents in themselves that are problematic, but what they mean to the person. For example, someone who is predominantly sociotropic may perceive the loss of a relationship to be significantly more distressing than would someone who is predominantly an autonomous character. Critical incidents can also lead to unhelpful internal attributions so, for example, someone who is made redundant may blame themselves rather than external circumstances, such as a downturn in the economy. From the critical incident, we can gain an insight into how long someone has been experiencing the distress and, by further questioning, what coping strategies they have employed.

Assessment of underlying psychological vulnerability

As stated previously, our views of ourselves, others and our world are generally determined by our early experiences. There are various ways in which to gain access to the underlying psychological mechanisms that lead to a vulnerability to depression.

Beck (1995) proposes some ways in which to access beliefs, as set out in the table below.

Strategy	Example
Provide the first part of an underlying assumption.	'If someone does not like you then … ?'
Using a downward arrow technique.	'If it were true that they did not like you, what would be so bad about that for you?'
Looking for common themes in someone's automatic thoughts.	For example, perfection, approval from others, failure and so on.
Asking the person directly if they have a specific rule about situations.	'I'm getting the feeling that it's important for you to present yourself as always being able to cope in these kinds of situations?'
Recognising when a belief is expressed as an automatic thought in relation to specific triggering events.	For example, 'I'm a loser', 'I'm worthless.'

In assessing someone who is depressed, it is important that practitioners undertake a thorough risk assessment. Although depression is not in itself a principle causal factor in suicide, it is important to recognise the impact of emotions and phenomena such as hopelessness – both of which can play a major role in eventual suicide. When undertaking a risk assessment, it is important to listen for certain clues or cues in relation to suicide and position these factors within an overall assessment.

Measures used in assessment and throughout the intervention

Measures for depression are used not only to determine whether the therapy is working or not, but also to help define depression in terms of nature and severity. They can also provide practitioners with information to inform and direct interventions. The Beck depression inventory, second edition (BDI II, Beck, 1996) is recognised as being a valid, reliable and sensitive measure of depression (see Chapter 3). This 21-item self-report measure can be used in a number of ways, including assessing whether or not a person is suicidal. Items 2 and 9 relate to pessimism and suicidal thoughts or wishes and are reliable indicators of the level of someone's hopelessness.

When items 2 and 9 are each scored at 2 or more, then it would be appropriate to measure the level of hopelessness using Beck's hopelessness scale (Beck et al., 1974). Then, if the client is suicidal, that needs to be addressed as a priority problem in its own right, which may require a risk management plan or be considered as part of the client's depressive experience.

High scores on certain aspects of the BDI are also useful pointers to a client's thinking, if they have difficulty in accessing specific automatic thoughts. These measures would ideally be employed on a weekly basis and help chart progress or not in relation to interventions. A significant and sustained reduction in BDI II scores may indicate a good time to address the underlying vulnerability factors of core beliefs and rules for living (see Chapters 2 and 4).

It is important to remember that measures such as the BDI II are not diagnostic tools and are only truly useful when a primary problem of depression is already established or when they are employed in conjunction with the practitioner's overall assessment. If the BDI II score is high and the mental health assessment gives no indication of clinical depression, then an axis II (APA, 2000) problem, such as borderline personality disorder, may be present (see Chapter 7).

Homework and depression

As stated in Chapters 3 and 4, the process of change in CB therapy is achieved by what the person learns as a result of prescribed activities outside the session. Beck (1995) points out that homework is an integral – not optional – component of the recovery process. Whereas therapy sessions are essential in helping the person to find new ways of understanding depression and, subsequently, more helpful strategies to deal with its impact, homework assignments – often in the form of behavioural experiments – represent the more potent agent in facilitating cognitive and behavioural change (see Chapter 4). Successful completion of homework assignments in depression tends to indicate better outcomes in therapy (Garland and Scott, 2002).

Behavioural interventions

Behavioural strategies for depression consist of monitoring activities, task analysis/graded task assignment and activity scheduling. Behavioural interventions can sometimes appear deceptively simple or simplistic to clinicians and clients alike. The general principle of being more balanced in activities that make us feel good (pleasure) or that reinforce our sense of personal achievement (mastery), when viewed from the outside, appear to be plain common sense. Within depression, however, the prospect of engaging in some behaviour can be processed as taking unacceptable risks. If someone believes that they will not attain a certain level of achievement and the outcome could mean a confirmation of themselves as a failure, then such tasks take on a different, emotionally laden aspect. Lowering of motivation levels is a common experience, which can lead to a pervasive sense of hopelessness and this makes it difficult to summon up the will and energy to do things that individuals truly believe will be of no benefit.

Behavioural interventions, therefore, may be the initial focus of interrupting the cycle of depressive responses. However, human beings tend not to do things without thinking. It is often necessary to work with the cognitive processes that prevent people engaging in helpful activities, so the concurrent use of thought diaries – introduced in Chapter 4 – is often appropriate. When people are enabled to make use of these types of interventions, the positive effect on someone's mood can be quite marked.

Assessing activity levels

We know from people's experiences of depression that they are likely to avoid activities that they may find to be overwhelming or unachievable (Greenberger and Padesky, 1995). This leads to behavioural patterns that reinforces inactivity and promote unhelpful cognitive processes, such as rumination. Rumination is believed to be an unhelpful attempt to solve our difficulties by exclusively focusing internally on our problems to the exclusion of other, perhaps more helpful, strategies (Wells, 1997). When depressed, we have a tendency to go over situations time and time again in order to find an elusive answer. When doing this, we can become preoccupied to the extent that this activity takes up so much space that it perpetuates psychological distress.

Prior to proposing behavioural interventions, it is useful to gather a baseline of someone's activity level. This is usually carried out as an initial homework exercise and provides recent accurate and relevant data. It is not uncommon for people to underestimate their levels of activity or for practitioners to see emerging patterns, such as someone devoting most of their time to activities that they derive little or no pleasure from. Understandably, when people are depressed they can find such tasks difficult to do. Practitioners need to be flexible in how they gather this information. Like all homework exercises, clients will do this more readily when they understand the rationale, which needs to be based on a collaboratively developed case formulation, feel able to complete it and believe it to be relevant in that it addresses their problems.

Practitioners need to help clients understand the rationale for activity monitoring within the initial sessions. Clients can dismiss or ignore certain activities as they do not see them as being personally meaningful – for example, getting out of bed or making a cup of tea. It is important to discuss what may hinder the process and work with any unhelpful thoughts the client may have about undertaking the task. The aim of the exercise is to gain a picture of the person's level of activity and then help them make the connection between the activity and their mood. The severity of the individual's depression will influence the amount of data that they are able to gather. For example, some people may be able to record their activity hourly in the course of a day. For others, it may be more relevant for them to record their activity during a morning in twenty-minute sections.

The table on pages 195–6 is an example of an activity-monitoring record for 'Lisa', where P = pleasure and M = mastery (or competence), both in relation to the recorded activity. She continues to work as a legal secretary and is generally active throughout her week. On examining her schedule, we can see that, at present, most of her time is spent in performing tasks that give her little pleasure, but, at work, she does feel a moderate degree of achievement or mastery. At home, she busies herself with household tasks and does not spend much time engaged in social or pleasurable pursuits. On seeing the extent of her engagement in the tasks that she didn't find pleasurable, she was able to make an instant connection between her behaviour and her low mood.

The table on page 197 is of an activity schedule for 'John', a 28-year-old man who suffers from a more severe form of depression. At the time of monitoring, he was an inpatient at an acute mental health unit. Rather than attempting to monitor a week of activity, we decided to reduce the task to fit with his biological and psychological resources. In John's case, this was for an afternoon. Prior to completing the task, John believed that he either 'stayed in bed' or 'did nothing all day.'

By monitoring his activity, John was able to see that he was being active but tended to discount this. Rating his mood enabled him to tentatively accept that his mood was influenced by his behaviour and that he tended to measure his 'performance' without taking into account the effect of his depression on his ability to recognise or appreciate when he was doing things.

Time	Monday	Tuesday	Wednesday	Thursday	Friday	Saturday	Sunday
7–8	Get self and kids ready, do breakfast.					Sleep.	Sleep.
8–9	Leave kids off to school. Drive to work.					Sleep.	Entertain kids. P6 M5
9–10	At work. P4 M5					Weekly laundry. P2 M6	Prepare Sunday lunch. P3 M7
10–11	At work.					Weekly laundry. P2M6	Church. P5 M0
11–12	At work. P4 M6					Drop kids off to friends/husband to golf club. P4 M0	Read Sunday newspaper. P5 M0
12–1	Half-hour break. P8 M2					Food shopping. P1M2	Play with kids. P7 M0
1–2	Work. P6 M3					Food shopping. P1 M2.	Lunch.
2–3	Work.					Collect kids from friends. Prepare snack.	Wash up. Vacuum.
3–4	Work.			Therapy session.		Mow the lawn.	Go over finances/budget for next week. Argue with husband.
4–5	Collect kids, drive home. P3 M2					Watch film on TV with the kids. P7 M1	
5–6	Prepare dinner. P2 M5					Collect husband from golf club.	
6–7	Dine and wash up. P0 M0	P0M0				Prepare and cook dinner. P0 M4	

(Continued)

(Continued)

Time	Monday	Tuesday	Wednesday	Thursday	Friday	Saturday	Sunday
7–8	Get kids ready for bed/review homework.	Get kids ready for bed/review homework.	Get kids ready for bed/review homework.		Listen to therapy tape. P1 M2	Clean the kitchen. P0 M2	Drive husband to local public house. Review kids' homework.
8–9	Do washing and cleaning.				Vacuum and clean living areas.	Watch television. P7 M0	Prepare family clothes for tomorrow.
9–10	Prepare kids stuff for a.m. Vacuum downstairs.				Put kids to bed.	Catch up with friends by telephone.	Collect husband from pub. Put kids to bed.
10–11	Bath, take sleeping tablet, go to bed.		Watch TV, chat with husband.			Few glasses of wine with husband. P5 M0	Retire to bed. Have sex. P1 M2

Time	Activity
1.00–1.20	Join queue and take medication.
1.20–1.40	Make and drink coffee.
1.40–2.00	Play pool with nursing staff.
2.00–2.20	Sit in lounge thinking.
2.20–2.40	Try to read the newspaper but can't.
2.40–3.00	Walk around the unit.
3.00–3.20	Sit thinking/have a smoke.
3.20–3.40	Join in quiz in the unit. Leave early.
3.40–4.00	Talk about problems with nurse.
4.20–4.30	Talk with nurse.
4.30–4.40	Play pool.

Task analysis and graded task assignment

Feeling overwhelmed by, and being unable to complete, everyday tasks previously taken for granted is a common feature of the depressive experience. Related to this is the tendency for people not to validate the disabling impact of depression. People tend to retain or have an increased expectation of themselves that fails to take into account the disruption and interference caused by phenomena such as insomnia or memory impairment. Everyday behaviour, such as brushing our teeth or preparing a meal, is made up of a series of actions that, when broken down into their components, are more complicated than they initially appear. When depressed, people can experience responses that inhibit their ability to sequence the actions needed in order to achieve their desired goal.

Mary, described earlier in this chapter, was someone who found it difficult to complete the tasks that she set herself. In the first few weeks of the intervention, she described how she did not go out unless it was a necessity. This resulted in her increased isolation and reduction in activity. On exploring the reasons for this, it became apparent that she could no longer find the energy or the inclination to wash her clothes. She had overcome this previously in a number of ways – by having others do it for her when she was incapacitated or buying new clothes or using the launderette, for example. Financial issues now meant that the latter two options where no longer viable and the former represented a further risk – that of confirming her inability to cope.

Mary spoke of how, on numerous occasions, she had tried but always given up in despair. It became apparent that Mary had attempted to do all her washing at once. She would set out her clothes in bundles, look at the 'mountain' she had to wash, become disheartened, then retreat to her bed, where she would berate herself for being useless and stupid.

We examined this in the light of her case formulation. Mary was able to identify her 'all or nothing' thinking, her assumptions concerning perfection and her beliefs about her worth being based on success (see Chapters 2 and 4). She was also able to recognise how her thoughts and behaviour after withdrawing to her bed reinforced her depressed mood.

This event – washing her clothes – was used to highlight the need to break tasks into smaller, more manageable parts. Below is an example of how Mary's therapist showed her that she was able to do this.

Therapist: OK Mary, we can see that there is a tendency to take things on in an 'all or nothing' way. When you do that, it ends up with you feeling pretty miserable and the perfectionist rule leads to you having a stream of unpleasant and unhelpful thoughts. How could we approach this differently?

Mary: I don't know. I've always been able to knuckle down and do things in that way.

Therapist: What's changed now so that way doesn't work for you?

Mary: The whole depression thing. It just stops me from doing what I need to do.

Therapist: Can I ask, what made you put the clothes into different bundles rather than put all your clothes into the machine at once?

Mary: Are you stupid? The machine couldn't take all my clothes at once. The colours would mix with the whites – it would be a disaster. The machine would break down and that would mean I had to buy a new washer.

Therapist: So it is important to fit the wash load to the machine's capability?

Mary: Yeah, course it is. Ah! I see what you're getting at. I don't expect my washer to do it all at once but I do me.

Therapist: Good. How do we make the mountain more manageable?

Mary: I need to wash clothes that will get me out over the next few days, that's all. I keep telling you I'm stupid. Why couldn't I see that?

The remainder of the session focused on Mary drawing up a plan of what she needed to do to get her washing done. She listed the processes from planning (making sure that she had powder and conditioner) through to implementation (what time of day, what she would do between stages – introduce short, pleasurable activities). We predicted possible impediments and rehearsed what to do. We agreed this homework assignment as a way of putting to the test which method (if any) was most helpful. This was not an experiment to explore ways of doing tasks as opposed to a measure of Mary's competency. She found out that she was able to complete her washing and maintained this achievement, which, in turn, enabled her to go out a lot more. Although she did not gain much pleasure from the activity, she achieved an increased, but not complete, sense of mastery. By increasing her contact with friends and spending less time on her own, her level of pleasure increased.

Activity scheduling

Once a baseline has been established for what someone is doing and how their activity patterns are influencing the maintenance of depression, the schedule can then be used to help reduce this. As with the monitoring process, it is essential that we match our expectations to the resources available. For example, John (the man in the inpatient unit) would not be expected to plan and complete a full week's activity schedule. Goals must be realistic and achievable.

Activity scheduling is a process that evolves in the course of therapy and is not a one-stop solution for unhelpful levels of activity or inactivity. It is a useful means of providing a daily structure or plan that enables people to have a sense of control and direction in their daily lives. It can also help to reduce periods of depressive thinking, decrease the need for repeated decision/risk taking and increase subjective experiences of pleasure and mastery. As stated previously, behavioural interventions also provide an opportunity to address unhelpful thoughts or beliefs that arise as a result of attempting behavioural change.

From the activity-monitoring process with Lisa we learned that the majority of her time was spent on tasks that gave her little or no sense of pleasure, so, at that point in the intervention, the dialogue turned to help Lisa explore alternative strategies to reduce her sense of burden. When asked what her partner could do to help out, she replied that 'it is not man's work', that 'I need to find a better system' and that her partner shared and encouraged these beliefs. Although Lisa was aware that she was 'overloaded', she felt that she would be unable to enlist the help of her partner.

At this point two theories about the situation were proposed, shown in the table below.

Theory 1 – Lisa's	Theory 2 – Mulhern's
All child and house care are my responsibility. If I reduce my level of burden by finding a better system, my mood will improve.	Both you and your partner have inherited rules and assumptions about home and child care. These include 'if I do not do everything for my child then I am a bad mother', and 'women must look after men.' Acting on those assumptions as if they are true helps to maintain your low mood. If you modify them, your mood should improve.

It was agreed that the next step was to test out both of these theories, with Lisa's being tried out first for a two-week period. The BDI was used as a measure of the effect on her mood and the pleasure and mastery scores on the activity schedule were used to judge the efficacy of the new system. It was further agreed that, if this proved unsuccessful, we would meet with Lisa's partner and explore the possibility of working with, and modifying, the shared rules and assumptions. This 'agreeing to differ' and testing out the theories route was used in order to avoid conflict and possible ruptures within the therapeutic alliance.

Testing out theory 1 actually increased Lisa's BDI score and resulted in an overall decrease in her level of mastery, with no gain in her level of pleasure. Lisa and her partner found testing out theory 2 quite difficult. Lisa had previously shown her partner a copy of her formulation. He had agreed with it in principle, but believed that Lisa's low mood was a matter for her to sort out. It was difficult for him to take on more 'work' as he was always exhausted on returning home.

By understanding where the rules about what constitutes 'women's work' came from (early experiences, society norms), how they are particularly helpful for men (abdication of responsibility, reduction in caregiving), that they do not take into account changes within society (women's desire or need to work outside the home) and that now they were having a direct impact on the family unit (Lisa being depressed, her partner worrying about her health and its effect on their children), they agreed to try out a shared activity schedule for a two-week period.

This experiment was uncomfortable for both of them initially. In the first two weeks there were slight gains, but, after they agreed to continue for a month, the gains for both were more substantial. Lisa's mood improved, as measured by a reduction in her BDI score, she was able to engage in pleasurable activities both inside and outside the home (meet with friends twice a week) and gained much greater pleasure from time spent with her children. Her partner also reported being less concerned about Lisa's health, feeling more energised when at home and more positive about the time he spent with his family. This example highlights the importance of matching specific interventions with the social and material environments within which they can be implemented.

Monitoring behavioural interventions

As we come to the end of this chapter, it is important to emphasise that behavioural interventions for depressed clients must be constantly monitored and scrutinised. Obstacles will, and frequently do, occur and it is the role of the practitioner to help the client uncover what they are, understand their helpful and unhelpful natures and enable the client to discover ways to overcome such difficulties. It is not the job of the practitioner to push the process forward, but, rather, help the client explore a range of options to test out and find the most helpful ways in which to do their usual activities.

As with Lisa above, it is sometimes difficult not to make value judgements and believe that there is an easy solution. Like all interventions, it is essential to develop a collaborative, detailed analysis of the problem, help the client to develop their own solutions, plan in detail for any obstacles and set the intervention up as a no-lose experiment.

This detail may seem unnecessarily pedantic, but should be considered with regard to an example from my own practice, when I failed to pay sufficient attention to detail as I was developing an activity schedule with a severely depressed client. She was planning to go to the cinema with her sister and we worked out time, place, transport and finances, but did not take into account the film she intended to see. When we met the day following the trip to the cinema, she stated how taking part in the activity had made her 'ten times worse' and that she couldn't stop thinking about the film and crying. It was *Schindler's List*!

SUMMARY

- Depression is a major worldwide health problem.
- The diagnostic classification of depression has strengths and limitations.
- The CB explanation of depression derives from the work of Beck and helps us to understand the relationship between unhelpful thinking, emotion and behaviour.
- Initial contact with a person suffering with depression calls for sensitivity on the part of the practitioner and underscores the significance of the therapeutic alliance.
- Careful assessment in helping a person with depression, includes exploration of underlying psychological vulnerability and measurement.
- Client homework is essential when helping someone with depression.
- The assessment of client's activity levels is also a pivotal therapeutic tool and offers opportunities with regard to task analysis, graded task assignment and activity scheduling.
- Matching interventions to client's environments, and carefully monitoring them are essential strategies.

Activities

- Attempt to undertake a behavioural activity monitoring schedule. Identify any problems you encounter with this and record them.
- Highlight unhelpful thoughts that inhibit the possible completion of the schedule and challenge these thoughts (using the methods described in Chapters 4, 5 and 16).
- Assess and conceptualise depression with one of your clients using a case formulation model from Chapter 2.

Further reading

Beck, A.T., Rush, A.J., Shaw, B.F., and Emery, G., 1979, *Cognitive Therapy for Depression*. New York: Guilford Press.
This introduces the reader to key, and still relevant, historical work on the development of the cognitive approach for depression.

Leahy, R.L., and Holland, S.J., 2000, *Treatment Plans and Interventions for Depression and Anxiety Disorders*. New York: Guilford Press.
The reader is able to consider the relevance of a range of assessment and intervention protocols, as well as guided reading, for depressed clients.

Fennell, M., 1989, 'Depression', in Hawton, K., Salkovskis, P.M., Kirk, J., and Clark, D.M. (eds), *Cognitive Behaviour Therapy for Psychiatric Problems: A Practical Guide*. New York: Oxford University Press.
An excellent and comprehensive overview of the cognitive approach to depression.

FOURTEEN Working with People Who are Anxious

Nigel Short, Alec Grant, Jem Mills and Ronan Mulhern

Learning objectives

After reading this chapter and completing the activities at the end of it you should be able to:

1 describe anxiety from a CB perspective
2 outline the role of behaviour in maintaining anxiety difficulties
3 describe some theoretical explanations of anxiety
4 outline key strategies and principles in beginning work with someone, including fostering hope
5 describe the ways in which individuals' fearful predictions serve to maintain anxiety
6 explain what is meant by 'fear of fear'
7 describe the role of avoidance in maintaining anxiety difficulties
8 understand the importance of behaviour experiments in helping someone with anxiety difficulties.

Introduction

The experience of anxiety is related to elaborate mechanisms that have been developed over the history of humankind to help us adapt to new situations and keep us safe from potential threats. This chapter considers what we mean by anxiety and explores what happens when it becomes a difficulty. Some theoretical explanations are described, along with simple behavioural experiments for the reader. The discussion broadens to focus on helpful ways in which to overcome or manage the distress associated with anxiety difficulties and the chapter concludes with three case examples representing common anxiety problems presented to mental health practitioners.

What do we mean by anxiety?

Anxiety is a normal human reaction in times of danger and stress. It becomes problematic when an anticipated or imminent threat or pervasive sense of vulnerability generates relatively long-lasting changes in mood, body sensations, thinking and behaviour. The aim of this chapter is not to show how anxiety can be banished from people's experiences, but more to describe how people can be helped to learn to manage their distress differently and feel more in control of their anxiety on the basis that:

> ... people are more likely to interpret situations as being more dangerous than they are because of their own particular assumptions and beliefs that have been previously learned. The second factor concerns the way the threat is appraised.
>
> Beck and Emery, 1985: 5

When trying to help people understand their difficulties, it is important to help them make links between their thinking, the physical sensations that accompany the thoughts and their subsequent behaviours. Helping people to identify these thoughts is discussed later in this chapter. For now, it is important to examine the role of behaviour in anxiety problems.

The role of behaviour

There is much discussion in the CB literature regarding the mechanism mediating anxiety. Salkovskis (1991, 1996) highlighted the importance of threat beliefs and safety-seeking behaviour. When someone experiences anxiety, their behaviour becomes linked with their perception of threat and may be coupled with anticipatory fears. These either lead them to want to avoid the feared situation or escape from it if they are in it.

Avoidance and escape have long been recognised in people experiencing anxiety and can be considered as gross forms of safety-seeking behaviour. More subtle forms include very discreet, often unseen behaviour. For example, someone who fears that they might collapse because of wobbly legs may tense their muscles in the supermarket to prevent this from happening. Equally, having the thought that an increase in heart rate means that one is about to experience a heart attack is likely to provoke safety-seeking behaviours, such as taking to bed or calling an ambulance. The difficulty with these behaviours is that the person concerned fails to find out whether or not their fears are warranted.

The important point here is how the person interprets their unique set of circumstances at any given time. These interpretations may not be accurate, but are reasonable responses on the basis of the person's attributions made in relation to their difficulties. Practitioners can use the individual's theory about this to help with initial engagement, as shown in the following example of dialogue between a client and a practitioner.

Client: When I get home, I can either go up to the third floor in the lift or I can walk up the stairs. I think if I get in the lift I will start to suffocate and will lose control, so I always take the steps.

Practitioner: That's not surprising then. If I believed I was going to suffocate and lose control I might do the same.

Let's look at another two examples to see what is being avoided – anxiety or the consequences of anxiety?

> My children ask me to get their bicycles out of the shed. My first concern is the spiders hiding in the roof of the garden shed. If I see them I know I will get very anxious. They frighten me. I try many different ideas to keep me away from my anxiety, such as 'I'm busy', 'There isn't much sunlight left today – perhaps tomorrow' or 'The tyres are punctured – I haven't got anything to repair them with.'

Here, the client is attempting to avoid the anxiety.

> I am driving home one evening. I notice I'm having odd, infrequent heartbeats. I think that there is something wrong. I pull over and stop the car. I make an appointment to see my GP. I take an aspirin and cancel the evening at the gym. I know that my dad died of a heart attack, as did his dad. With this historical information it may not be surprising that I try to prevent a heart attack from occurring. If I do not experience a heart attack, I may believe that the behaviour I perform prevent it from occurring.

The types of behaviour described are performed to avoid the feared outcome – that the client might have a heart attack.

As highlighted in Chapter 2, it is useful to consider the relationship between thinking styles and different types of emotions. When people experience anxiety, the content of their thoughts usually focus on a perceived threat – 'If I go into the supermarket I will get anxious.' Alternatively, they may make a prediction about what might happen if they confront a perceived threat – 'If I don't get out of this supermarket my heart will explode.'

Practitioners using the CB approach to anxiety gently help their clients to consider alternative explanations for their particular difficulties. Sadly, it is not unusual for clients to experience unhelpful suggestions from practitioners, such as 'try to stop thinking your thought', 'your thinking is irrational' (Short et al., 2003). CB interventions help them to identify where they may have become unhelpfully caught by the ways in which they think and behave and offer opportunities to discover other ways to approach their difficulties. Before exploring those, it is necessary to describe some theories of the significance and function of anxiety for human beings.

Some theories of anxiety

Evolutionary psychologists examine the role of evolved psychological mechanisms in shaping human behaviour and experience. These mechanisms have developed into their current form as a result of our ancestors having successfully solved specific adaptive challenges. Generally, an adaptive solution is one that increases the chance that genes will be transmitted on to subsequent generations as these people will survive as a result (Hofman et al., 2002).

It has been argued that our evolutionary biological legacy may well influence psychopathology (Marks and Nesse, 1997; Gilbert, 2002; Leahy, 2002). In the course of the history of humankind, this legacy has developed to keep us safe, promote survival and assist in reproduction. Leahy (2002) argues that our brains evolved to select specific strategies that help us engage with the world. The precise details of these may not always be readily available to the conscious mind and so may not be addressed by logic alone. Once chosen, the strategy or strategies help us to find reasons to avoid or escape and are essentially motivated by a desire to reduce risk.

There are many different types of problems for an individual to solve – for example, finding food and keeping safe. Evolutionary psychologists have suggested that different programmes have developed to help solve these problems. Tooby and Cosmides (1992) have proposed using the notion of the 'modular mind' to describe these different and separate activities. The modular mind aims to protect whatever 'investments' in their genes the individual will make.

Developing from earlier theories of conditioning, the proposal was made in the early 1970s that psychological difficulties could usefully be thought about in relation to three interacting systems: verbal, behavioural and physiological (Rachman and Hodgson, 1974; see also Chapter 2). This account supported the idea that psychological difficulties are mediated by the meaning of the overall experience for the person. Beck and Emery (1985), similarly, suggested that the core problem in anxiety difficulties is in the cognitive processing of the situation, so that interventions should attempt to modify existing or anticipated difficulties by virtue of altering cognitions or cognitive processes.

The general focus of the CB intervention

As was made evident in Chapter 2, it can be very helpful for some people to have an understanding of the development of their problems. However, the main concern of an intervention should be on how people are thinking, feeling and behaving today, rather than focusing too much on early experiences (Leahy and Holland, 2000). It is not essential for people to know how and when their problems started in order to overcome them now – a point made by Laing (1960: 87): 'Imagine you wake up one morning in a prison cell and the door is open. Do you spend time finding out how you got in there or do you walk out of the door?'

Barker (2000), in support of this theme, asserted: 'Imagine someone stops you in the street and asks for directions. We would not routinely ask them where they have just come from.'

Beginning to work with someone

When helping people to understand their distress, it can be useful for them to consider their experiences as something that can be tackled and managed. It is not unusual for people to make statements such as, 'I am just waiting for the panic to happen' or 'the attacks come out of the blue.' Clearly these descriptions sound like the person thinks that they have little or no control over their difficulties. This appraisal can be helped using CB interventions.

Many people describe their anxiety difficulties as physical experiences, reporting, for example, a dry mouth, increased heart rate, increased breathing and sweaty hands. CB approaches use this important information to draw attention to the importance of the thoughts the individual has about such physical experiences. This can be achieved by, for example, asking the person to discuss in detail a recent example of their difficulties. If they are unable to do this, then it may be helpful to encourage them to monitor their thoughts the next time they experience these problems.

However, people often have difficulties identifying their thoughts when they are not experiencing anxiety, so it is not surprising that this may be all the more difficult to pin down when they do have distressing sensations. It is helpful for the person to realise that this is not unusual. People do not necessarily pay attention to what they are thinking, particularly their automatic thoughts. Thinking about thinking – so-called metacognition (Wells, 1997, 2000) – may be an unusual idea for people, so they may need some help to find out what they think about and how this relates to physical sensations and behaviour. Consider the following example.

'Kevin' is in a lift. He notices his hands getting warm and his heart rate increasing. He thinks that he is going to suffocate. His heart rate continues to increase and he can feel it pounding in his chest. He begins to think that he is going to have a heart attack. He gets out of the lift on the next floor and his bodily sensations begin to reduce.

Here, Kevin began by thinking that he was going to have heart attack. It is not surprising that he did whatever he thought necessary to prevent this from happening. Clearly, in this situation Kevin knew what his thoughts were and acted on them.

Let's take another example.

'Lucy' is at home with her young children. She sees her two-year-old daughter pick something off the floor and play with it. Lucy becomes anxious and takes the item away from her daughter, washes her child's hands and then washes the floor. Her anxiety reduces.

Lucy had no idea what was going through her mind. Her immediate goal was to remove the item from her daughter and clean the floor, knowing that this action would reduce her anxiety. It is not unusual for people experiencing these types of anxiety difficulties to fail to notice or recall what was going through their minds at the time. However, with some help, Lucy was able to identify her thoughts, as the following dialogue illustrates.

Practitioner:	I wonder if we can look at the situation you described in more detail. You said that you saw Rebecca pick something off the floor and start playing with it. Is that right?
Lucy:	Yes. I saw Rebecca pick something up from the floor. My heart rate went up and I panicked.
Practitioner:	Can I just check this out further? You saw Rebecca pick something up from the floor, your heart rate increased and you panicked. Can you remember what was going through your mind at the time?

Lucy:	I thought, 'If I don't take that from her she might get germs and then become ill.'
Practitioner:	I see. So, if you hadn't taken it away from her, she might have become ill. What would happen then?
Lucy:	She could have died and it would be my fault.

In this example, Lucy needed some help to identify what was going through her mind at the time, which was that she thought her daughter might become ill and possibly die. The important component here is that, at the time, she believed this. This belief then affected Lucy's behaviour, emotions and physical sensations.

Thinking about thinking

Activity – an experiment
Ask your colleagues at work or some of your friends if they will help you with an experiment. If they agree, ask them the question, 'What's going through your mind right now?'

What did you find out?
I suspect that they may have said things such as, 'I don't know' or maybe, 'What shall I have for supper tonight' or 'I must get those holiday photos from the chemist.' The list of possibilities is endless. It would be very surprising if anyone said, 'I was just thinking about what I was thinking about.'

Activity – another experiment
Now try repeating the question, followed by the question, 'What went through your mind when I asked you to tell me what you were thinking about?'

What did you find out this time?
You may have had responses such as, 'What are they asking me that for?', 'What are they going to do with the information', 'What a crazy idea', 'That's an interesting idea.' Again, the list is potentially endless.

If people you are working with or friends have difficulty with the idea of thinking about thinking, try the following.

Practitioner:	I appreciate that the types of questions I am asking you may sound unusual – asking you to think about the way you think. Have you ever been asked to think about your difficulties in this way before?
Client:	No, I haven't.
Practitioner:	So, maybe it's not surprising, then, that you may have to think about this idea. Let's see if we can help each other out more. You know when you were waiting to see me today, can you remember what sorts of ideas were going through your mind at the time?

Please note that, by saying 'ideas', we are giving the person the opportunity to tell us about images that they might have experienced as people often experience images in addition to, or instead of, verbal thoughts.

This may elicit important automatic thoughts that can be used to help people see how the CB model might work for them. Here are some examples:

- 'I wondered what you might ask me today.'
- 'I thought about the last time I met you.'
- 'I know nothing about why I'm here.'
- 'I had an idea that you would be short and wearing a suit.'

At this early stage you may want to try additional questions, such as those in the following continuation of the conversation between a practitioner and their client.

Practitioner:	Did you notice whether any of those ideas changed the way you were feeling?
Client:	Yes I did. When I thought about what you were going to ask me, my heart rate increased. I then thought that you might think I'm silly.
Practitioner:	That's interesting. So when you thought, 'I wonder what he is going to ask me', you thought I might think you were silly and your heart rate increased. What happened next?
Client:	I picked up a magazine and started looking at the pictures.
Practitioner:	What happened when you looked at the pictures?
Client:	It took my mind off things.
Practitioner:	I see. That sounds like a good example that fits with our model and might help us make sense of your difficulties. So the automatic thought, 'I wonder what he is going to ask me today?', brought along a change in body sensations. Your heart rate increased and then you did something – you looked at the pictures in the magazine to take your mind off things. What happened to your heart rate?
Client:	It went down.

At this stage it is useful to draw a diagram of what the client has described to you. (see Chapters 2 and 3). Doing this with the person can help them to appreciate more how a CB model can apply to their difficulties and distance them from their worries. In the example below, the three systems diagram is extended to incorporate the behaviour that reduces the client's physical sensations, offering relief.

This might help the client to begin to consider that what they are doing may be maintaining their difficulties. In this example, they may have learned that doing something else, such as looking at pictures, helps them to manage their anxiety. In addition, if you see any changes in the person's mood when you are talking with them, ask them at that moment, 'What was going through your mind just now?' This process may be used to help them realise that their thinking influences their emotions.

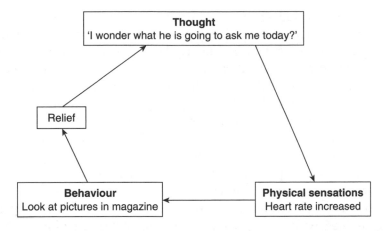

Predictions driven by, and maintaining, anxiety

Many of the fears that people worry about do carry some risk. For example, there is a risk of dogs biting us or having an accident in a car, so some fears are not completely irrational or unhelpful. However, CB interventions for people suffering from anxiety-related problems adhere to the central idea that people often misinterpret danger and underestimate their ability to confront feared objects or situations. When we experience anxiety, our thinking often becomes extreme and biased. The most common biases are:

- overestimating the likelihood that something bad will happen – 'If I see a dog in the park it's bound to come over and bite me'
- overestimating how serious an event will be – 'If I get stuck in the lift, it will take hours for someone to come and help'
- underestimating our ability to cope – 'If a spider comes near me I will go mad and be taken to hospital'
- underestimating other people's abilities to help and not trusting them to help – 'If I faint in the supermarket, everyone will start laughing at me.'

These ways of thinking then make the danger seem much worse than it is, with the thoughts making individuals feel even more frightened. In turn, the more frightened they are, the more fearful their thoughts become. It follows that behavioural experiments, collaboratively designed between practitioner and client, are helpful in testing out the beliefs that actually serve to maintain anxiety (see Chapter 4).

Fear of fear

When people are confronted with a feared object or situation, anxiety can develop very quickly, generating a range of uncomfortable physical sensations.

These sensations, including increased heart rate, sweaty palms and breathing heavily can be uncomfortable and may be misinterpreted in catastrophic ways. For example, an increase in heart rate may be attributed to an impending heart attack. Becoming disorientated can lead us to think that we are going mad. Thoughts such as, 'I feel bad, so something horrible is going to happen', are not unusual. It is understandable and not surprising that when people feel like this they will avoid the object or situation and associated worries. If the uncomfortable feelings are associated with an object or situation, then fears about those objects or situations may become more pronounced. People may then avoid anything that may prompt or trigger these physical sensations.

When we become anxious, it seems reasonable to try and keep ourselves safe. As discussed earlier, this may have an evolutionary underpinning as well as being influenced by the person's appraisal of the situation at the time. However, some of the strategies that people use to keep safe may make their difficulties worse. Consider the following examples.

Imagine someone who is frightened of driving. When they are in their car, driving, they grip the steering wheel tightly, causing tension in their muscles. They concentrate on their feelings and not the road or other road users, ensuring that they keep well within the speed limit.

Next, imagine a person who is worried about being in social situations. They are concerned that people may think they are boring. They then concentrate so much on what they are going to say that they may appear disinterested and possibly bored. They may also worry that their hands will shake. They hold their glass or teacup really tightly. The consequence of this is that their hands shake.

These types of behaviour may provide temporary relief from the situation, but they do not reduce the fear in the long term.

Avoiding fears

People with different types of anxiety go out of their way to avoid what they are afraid of. Avoidance is one of the main factors maintaining anxiety. People will use this word when describing their difficulties, saying, for example, 'I avoid having blood taken unless absolutely necessary.' While avoidance makes sense to people, we can understand from a CB perspective that it is one of the main factors that keep people's difficulties going. Avoidance leads to the fear becoming exaggerated and does not allow the person to test out their anxiety-driven beliefs. For example, if someone is worried about needles, their continued avoidance of injections and possible reliance on anxiety-reducing medication will prevent them from discovering that they may well feel uncomfortable but will not go crazy.

Safety behaviour and phobic anxiety

These types of behaviour have been discussed before but are worth considering again here when thinking about phobias (Butler, 1989). As a form of avoidance, safety behaviour works in the short term, but maintains the fear in the long term, as the following examples demonstrate.

Imagine someone who is fearful of spiders. They may check every room they enter, look behind curtains, avoid going on holidays and be unable to get their children's bikes out of the shed. They are on their guard all the time and attentive to the dangers of coming across them.

Equally, imagine someone who is fearful of fainting in a supermarket. They can only go when a friend is able to accompany them. They may take talismans with them, such as a lucky charm. They may suck on sweets so their mouth remains moist. They may have to hold on to the supermarket trolley.

These examples of safety behaviour may help temporarily. However, they may also leave people thinking that the only reason they have been safe is because of what they have done. They do not have an opportunity to find out if their fears were unrealistic.

Looking for danger or threats

When people have a particular fear, they tend to be on the lookout for their feared object or situation. Being constantly alert in this way contributes to the experience of anxiety and is also very tiring. By attending to the possibility of feared objects or situations, people are on edge most of the time. These threats also mobilise our bodies' physical systems to stay alert to danger. Unfortunately, this attention to danger means that people often unnecessarily trigger their responses to innocuous objects or situations, as the following examples show clearly.

Imagine someone who has a fear of snakes. They may misinterpret a piece of string on the grass as being a snake.

Further, imagine someone who has a fear of spiders. When they enter a room, they scan the environment for spiders. They often mistakes small marks on the carpet, chipped paint on the wall and so on for spiders.

Also, imagine someone who has a fear of being trapped in an enclosed space. They may become highly anxious of the sliding doors on a train if they do not open immediately the train has stopped.

There are many different types of anxiety and it is beyond the scope of this book to discuss them in detail (see the Further reading section at the end of this chapter for sources of more information), but the principles of helpful interventions remain similar for different anxiety disorders. Overcoming fear essentially involves understanding it and gradually testing out whether or not it is reasonable or accurate by means of behavioural experiments. In preparation for this work, thought diaries are extremely useful (see Chapter 4).

Behavioural experiments

The stages of a behavioural experiment to help with an anxiety problem are as follows:

- be attentive to your anxious thoughts and predictions
- describe your coping strategies and safety behaviour
- think through and re-evaluate your predictions
- be aware of your physical sensations
- develop an experiment to test out your anxious predictions, such as coming face to face with your fears
- start with a situation that you think you will have success with
- move on to gradually more and more difficult situations.

One useful way to help someone formulate a behavioural experiment (Greenberger and Padesky, 1995; see also Chapter 2) is to develop a sentence that contains an 'If …, then' statement. For example:

- '*If* I enter the supermarket, *then* people will start laughing at me'
- '*If* I don't take my mobile phone with me, *then* I will become anxious'
- '*If* I have an injection, *then* I will pass out'
- '*If* I sit that exam, *then* I'm bound to fail.'

Once these predictions have been made, the practitioner can enquire how much the client believes the statement. A scale of 0–100 can be used. The following dialogue is an example of this process in practice.

Practitioner: So you think that 'If you go into the supermarket, then people will start laughing at you.' Is that correct?
Client: Yes, that's it.
Practitioner: If we use a scale of 0–100 – where '0' means no belief and '100' means total belief – where would you score your belief now?
Client: At 90 per cent.

The client is then gently encouraged to test this belief out by, in this case, going into the supermarket. A discussion takes place before entering the shop and focuses on how the client might find out whether or not people will actually laugh at him. It is agreed that looking at the other people in the shop will help. The client acknowledged that it has been difficult to see if people are looking at him because he usually stares at the floor (safety behaviour).

The client managed to stay in the supermarket for 20 minutes. During this time he looked at the other people in the shop.

Practitioner: So, what happened?
Client: I was able to stay in the supermarket for about 20 minutes. I did get anxious to begin with, then I felt more comfortable.
Practitioner: What were the other people doing?
Client: They seemed to be getting on with their own shopping.
Practitioner: Did any of them laugh at you?
Client: I didn't see anyone laugh at me.
Practitioner: Before we went in there you said, 'If I enter the supermarket, then people will start laughing at me.' Can you remind me how much you said you believed this?

Client: I said 90 per cent.
Practitioner: So how much do you believe that statement now?
Client: About 5 per cent.

When developing collaborative goals as experiments, it is important that these are done within a realistic hierarchy, as a gradual approach to anxiety difficulties is more likely to be acceptable to the client than some major change or challenge (Kirk, 1989). The metaphor of learning to swim is a useful example. Most people learn to swim by starting in the shallow end and make their way to the deep end. CB experiments can be seen in the same way. In metaphorical terms, the practitioner can be seen as the therapeutic armbands and, as the person becomes more confident in their ability to tackle their problems, the practitioner can slowly begin to reduce their involvement.

Putting Ideas into practice

To conclude this chapter, the following three case examples serve to illustrate the points developed above.

'Jane'

Jane is a 38-year-old, married woman.

She experiences anxiety when confronted by needles and, in particular, if some blood needs to be taken for investigations. She has avoided situations where she may have to have blood taken. When it has been necessary, she has been prescribed anxiety-reducing medication.

Jane and her husband are trying for their third child. She has been told that she will probably need to have blood taken during her pregnancy, because of her age.

Jane was unable to remember the first time she became frightened of needles. She did say that she remembered watching her mother (who was dependent on insulin) being frightened of needles.

Please note that it is not essential for people to remember when their difficulties started in order to help them but it may enable them to understand their difficulties and help with the question, 'Why am I like this?'

When Jane described the last time she experienced her difficulty, it became clear that using the three systems approach might be helpful for an early case formulation (see the diagram below). She described the thought, 'It's disgusting – having a needle stuck in your arm.' This thought brought along physical changes – increased heart rate, sweaty palms and heavy breathing. In order to manage her anxious sensations, Jane left the GP's surgery. The distress of the anxiety quickly lapsed and she felt relieved.

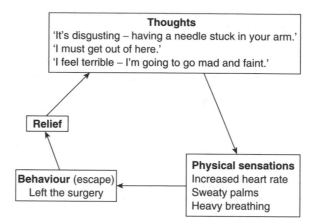

Please note that this three systems model has been extended to include the relief that Jane experiences when leaving the situation. This may help us both when considering what might be maintaining her problem. Jane has learned that what makes her difficulty easier is escaping from the perceived threat.

Many people with these types of difficulties know that their fears are out of proportion to the actual threat. Interestingly, many have made contact with their feared object or situation a number of times and survived the experience, but the fear still remains. So, what keeps the fears going, even when people know that they are unfounded?

In the diagram above, Jane's difficulties are expressed as a vicious cycle that maintains the problem. Her thinking includes predictions such as, 'I'm going to go mad and faint.' This relates to a fear of fear, influenced by the physical sensations she experiences in such a situation (see also Kirk, 1989; Ost et al., 1992). Leaving the surgery results in a reduction of her fears, which of course does not allow her to put her fearful predictions to the test.

A further difficulty for Jane is that she tends to look out for her danger. So, for example, if one of her teeth momentarily aches, she will begin to think about the consequence of visiting the dentist, which will possibly involve an injection. She will be unable to think about the possible benefits of such a visit – for example, recommending different toothpaste. Ironically, if Jane keeps avoiding the dentist, the eventual outcome may turn out to be dental treatment that does require an injection.

Therapy plan

The following behavioural experiments were developed collaboratively with Jane:

- talking about needles
- talking about having an injection

- looking at a video of people having blood taken
- watching the therapist having blood taken from their arm
- holding a needle against her skin
- pricking her fingertips with a needle
- having an injection in her arm
- having blood taken from her arm.

'Paul'

Paul is 23, single and lives at home with his mother.

He was referred by the local mental health team for a CB assessment. He describes his main problem as that of experiencing unwanted intrusive thoughts. When he experiences these, he becomes very anxious. His heart rate increases, his breathing becomes rapid and he becomes restless. In response to these thoughts, Paul then feels as if he *has* to complete certain behaviour (checking). Once he has completed those he feels better and is able to settle down again.

Paul's difficulty occurs in different situations.

Examples of his unwanted thoughts are:

- 'Is that mark on the door a sign of fire?'
- 'Did I lock all the car doors?'
- 'Did I wash my hands?'
- 'If I carry the lighters with me, then they won't ignite.'
- 'What's that crackling? Is the television on fire?'

Here are some examples of Paul's behaviour:

- checking that any marks on walls, skirting boards and so on are not the start of a fire
- checking the doors on the car
- turning water taps off with a towel
- if no towel is available, turning water taps off with his feet
- carrying four cigarette lighters with him all the time
- checking that the television is not on fire
- seeking reassurance that he has done the above.

The diagram below sets out Paul's case formulation.

Intrusive thoughts and safety-seeking behaviour

Most people experience intrusive thoughts and those can be, for example, sexual or relate to harming themselves or others. However, the way in which intrusions are interpreted or appraised can lead to obsessive – compulsive

Intrusive thoughts
'Is that mark on the door a sign of fire?'
'Did I lock all the car doors?'
'Did I wash my hands?'
If I carry the lighters with me, than they won't ignite.
'What's that cracking? Is the television on fire?'

↓

Interpretation/Appraisal of intrusive thoughts
'I'm responsible.'
'If I don't check and it is a fire, then I'm irresponsible.'
'If I didn't wash my hands, then my Mum will become unwell.'

Safety-seeking behaviour
Checking that any marks on walls, skirting boards and so on are not the start of a fire.
Checking the doors on the car.
Turning water taps off with a towel.
If no towel is available, turning water taps off with his feet.
Carrying four cigarette lighters with him at all times.
Checking that the television is not on fire.
Seeking reassurance that he has done the above.

↓

Relief from anxiety.

Anxiety and discomfort
Heart rate increases.
Hyperventilation.
Becomes restless.

anxiety problems in individuals (Rachman and De Silva, 1978). Associated with an elevated sense of responsibility (Whittal et al., 2002), Paul's case formulation illustrates the common appraisal, 'I am responsible for potentially avoidable harm to myself or other people.' An understandable response to these appraisals for people such as Paul is to respond by checking or taking the kinds of precautions described in his formulation above.

Therapeutic aims

The aim of the CB intervention is not to rid the person of their intrusive thoughts, but to change the significance they attach to them. The worker and client collaboratively develop and agree a comprehensive CB formulation of the client's difficulties. This is achieved by identifying the key responsibility assumptions and appraisals and then the construction of a non-threatening alternative account of their experiences. The aim is to help the person explicitly test these non-threatening alternatives.

Therapy plan

The aim of the intervention is to help the person conclude that their unwanted intrusive thoughts, however distressing, are irrelevant to further action in the form of safety behaviour. In order to achieve this, it is essential that a comprehensive formulation – such as Paul's above – be developed. The client is then helped to create a list of the strategies that are currently employed to reduce discomfort – in Paul's case, avoidances, safety behaviour and reassurance-seeking. This list then becomes the target of behavioural experiments, with the client being gently and sensitively helped to confront the situations or objects that they find distressing. This may increase their anxiety in the short term, but will help them to find out, over time, that nothing dreadful happens (Salkovskis and Kirk, 1989).

Behavioural experiments developed collaboratively with Paul

These had as their objectives to:
- resist the urge to check the back of the television
- leave the four cigarette lighters at home
- deliberately open and shut the back door and not wash his hands
- deliberately wash his hands and not use his feet or towels to turn the taps off
- resist the urge to return to his car to re-check that he'd locked the doors.

'Jonathon'

Jonathon, a 46-year-old mature student in his second year at university, was referred by the local community mental health team for an assessment. They wanted to know if his difficulties were suitable for a CB approach.

Jonathon described his main problem as that of 'experiencing panic attacks'. As a result, he was unable to travel in cars or on public transport. He believed that if he did, he would experience an attack and this would then lead to sudden death as he thought that he would have a heart attack.

Jonathon had experienced his first panic attack some three months earlier. He had been travelling as a passenger with a friend to college when they had to wait at a level crossing. Jonathon became hot and sweaty and began to think that he would soon be unable to breathe. He then began to hyperventilate (to breath quickly, with short intakes of breath) and think that he would soon be unable to breathe. He then noticed that his heart rate had increased, and thought that he was going to have a heart attack.

In response to his thinking, Jonathon got out of the car and his physical sensations began to reduce. Soon after, he asked his friend to take him to the local accident and emergency department. He was prescribed a small dose of Valium (an anxiety-reducing drug) and was taken home.

It is important to note here that Jonathon's belief regarding having a heart attack is strongly held. Therefore, it is not surprising, when faced with this imminent risk that he tries, logically, to prevent this from happening. (See Salkovskis, 1991; Wells, 1997.)

Using Greenberger and Padesky's (1995) model (see also Chapter 2), let's try to develop an understanding of Jonathon's difficulties – in particular, paying attention to what might be maintaining them.

The diagram below shows Jonathon's five aspect case formulation.

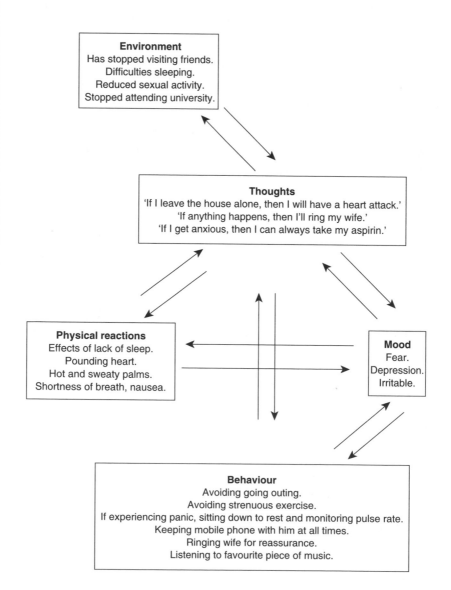

Environment
Has stopped visiting friends.
Difficulties sleeping.
Reduced sexual activity.
Stopped attending university.

Thoughts
'If I leave the house alone, then I will have a heart attack.'
'If anything happens, then I'll ring my wife.'
'If I get anxious, then I can always take my aspirin.'

Physical reactions
Effects of lack of sleep.
Pounding heart.
Hot and sweaty palms.
Shortness of breath, nausea.

Mood
Fear.
Depression.
Irritable.

Behaviour
Avoiding going outing.
Avoiding strenuous exercise.
If experiencing panic, sitting down to rest and monitoring pulse rate.
Keeping mobile phone with him at all times.
Ringing wife for reassurance.
Listening to favourite piece of music.

From the assessment, Jonathon and his worker agreed that it was not necessary to include his early life experiences in this formulation. As mentioned in Chapter 2, a good case formulation should use the minimum amount of information to explain someone's difficulties (Persons, 1989).

Intervention plan

The intervention was developed as a result of gathering information in the form of a diary (see Chapter 4). Directly relevant to the case formulation, it is helpful to know where the person is experiencing their difficulties, the physical symptoms that emerge, what they were thinking, as well as what they do in response to it (behaviour) in order to cope (for example, avoidance, escape and safety behaviour). This early intervention can help the person to see that their panic difficulties are linked to their bodily sensations, their appraisal of these and how their behaviour may be maintaining their distress. At this point, standardised measures were taken of mood, level of anxiety and work and social adjustment (see Chapter 3).

Panic provocation

When working with people suffering from panic disorder, it can be enormously helpful for them to be encouraged to engage in behavioural experiments that deliberately evoke sensations similar to those experienced during distressing panic experiences.

Jonathon agreed to several 'panic provocation tests' (Wells, 1997), which enabled him to produce and experience sensations closely resembling those that occur during his panic attacks.

Hyperventilation provocation test
People are asked to breathe through their nose and mouth quickly for up to two minutes, although they are advised that they can stop before then if they wish. There is minimal discussion before the test is carried out.

Once the test has been completed, people are asked to compare the differences between the sensations produced during voluntary hyperventilation and during one of their panic attacks.

Physical exercises test
This test is useful for people actively avoiding strenuous exercise because they think that this may induce a heart attack. Tests should be creatively and pragmatically linked to the client's fears about the

consequences of exercising and may, for example, include jogging or walking briskly.

Inducing visual disturbances

A further test is to encourage someone to stare at a particular object for a few minutes. This can produce unusual visual effects, similar to those that occur when people experience their distress.

Verbal reattribution discussions

A detailed analysis of the person's difficulties, subsequent feared consequences, safety behaviour and avoidances is crucial. It is perhaps understandable that if someone believes they will faint or have a heart attack, they will do whatever they can to prevent this from happening. Reattribution helps the person to consider that their responses to their thinking may be maintaining their difficulties.

This strategy uses questions that help the client to evaluate specific cognitive misinterpretations. It is particularly helpful to use the questions before a behavioural experiment is undertaken. For example, 'What do you think might happen if you were to jog around the car park?' The person is then asked to rate this belief on a scale from 0 to 100, then asked to re-measure and compare this new score with the original one after the experiment has taken place.

Jonathon found that engaging in all of the above provocation experiments served to disconfirm his predicted feared consequences.

Behavioural experiments

Behavioural experiments are designed specifically to help people re-evaluate their unhelpful, belief-driven thinking. Let's consider this example from work with Jonathon:

Practitioner: OK, Jonathon. What do you think would happen if you went outside your house without your mobile phone?
Jonathon: I think I would have a heart attack.
Practitioner: Let's see if we can measure this somehow. Let's try a scale where 0 represents no belief and 100 means total belief. Where would you rate yourself now?
Jonathon: About 90 per cent.
Practitioner: In terms of our understanding of your difficulties – and in particular the idea that you may be innocently maintaining your problems – can you think of anything that you can do to find out if this prediction is accurate or not?
Jonathon: ... Yes.

Jonathon then left his house without his mobile phone. He managed to spend a period away from his house. The next time he saw the practitioner, they discussed the results of this experiment.

Practitioner: OK, Jonathon, can you tell me what happened?

Jonathon: Nothing. I managed to walk away from the house. I noticed that my anxiety eventually reduced. I was a little worried at first.

Practitioner: How much do you now believe that you are going to have a heart attack when you leave your house without your mobile phone?

Jonathon: About 5 per cent.

This experiment provided Jonathon with an opportunity to disconfirm his original prediction. Subsequent experiments were designed using similar principles.

Subsequent behavioural experiments developed collaboratively with Jonathon

These included:

- leaving the house accompanied by the practitioner
- leaving the house with the practitioner, then separating – the practitioner walking along the other side of the road, still in view
- leaving the house unaccompanied
- leaving the house for increasing periods, unaccompanied and without his mobile phone
- attending clinic for therapy session unaccompanied.

SUMMARY

- From a CB perspective, anxiety difficulties can be understood in terms of the meaning they have for the individual.
- Meaning influences behaviour, which also serves to maintain anxiety difficulties.
- Evolutionary explanations of anxiety complement cognitive theories.
- There are key strategies and principles for beginning to work with someone with anxiety.
- Behavioural experiments are central to helping someone with anxiety difficulties.

Activities

- Think about your own fears and consider to what extent they are maintained by the way you think about them and behave in relation to them.
- Ask one of your clients who has anxiety difficulties to read and comment on this chapter.
- Consider how individuals with anxiety problems are helped in your workplace. Could the examples and strategies described in this chapter be helpful?

Further reading

Craske, M., 1999, *Anxiety Disorders*. Oxford: Westview Press.
As with Wells' book, listed below, this constitutes an excellent, in-depth study of all specific anxiety disorders and related CB interventions.

Hawton, K., Salkovskis, P.M., Kirk, J., and Clark, D.M. (eds), 1989, *Cognitive Behaviour Therapy for Psychiatric Problems: A Practical Guide*. New York: Oxford University Press.
See the chapters on panic and generalised anxiety disorder, obsessive–compulsive disorder and phobic anxiety.

Wells, A., 1997, *Cognitive Therapy of Anxiety Disorders: A Practice Manual and Conceptual Guide*. Chichester: John Wiley.

FIFTEEN # A Critique of Evidence-Based Mental Health and its Relationship to Cognitive Behavioural Psychotherapy

Alec Grant, Jem Mills, Ronan Mulhern and Nigel Short

Learning objectives

After reading this chapter and completing the activities at the end of it you should be able to:

1 outline the main features of evidence-based practice in mental health
2 describe what constitutes 'evidence' from the perspective of the evidence-based movement
3 understand key issues in the contemporary development of evidence-based mental health practice
4 describe the implications for changing customary, but non-evidence-based, existing work practices
5 understand the ways in which the evidence-based movement has influenced psychotherapy practice generally and the significance of this for CB practice
6 consider the limitations of the evidence-based movement, in its current form, for the CB approach
7 describe the links between those limitations and the historical roots and assumptions driving the evidence-based movement in its current form and more recent complementary worldviews
8 understand what is meant by 'paradigm entrapment'
9 identify the ways in which qualitative research would lend balance to the evidence-based CB agenda.

Evidence-based practice in mental health

Evidence-based healthcare

The development of evidence-based mental health needs to be viewed within the broader context of evidence-based healthcare. Muir Gray (1997) argued that decisions about the management of client groups and populations should derive from the combination of three factors:

- the best available evidence
- the values of society
- the resources available.

Gray then went on to describe three stages in the practice of evidence-based healthcare. The first is the production of evidence by researchers. This may occur either in the context of research commissioned by government or research councils or within an area or topic chosen by the researcher and supported by funding bodies if the research proposal is deemed to be of sufficiently high quality. The second stage is making evidence available and accessible. The third and final stage is the use of evidence to improve clinical practice.

What counts as 'evidence'?

The practice of evidence-based healthcare is conducted on the basis of an established hierarchy of strength of evidence, described below, where 1 is assumed to be the source of evidence that clinicians can place the most confidence in (Muir Gray, 1997):

1 strong evidence from at least one systematic review of multiple and well-designed randomised control trials
2 strong evidence from at least one properly designed randomised control trial of an appropriate size
3 evidence from well-designed research trials that do not contain randomisation – single group, pre-post, cohort, time series or matched case-control studies
4 evidence from well-designed non-experimental studies from more than one centre or research group
5 opinions of respected authorities, based on clinical evidence, descriptive studies, reports or expert committees.

At this stage, it may be helpful to briefly unpack some of the terminology used above. A 'randomised control trial' (RCT) is an experimental procedure, the core feature of which is the random allocation of all research participants to either control or experimental groups. Random allocation allows for the optimal reduction of potential sources of bias, including client preference, clinicians' expectations and personal characteristics. The RCT is generally accepted as the 'gold standard' of research procedures, in terms of being the best (although not the sole) method of evaluating treatment efficacy (Trinder and Reynolds, 2000). 'Efficacy' means how well a treatment performs under experimental conditions.

'Systematic reviews' aim to decrease the bias and increase the power of research findings and have the following characteristics. They are based on an exhaustive search of all relevant literature, using explicit and previously validated criteria for excluding evidence of inadequate quality. All evidence that has been included and excluded is cited in the review and valid and explicit methods for combining data are used – a process referred to as 'meta-analysis' (Muir Gray, 2000).

Finally, 'non-experimental studies' means research that is conducted using qualitative approaches (to be discussed later in this chapter).

The contemporary development of evidence-based mental health

The process of evidence-based mental health has been aided by a combination of recent developments in the types of research practice described above and information technology (Geddes, 2000). In turn, this has enabled resources to be put in place so that both clients and practitioners can have both quick and easy access to the best available evidence to support the use of defined interventions. In recent years, increasingly sophisticated ways of producing systematic reviews of randomised control trial research have resulted in a number of available review resources in mental health (Geddes, 2000). For example, the Cochrane Collaboration's review groups (visit its website at www.cochrane.org), an international resource for practitioners, has produced a range of systematic reviews. The longest established group is the Cochrane Schizophrenia Review Group. Other groups include the Cochrane Depression, Anxiety and Neurosis Group and the Dementia and Cognitive Functioning Group. Equally, the Centre for Evidence-based Mental Health (visit its website at www.cebmh.com) also aims to promote and support the dissemination and practice of evidence-based mental health internationally. It hosts the electronic version of *Evidence-based Mental Health* – a journal that brings clinically relevant developments in research to the attention of practitioners.

Using the evidence: changing training practice

The British Department of Health recently called for a greater investment in staff training to ensure that effective interventions are offered where they are most needed and will be likely to achieve the most impact (DoH, 1998). However, as reported in Chapter 1, Brooker et al. (2002) concluded that the provision of training and education in evidence-based practices generally, and in cognitive-behavioural approaches specifically, seemed to be the exception rather than the rule in university mental health teaching departments.

However, Geddes (2000) reported that the contemporary evidence-based movement in mental health has had a positive impact on professional training courses in psychiatry and clinical psychology in recent years. In Britain, this includes the need to train psychiatrists in how to critically appraise research reports. In the USA and Britain, clinical psychology training is more explicitly linked to both understanding the design of empirically supported psychotherapeutic research and achieving competence in empirically supported psychotherapies. With regard to mental health nursing, Newell and Gournay's (2000a) text constituted the first British book on evidence-based mental health nursing practice, an aim of which was to counter the hitherto non-evidence-based trends in mental health nurse training.

Using the evidence: changing clinical practice

Critics of evidence-based mental health practice argue that it is not a new thing as good practitioners always try to keep abreast of the best available evidence. Geddes (2000) pointed out, however, that the sheer volume of accumulating research in mental health would make it impossible for practitioners to keep up to date with such knowledge in the absence of systematic reviews.

Newell and Gournay (2000b) highlighted other criticisms, including the perception of some mental health professionals that evidence-based mental health practice is either a threat to their long-held investment in clinical judgement or client-centredness as systematic reviews pertain to groups of clients rather than individuals. In response to these criticisms, the authors:

> ... strongly refute both these suggestions; evidence-based care is a framework ... designed to support individual clinicians' decision making in response to the unique profile offered by each client ... Evidence-based care and clinical effectiveness provide the best possible evidence to enhance our decision making, rather than supersede it. Since good information about efficacy reduces our reliance on custom, precedent and so-called expert opinion, it increases client-centredness, rather than reducing it.
>
> Newell and Gournay, 2000b: xii

The evidence-based movement and CB approaches

Evidence-based psychotherapy

Before looking at CB interventions specifically, it is useful to outline contemporary trends in the evidence-based practice of psychotherapy generally. The American Psychological Association's Division 12 task force reported on the promotion and dissemination of psychological interventions (Chambless and Hollon, 1998). Geddes (2000: 77) argued that this report was the response to 'intense social, economic and political forces to identify which psychological treatments were supported by high-quality evidence'. A parallel process occurred in Britain in the 1990s, with the National Health Service Executive commissioning a review of the effectiveness of psychotherapy. This resulted in a similarly positive response to the need for empirically supported psychotherapies (Roth and Fonagy, 1996; NHS Executive, 1996).

The evidence-based movement and the CB approach

Prior to the development of the evidence-based movement – indeed, from its inception – it has always been asserted that behavioural and cognitive interventions have a solid scientific underpinning (Hawton et al., 1989; Gelder, 1997; Rachman, 1997). On this basis and, at this time in their development, aided by the evidence-based movement, claims can confidently be made, for example, that, while not necessarily the only effective approach for anxiety- and depression-related problems, the CB approach is the most thoroughly researched (Leahy and Holland, 2000). The extensive and longstanding empirical support enjoyed by CB psychotherapy does give it a clear (and, some say, perhaps unfair) advantage over other psychotherapeutic approaches.

Limitations of the evidence-based movement for the CB approach

From the discussion so far, we can see that what counts as evidence-based CB practice generally, based on randomised control trials and systematic reviews, is immensely helpful to practitioners and clients alike. However, it may be equally evident that the evidence base, in its current form, has little to say about some important aspects of the practice of the approach.

A criticism of evidence-based healthcare practice is that it gives the impression of being value-free and neutral when, in fact, it is an approach resting on an identifiable set of assumptions and values (Trinder, 2000). As an illustration of this, under the heading 'Evidence-based healthcare' earlier in this chapter, a potential contradiction may be spotted in the core values of the movement. This is between the emphasis given to researcher-led or government/committee-sponsored research and societal values. Trinder (2000: 228) pointed out that 'the quantitative foundation of evidence-based practice ... requires the selection of outcomes that are measurable, thus including some questions and excluding others.' What may be excluded in many cases are questions that are of arguable importance to clients and other members of society, which do not lend themselves readily to quantification and are thus disregarded as not of sufficiently 'high quality'.

Because of this, it comes as no surprise that the research literature fails to, for example, help us appreciate the specific and unique experiences of clients in relation both to the approach used and their relationship with practitioners. With some notable exceptions (Padesky, 1996b; Bennett-Levy et al., 2001, 2003) it also has little to say about the experiences of practitioners learning the approach or the ways in which the individual practice of the approach may change in many and, ironically, deviant ways over the course of a professional's working career (see, for example, Nezu and DelliCarpinni, 1998).

To be fair, the intention to incorporate the views of actual and potential clients as consumers of research in the evidence-based movement is evident in the Cochrane Consumer Collaboration Network (visit its website at www.informedhealthonline.org). However, the extent to which real, as opposed to tokenistic, involvement is possible within the current parameters and assumptions of what constitutes evidence-based practice is still unclear. In support of our perception of what we will describe below as 'paradigm entrapment' in evidence-based CB practice, Bastion (1994: 8), writing on the Cochrane Consumer Collaboration Network website, asserted that:

> People's views in pluralistic communities cannot, and should not, be squeezed into unidimensional frameworks to meet demands for mathematical order. Values cannot be measured with a ruler, and the pain of people's struggles with ill health should not be homogenised till it is no longer recognisable. That something is useful, does not necessarily make it right. It should not be forgotten that utility does not equate with value, and that utilitarian decisions – 'the greatest good for the greatest number', by definition discriminate against minorities.

Because research conducted in the name of evidence-based practice into the CB approach is mostly done *to* rather than *with* clients, the focus is mostly and inevitably on clinical outcomes. This focus is, in turn, based on a consensus in the research and practice communities of the universal nature of types of psychological disorder. With few exceptions, in the areas of culture and ethnicity (for example, Iwamasa, 1996; Tanaka-Matsumi and Seiden, 1996; Mathews, 1997), it is therefore not surprising that issues concerning minority groups, gender and sexuality are marginal to the CB evidence-based agenda.

These issues are most appropriately explored by qualitative (to be discussed below) rather than quantitative designs. However, because of the dearth of qualitative research to date, illustrating its relative unimportance in the evidence-based movement (see its low rating in Muir Gray's 1997 hierarchy of evidence-based practice described above), the net effect of all of this is the representation of disorders rather than human experiences. In the mainstream CB literature, this is reflected in the frequent use of inappropriate medical terms to describe aspects of human experience, such as 'symptoms' and 'disorder', with people needing help often being referred to as 'patients' and therapy as 'treatment'.

Reflecting, in our view, an uncritical acceptance of the sufficiency of the current form of evidence base for CB practice, we have, for many years, witnessed students emerging from British courses who have been trained to assume that the randomised control trial is the only window on their clients' worlds worth looking through, rather than educated to consider how the paradigm context of different research approaches influences the relative strengths and weaknesses of these approaches. We will now explore this area.

Evidence-based mental health: historical roots and assumptions

In considering the unfortunate spin-offs from evidence-based CB practice, which lead to the neglect of important areas of experience and reductionist, medicalised language, it is important to explore the historical backdrop to evidence-based mental health. The movement is rooted in a long-standing assumption that, in the human psychological sciences, there are objective truths that can be known about, subject to careful and controlled observation. Scientific activity thus strives towards the uncovering of, or moving closer towards, the truth. This makes for a circular argument in which good scientific practice is seen to depend on careful, controlled observation and vice versa.

This particular view of the function and purpose of science is historically locatable in 'the Enlightenment project' or 'modernism' (Rolfe, 2000). By a consensus initiated in the late seventeenth century, the essence of the Enlightenment project was social progress and emancipation from suffering through scientific understanding. In the social and psychological sciences, the research stance came to be associated with the paradigm (pattern or patterning of worldview) term 'positivism'.

A positivist worldview is directly related to the activity of quantitative research designs. Quantitative research is useful for isolating causes and effects and quantifying phenomena. Hypotheses (carefully specified propositions) are tested out, using numerical and statistical methods, on the basis of the manipulation of independent (input) and dependent (outcome) variables. The positivist paradigm influences quantitative researchers to employ the language of objectivity, control and distance because these are seen as key to the conduct of good social scientists (Greenwood and Levin, 2000). As has been made apparent in the above discussion, the CB approach is almost exclusively grounded in quantitative research.

Complementary paradigms

However, the twentieth century has witnessed the emergence of a number of additional and complementary paradigms for making sense of other important aspects of human experience. The development of the 'interpretivist' (Schwandt, 2000) and 'social constructionist' (Gergen, 1999; Schwandt, 2000) paradigms is associated with qualitative approaches to research.

Qualitative approaches generally do not aim either to test hyphotheses or employ numerical or statistical measurement or replace this valuable approach. Instead, they aim to explore, discover and describe human experiences and meanings in order to accord full respect to them (Maione and Chenail, 1999).

Whereas the aim of quantitative research is prediction and careful control, the aim of interpretive, qualitative research is to understand people individually and collectively in terms of the meanings of their experiences. The aim of social constructionist qualitative research is to find out how individuals relate to those meanings in the active construction of their life worlds.

Emerging implications: paradigm entrapment

An argument emerging from this discussion is that many CB practitioners and researchers are trapped within assumptions deriving from the dominant, positivist research paradigm underpinning their craft. These assumptions – about what is and is not important knowledge and research activity – contribute to the social construction of clients and their experiences in particular ways. As has hopefully been made clear, there are clear advantages for clients and practitioners operating within the worldview of current, positivist constructions of evidence-based CB practice. However, the flip side of this is the neglect of, and stifling of debate about, other aspects of the experience of clients and practitioners that may be considered important to both groups.

In an important paper summarising the major achievements and challenges to qualitative research, Atkinson et al. (2001: 6) argued that:

> It is singularly unhelpful to all concerned if disciplines become too tightly classified and circumscribed according to styles of research. It is too easy to assume that disciplines like economics or psychology are exclusively characterized by quantification and positivist epistemologies.

As far as we can see, this unfortunate state of affairs characterises mainstream contemporary CB practice. The long tradition of scientific underpinning of CB interventions, described by Gelder (1997) and others, coheres with the concerns and focus of the evidence-based practice movement. However, this tradition rests squarely – and, to date, almost exclusively – within the positivist paradigm.

The need for more qualitative research to balance the evidence-based CB agenda

With the notable exception of the work of Bennett-Levy and his colleagues (Bennett-Levy and Taylor, 2000; Bennett-Levy et al., 2001, 2003), a trawl through the mainstream CB journals will confirm to the interested reader that qualitative studies are hardly ever given editorial space. In large part, this is because of what Bennett-Levy and Taylor (2000: 1) describe as 'paradigmatic antipathy'. Put more simply, this refers to CB journal boards assuming that qualitative studies are not scientific enough to merit publication.

However, there is some evidence that this picture may be beginning to change in Britain, and recent developments stand out as having possible significance. First, the emergence of the Cochrane Qualitative Methods Network (visit its website at www.iphrp.salford.ac.uk/cochrane) indicates a growing interest in the evidence-based movement about how qualitative research can be incorporated into systematic reviews. Second, the Government's approach to evidence-based policy making in the delivery of public services, including healthcare, has recently resulted in the development of guidance on quality standards in qualitative research (see its website at www.policyhub.gov.uk). This has been viewed with interest by the Mental Health Qualitative Research Network – another recent British development. Finally, an e-mail to all members of this network recently called for members to volunteer themselves as 'expert reviewers/assessors' in response to a request from the new editor of the *British Journal of Psychiatry* who wished to correct the situation of a dearth of qualitative papers being published in the journal in recent years (Quirk, 2003).

Although all of the above may well signal a positive development, in that qualitative approaches seem to be beginning to be taken more seriously in evidence-based healthcare, a note of caution should be stressed as such trends may reflect a more sinister strategy of 'capture and tame'. Readers should be aware that the centuries-long assumptions underpinning evidence-based practice influence the fact that qualitative research has long been viewed as, at worst, low-strength evidence or, at best, as a kind of auxiliary form of 'evidence', the function of which is simply one of support for gold standard RCT designs (Muir Gray, 1997). In a strangely contradictory way, Muir Gray (1997: 100) wrote:

> Qualitative research should not be regarded … as a method that merely complements and supplements quantitative research. It can often be used to generate hypotheses for the solution of a problem which can then be tested using either quantitative research, by building on the findings of the qualitative research, or a combination of qualitative and quantitative methods.

The above quote may indicate both the extent to which the approach has been really allowed to exist as an equal in scientific activity and its reduction to a method, stripped of its rich paradigmatic context (Lincoln and Guba, 2000). It is not surprising, therefore, that qualitative studies accepted for evidence-based journals are usually of the traditional variety (Holliday, 2002; Bennett-Levy, 2003), in that they conform to the values of positivistic research rigour in their attempts to demonstrate degrees of 'reliability' and 'validity' more relevant to quantitative designs. 'Progressive' paradigm qualitative research studies – long established in the social sciences (Denzin and Lincoln, 2000; Holliday, 2002), where the credibility and trustworthiness of the experiences represented are accorded more significance than their universal and generalisable truth – are unlikely to be well received by evidence-based journals in the mental health field at this present time.

How things could be different

It seems improbable that the current 'enthusiast' evidence-based practice establishment (Trinder, 2000) will allow for the absorption of progressive qualitative approaches of the more dramatic or poetic variety (see the Activities section at the end of this chapter) into a revised sense of what constitutes 'evidence-based'. However, a long-established respect has been accorded to more scientifically formal qualitative research within, for example, counselling psychology and marital and family therapy (Maione and Chenail, 1999). With a clear focus on different, but equally important, areas of concern as those of the evidence-based CB movement at present, the inclusion and development of a greater range of qualitative studies would undoubtedly enrich research and practice.

An evidence-based agenda amended and broadened to redefine what counts as 'evidence' would, we believe, repair the 'restricted methodological vision' (Atkinson et al., 2001) currently characterising evidence-based CB practice and, indeed, evidence-based mental health more generally (Trinder, 2000). In addition, it would speed the paradigm advancement of CB psychotherapy towards an evolving position where the personal meaning-making and narratives of clients and practitioners are accorded much greater respect than is presently the case (Lyddon and Weill, 1997; Russell Ramsay, 1998).

In conclusion, we believe that the words of Maione and Chenail (1999: 77) have resonance for research and the practice of CB interventions, where an increased, less defensive, welcoming of qualitative approaches would constitute:

> [A] development [that] will also include more collaborative efforts between qualitative and quantitative researchers as their appreciation of the differences each other brings to the study ... grows. In all of its shapes, qualitative research will continue to help the stakeholders in clinical work – the researchers, the therapists, and the clients, to describe, to interpret, and to discover their understandings of the patterns which make a difference in this process of change.

SUMMARY

- Evidence-based CB practice derives from evidence-based mental health and the broader context of evidence-based healthcare.
- 'Evidence' is defined according to a hierarchy of the relative strength of research approaches.
- Recent developments in research practice and information technology allow for relatively easy access to what is currently defined as the best available evidence.
- The evidence-based practice movement has key implications for mental health education and work practice.
- The evidence-based movement has influenced psychotherapy practice generally, and CB practice emerges as the approach with the best evidence-base.
- Evidence-based practice, in its current form, influences and limits the kinds of questions and issues that are assumed to be important in CB research and practice.
- There are clear links between those influences and limitations and the historical roots and assumptions driving the evidence-based movement in its current form.
- Those longstanding assumptions lead to 'paradigm entrapment', whereby researchers and practitioners construct clients, client groups and interventions in particular, sometimes disadvantageous, and partial ways.
- This state of affairs would be remedied by a broadening of what constitutes 'evidence-based practice' to include additional paradigms for constructing and making sense of human experience.
- Such additional paradigms link to qualitative approaches already used extensively in some forms of psychotherapeutic practice.
- This would give balance to the evidence-based CB agenda.

Activities

- Explore attitudes towards evidence-based practice in your own organisation.
- Access the Cochrane Consumer Collaboration Network and the Centre for Evidence-based Mental Health websites cited earlier in this chapter.
- Compare the extent to which you are moved and engaged by works such as Kane's (2000) *4.48 Psychosis* or Fee's (2000) *Pathology and the Postmodern* compared with the style of infrequent qualitative research articles appearing in evidence-based journals.

Further reading

Bennett-Levy, J., Lee, N., Travers, K., Pohlman, S., and Hamernik, E., 2003, 'Cognitive therapy from the inside: enhancing therapist skills through practising what we preach', *Behavioural and Cognitive Psychotherapy*, 31, pp. 143–58.
In this pioneering article on the use of qualitative approaches in CB research, Bennett-Levy and his colleagues demonstrate the importance of self-practice by CB practitioners.

Muir Gray, J.A., 1997, *Evidence-based Healthcare: How to Make Health Policy and Management Decisions*. New York: Churchill Livingstone.
Although written for healthcare managers, this is an important book on the assumptions underpinning the evidence-based healthcare process.

Trinder, L., and Reynolds, S. (eds), 2000, *Evidence-based Practice: A Critical Appraisal*. Oxford: Blackwell.
This excellent book critically explores evidence-based practice, and its underpinning assumptions, in a variety of contexts – including mental health, nursing, social work and human resource management.

SIXTEEN Organisational Factors Impacting Cognitive Behavioural Practice

Alec Grant, Jem Mills,
Ronan Mulhern and Nigel Short

Learning objectives

After reading this chapter and completing the activities at the end of it, you should be able to:

1   describe the relevance of organisational studies for CB practice
2   understand the concept of organisations as sites of meaning-making
3   describe the meaning of backstage and frontstage organisational activity
4   describe the main features of the organisational unconscious
5   identify the possible links between this and organisational resistance to evidence-based practice
6   describe how organisational custom and practice is maintained
7   consider the argument that there may be links between such maintenance and more sinister organisational dynamics.

Introduction

Having got to this part of the book, many readers may feel confident in their intention to try out the CB approach with supervised help. Some may have worked through their own forms of resistance and feel that they have anticipated and dealt appropriately with resistance from work colleagues with the help of Chapter 3. Having read Chapter 15, those with access to the Internet may also feel increasingly secure in developing skills in the approach because it is supported by evidence-based systematic reviews.

This might leave such readers puzzled as to why we have included a chapter on how organisational factors might impact CB practice. Surely any rational individual, having progressed this far into the book, will agree that it behoves mental health organisations to support the practice and development of the CB approach within its work settings? Yet, we have hopefully made it clear that winning the hearts and minds of colleagues to change their work practices is not a straightforward business and not all will support the evidence-based practice agenda. This is just the tip of the organisational iceberg as, it will be argued, organisations do not behave rationally!

Our perspective on the relevance of organisational studies for CB practice

Psychological treatments have been around for decades, but while the research evidence for their effectiveness continues to grow, so too does the litany of reports of half-hearted or failed implementation in non-research settings.

Grey, 2002: 465

All four of us wear several hats. We are all practising CB psychotherapists. All of us are experienced teachers of the approach. One of us (Mulhern) is a mental health nurse consultant who has a brief to facilitate and support the development of evidence-based practitioners. As qualitative researchers, two of us (Grant and Mills) have recently completed organisationally focused research in areas of mental health practice relevant to the thrust of this text. Grant's (2001) doctoral research analysed the ways in which key organisational factors undermined the uptake of clinical supervision among mental health nurses. Mills (2003), using a discourse analytical social constructionist approach, explored the non-uptake of evidence-based approaches as a function of local and national influences on accounts of mental health practice. At the time of writing, Short runs courses at the Institute of Psychiatry, London, for staff working with clients in hospital settings. As a user of mental health services, he actively encourages staff to consider pragmatic, sensitive and useful CB interventions.

Concerns about the ways in which organisational factors get in the way of well-intentioned and sensible agendas of positive change and innovation represent a slowly developing but steady interest for all four. In addition to the research texts of two of us (as mentioned above), this interest is based on our frustrations, developing over many years, with the power of British organisations to hamper attempts to train and support practitioners in evidence-based and related approaches (see also Liberman and Corrigan, 1994; Tarrier et al., 1999; Grant and Mills, 2000; Grey, 2002).

Organisations

At this stage we should perhaps define what we do and do not mean by 'organisations'. We are not referring to bricks and mortar structures. Nor are we referring to rational domains, where decisions are made on the basis of good sense and accumulating evidence. Were that the case, there would be no need for this book as international mental health services would, by now, have enjoyed a long history of contextually relevant CB practice. We are, instead, referring to (in mental health, usually bureaucratic) organisations as socially constructed entities – as sites of negotiated meaning-making (Wright, 1994; Fineman, 1996a; Morgan, 1997).

Meaning, emotion and behaviour in organisations

Goffman (1969) analysed the process of meaning-making in social and organ-isational life using the metaphor of the stage. 'Frontstage' activity is public and subject to scrutiny, thus must be carefully scripted and crafted to satisfy public need. 'Backstage' activity, on the other hand, is more relaxed – organisational 'actors' can take off their masks and be themselves, even to the point of criticising their frontstage acts.

Meaning-making in organisations is characterised by the appearance of frontstage rational activity devoted to the client groups the organisation pur-ports to serve, reflected in public statements of mission and purpose. However, in reality, this rational front is always inevitably related to, and threatened by, an emotional backstage (Fineman, 1996a).

The emotional agenda of organisations can be played out in various forms of resistance, as indicated in Chapters 5 and 15. This agenda also takes the form of various ways of influencing the behaviour and attitudes of organisational members (Fineman, 1996a), carried out at both organisationally conscious and unconscious levels (Morgan, 1997) in the service of the maintenance of corpo-rate custom and practice (Pfeffer, 1981; Purser and Cabana, 1998). In turn, this may result in innovations to practice, such as the CB approach, being seen as a threat to the 'way things are done around here'.

We devote the remainder of this chapter to mapping out some of the ways in which the 'hidden' factors of the organisational unconscious and the mainte-nance of organisational customs and practices may undermine the successful organisational uptake of the CB approach. Although it may seem strange to devote part of a CB book to a consideration of unconscious factors, we consider it to be justified for the following three reasons:

- the need to broaden the dialogue in the (certainly British) CB community about the relative failure to disseminate CB approaches
- the integrative nature of CB psychotherapy, incorporating strategies, con-cepts and insights from other schools of psychotherapy – especially appar-ent in the work of Aaron Beck, Christine Padesky, Robert Leahy and Jeremy Safran
- the pioneering work of Leahy (2001) in unashamedly using the uncon-scious, and related psychoanalytical concepts, in developing our under-standing of schema, rule and self-consistency-driven forms of resistance in CB psychotherapy.

Regarding this last point, it may become apparent to interested readers, especially after consulting Leahy's book, that his model of individual resistance in CB psychotherapy is a useful metaphor for considering the forms of corporate, organisational resistance that we discuss in this chapter. For example, Leahy's concept of 'sunk costs', used in the service of the maintenance of 'self-consistency' by clients, can arguably be seen to roughly equate to Pfeffer's notion of investment in organisational custom and practice (see below), which serves the interest of organisational identity consistency.

In contrast to the relatively upbeat flavour of the rest of this book, our aim in this chapter is to provide food for thought rather than easy solutions. We also hope the chapter will encourage practitioners to look beyond blaming themselves to systemic reasons for problems concerning the uptake of CB approaches. In planning the text initially, we felt that it was essential to present the beginnings of a framework by means of which readers could make some sense of aspects of the 'dark side' of organisational life, to the extent that this can, and often does, interfere with the best of CB intentions.

The organisational unconscious

> If this psychic underworld be the case, organisations will be shaped, in part, by the unconscious concerns of their members. People's actions will have an internal rationality which reflects their own personal, hidden, emotional dramas. Some of these will be in tension with the more formal agenda and structure of the organisation; sometimes they will determine it. It is a process that may be observed in both individual and collective action.
>
> Fineman, 1996b. 25

In support of Fineman's position on organisational unconscious motivation, Morgan (1997) discussed the usefulness of considering organisations as 'psychic prisons'. By this he meant that (socially constructed) organisations tend to develop lives of their own, within which their members are caught up. Organisations come to exercise control over their creators, specifically with regard to what is consciously taken for granted as right and proper and what is unconsciously conducted by organisational members in the day-to-day ongoing negotiation and creation of 'business as usual'.

Morgan argued that organisational members can become trapped within favoured ways of thinking, quoting the observation made by the communications theorist Marshall McLuhan, that the last thing a fish is likely to discover is the water it is swimming in! The point is that individuals who are well-socialised in organisational ways of thinking and behaving are less likely to see organisational norms as problematic:

> Such is the nature of psychic prisons. Favoured ways of thinking and acting become traps that confine individuals within socially constructed worlds and prevent the emergence of other worlds.
>
> Morgan, 1997: 219

Groupthink

It is not uncommon for favoured ways of thinking to be so strong that organisational members may continue to share a particular viewpoint in spite of strong, often contradictory, messages from outside the organisation. Morgan (1997: 219) argued that this 'groupthink' phenomenon 'has been reproduced in thousands of decision-making situations in organisations of all kinds'. This concept might help us better understand why most English university mental health teaching departments continue to resist teaching evidence-based approaches (Brooker et al., 2002). Equally, it may throw some light on organisational resistance to the uptake of the approach in mental health work settings.

Yet, in the face of, by now, a considerable history of evidence-based practice, how can mental health organisations – educational or clinical – continue to sustain practices that are not evidence-based and, inevitably, may actually be unhelpful to client groups?

Morgan's framework allows us to consider two possible answers to this question. First, organisations use corporate defence mechanisms to get around the dissonance, or mismatch, between beliefs and corresponding practice and contradictory evidence. Second, organisations often fail to learn from their mistakes.

Organisational defence mechanisms

Drawing from the Freudian and neo-Freudian literature, Morgan described the kinds of defence mechanisms at play in sustaining organisational ways of thinking. In the table below, we have adapted some items on his list for the purposes of understanding unconscious organisational resistance to the CB approach using examples from our own experiences.

Single- and double-loop learning

If the above framework is accepted as useful for understanding organisation-level resistance to the CB approach, it is perhaps not surprising that, often, organisations fail to learn from experience.

'Single-' and 'double-loop learning' mean an organisation's ability to learn and to learn about learning, respectively (Morgan, 1997). An example of single-loop learning would be an organisation learning from the mistakes that it had made. Double-loop learning would be its ability to question and change the assumptions driving its thinking and behaviour.

The possibility of double-loop learning taking place seems remote in organisations that fail to recognise patterns of corporate unconscious resistance. Morgan argued that this picture is especially true of bureaucratic organisations, which have the double disadvantage of fragmented patterns of thinking and action:

> ... the ability to achieve proficiency at double-loop learning often proves ... elusive. Although some organizations have been successful in institutionalizing systems that review and

Defence mechanism	Defence mechanism defined	Examples of organisational resistance to the CB approach
Repression	Pushing unacceptable ideas and impulses into the unconscious.	Organisation's members consistently tell you that they support evidence-based practice, but, as a group, appear to be unaware of the ways in which they fail to acknowledge the mismatch between the way they practise and how they could or should practise. You give them evidence-based papers to read and many then either lose them or say that they are too busy to read them. You note that this does not happen with other papers agreed by the members to be 'very important'.
Denial	Refusing to acknowledge a disturbing fact, feeling or memory.	You point the above out to them and they deny that they have not accorded the same respect to evidence-based papers.
Displacement	Shifting disturbing feelings aroused by one person on to a safer target.	They say that, while it is their responsibility to keep up to date with evidence-based practice, it is the responsibility of some other person or group in the organisation to get it 'up and running'.
Rationalisation	The creation of elaborate or unconvincing schemes of justification to disguise underlying motives and intentions.	They say that, while evidence-based approaches are, of course, extremely important, there are other things that must take precedence at the moment, but 'we'll get there in time, rest assured.'
Regression	Adopting behavioural patterns found satisfying and effective in childhood in order to reduce the effect of current uncomfortable demands.	They fail to accept ownership of their own need to support evidence-based practice. You find yourself being pushed into accepting the 'hero innovator' role (see Chapter 5). This can be seductive and enticing – 'We totally depend on you', 'We can't do it without you', 'We see you as spearheading this' and so on.
Splitting and Idealisation	Inappropriately separating different elements of experience and talking up the good aspects of a situation to avoid facing the bad ones.	Organisational members maintain a stance of identifying good practice in areas other than evidence-based practice and neglect to talk about the latter.

challenge basic paradigms and operating norms, many fail to do so. This failure is especially true of bureaucratized organizations, whose fundamental organizing principles often operate in a way that actually obstructs the learning process. ... For example, bureaucratization tends to create fragmented patterns of thought and action. Where hierarchical and horizontal divisions are particularly strong, information and knowledge rarely flow in a free manner. Different sectors of the organisation thus often operate on the basis of different pictures of the total situation, pursuing subunit goals almost as ends in themselves. ... The existence of such divisions tends to emphasize the distinctions between different elements of the organization and fosters the development of political systems that place yet further barriers in the way of learning. ... Employees are usually encouraged to occupy and keep a predefined place within the whole, and are rewarded for doing so. Situations in which policies and operating standards are challenged tend to be exceptional rather than the rule. Under these circumstances, single-loop learning systems are reinforced and may actually serve to keep an organization on the wrong course.

Morgan, 1997: 88–9

In summary, it may be conceptually useful to think of organisations as often operating at a largely unconscious level, within which organisational members corporately fail to learn both from mistakes or to challenge their own assumptions. This picture is made worse by the fact that bureaucracies are often composed of organisations within organisations, which block the free flow of knowledge and development. There seem to be fairly obvious threats to organisational development and the uptake of evidence-based and CB approaches within such a picture. These include:

- difficulties with the free flow of vital information on the CB approach between organisational departments
- a bureaucratically sanctioned risk-aversive style among organisations' members
- an unwillingness to challenge the kinds of policies and operating standards that inhibit the free development of the CB approach
- an unwillingness to question too deeply the usefulness of current interventions carried out in the name of mental health practice, in the context of organisational learning and development.

The maintenance of organisational customs and practice

In view of the above discussion, we are still left with the question by what mechanisms are mental health practitioners trapped in the psychic prison of the organisations that employ them?

From a CB perspective, all of us are socialised into particular ways of viewing ourselves, others and the world and developing corresponding rules for living. By an analogous process, according to Pfeffer (1981), organisations' members are socialised into favoured 'custom and practice' ways of thinking and doing within the socialising process of 'structural power'.

Pfeffer argued that structural power is built into the interpersonal and material life of organisations and is most effective when it is least apparent to organisations' members. Pfeffer did not mean to imply a picture of absolute consensus among group members about day-to-day issues as people do argue and disagree on issues. Rather, his position was that, at a more general level, the edifice of structural power is held together by the cement of customs and practices that bureaucracies come to rely on. Over time, these contribute to the formation of repeated patterns of behaviour and attitudes among organisations' members. In turn, this results in the establishment of patterns of expectation and the influence of 'the way things are done around here, and by whom'. The resultant patterns of power and authority are, in a circular way, made legitimate and maintained as a result of such customs and practices. New members are socialised into a generally shared organisational worldview where the active exercise of power is not particularly apparent.

However, because bureaucracies are, by nature, fragmented structures, the appearance of general consensus is a useful camouflage for more sinister organisational dynamics (Purser and Cabana, 1998). These include:

- conflict between departments or in relation to function or purpose
- the exercise of power in decision making, unrelated to knowledge or expertise
- a lack of cooperative behaviour and reluctance to change practices or procedures
- hoarding knowledge for political gain, secrecy or one-upmanship.

In conclusion – giving knowledge away

Having developed a framework in the preceding discussion for making sense of the first three of the above bulleted points, we conclude this chapter with a comment on the last one. In Britain, the dynamic of CB knowledge hoarding is, for us, an all too familiar pattern. We have known many work settings and groups of workers in the past who developed expertise in CB practice and were subsequently unwilling to give their skills and knowledge away.

In the past 30 years, the few British mental health nurse specialist practitioners of the CB approach were only 'special' at the expense of the many generic practitioners, who were not (Newell and Gournay, 1994). Notwithstanding its difficulties (discussed in the Chapter 15), the development of the evidence-based mental health movement may signal a change to this state of affairs. In this context (at least at a conscious level), our aim in writing this book has been to support the urgent need to disseminate good, well-researched psychotherapeutic practice, in spite of the dark side of mental health organisations. May the passage of time demonstrate a triumph of hope over experience.

SUMMARY

- Selected aspects of the literature on organisational practice are useful for inclusion in a CB book, to give a conceptual framework for understanding organisational problems concerning the uptake of the CB approach and other evidence-based approaches.
- Organisations can be defined as socially constructed sites of meaning-making.
- A distinction can be made between backstage and frontstage organisational activity.
- It is useful to consider organisations as 'psychic prisons'.
- Within these, workers can become trapped in organisationally favoured ways of thinking.
- Extreme versions of this can be understood in terms of the 'groupthink' concept.
- This may partly explain organisational resistance to evidence-based practice.
- Corporate organisational resistance can also be helpfully addressed using the concept of defence mechanisms and single- and double-loop learning.

- There are at least four implications emerging for the uptake of the CB approach.
- The maintenance of organisational customs and practices maintains and makes legitimate structures of organisational power, expectation and influence.
- Bureaucracies also give rise to sinister organisational dynamics, including knowledge hoarding.

Activities

- Explore what attitudes and values are taken for granted in your workplace or organisation.
- Ask organisational members why and how they came to hold those attitudes and values.
- Consider what tensions are apparent in your organisation between backstage and frontstage activity.

Further reading

Morgan, G., 1997, *Images of Organisation* (2nd edition). Thousand Oaks, CA: Sage.
A wonderful and ground-breaking book that will help readers to gain a comprehensive, flexible framework for understanding organisational life and their place within it.

Fineman, S. (ed.), 1996a, *Emotion in Organisations*. London: Sage.
This is an introduction to the ways in which emotion affect several key areas of organisational life, including power, gender, identity and language.

Epilogue

Technique versus formulation

The varieties of practice subsumed under the umbrella of mainstream CB approaches might be plotted along a continuum between two poles. One end represents an explicitly technique-focused style, where concern is given to standardised interventions based on experimental and randomised control research methods. At this end sit computerised CB packages or highly structured manual intervention protocols that can be disseminated to a wide range of healthcare professionals at relatively low cost.

Formulation-based approaches are located at the other end of the continuum, where the richness of individual experiences is celebrated and valued. At this end can be found highly trained and experienced therapists, working with individuals who have very complex needs and giving more of an explicit, moment-by-moment focus to therapeutic alliance factors. Eventually, the same or similar techniques will be deployed as those used by practitioners at the other end of the continuum, but this will happen at a later stage in what will no doubt be a longer and relatively more expensive process.

Implications for the developing CB practitioner

Some interesting issues emerge from the above polarisation of CB approaches, including the issue of personal therapy. 'Technicalists' might argue that there is little quantitative research to show that CB practitioners who have undergone personal therapy achieve a better outcome with their clients. On the other hand, 'formulationists' might reply that it is essential for therapists to have a good grasp of their own self, other and world core beliefs and related rules as these will inevitably contribute to, and interact with, those of their clients in, for example, therapeutic ruptures.

A related issue of conflict to emerge is in the area of philosophy of knowledge. At the technical end of the continuum can be found 'realists' who are likely to see their job as engaging clients in the process of overcoming their disorders, using the best possible evidence from the gold standard research of the randomised control trial. Many will disparage the notion of personal therapy on the basis that, unlike their clients, they are on the other, non-disordered, side of the fence. In contrast, 'constructivist' CB practitioners, influenced by interpretive, postmodern and social constructionist paradigms, are more likely to reject the realist pathology-in-the-individual worldview and be concerned instead about the ways in which they are inscribed within the process of meaning and narrative construction with their clients.

The branding of CB psychotherapy

The above panorama of practice and assumptions governing practice is obscured from public view in Britain. Much of the literature emerging from government and academic sources describes the CB approach as if it were a uniform and unilateral knowledge and practice domain. This branding process is made more attractive by the vocabulary of evidence-based healthcare. The CB world is imbued with power by association, with words and phrases such as 'evidence-based', 'effective', 'low cost' and 'easy to disseminate'. Clearly, as in national politics, in some ways it profits the CB community to maintain this simplistic image of itself.

However, we hope that readers will have gained sufficiently from our work to engage intelligently with the branding of CB practice dialogue and be better placed to resist simplistic representations of both themselves and the broader CB community as a result.

Alec Grant, Jem Mills, Ronan Mulhern and Nigel Short
February 2002–January 2004

Bibliography

Alcohol Concern, 2002, *State of the Nation 2002*. London: Alcohol Concern.

Andersson, G., and Yardley, L., 1998, 'Combined cognitive behavioural and physiotherapy treatment of dizziness: a case report', *Behavioural and Cognitive Psychotherapy*, 26, pp. 365–9.

Andrade, L., Caraveo-Anduaga, J.J., Berglund, P., Biji, R.V., De Graff, R., Volleberg, W., Dragomirecka, F., Kohn, R., Keller, R.C., Kawakami, N., Kilic, C., Offord, D., Ustan, T.B., and Wittchen, H.U., 2003, 'The epidemiology of major depressive episodes: results from the International Consortium of Psychiatric Epidemiology Surveys', *International Journal of Methods in Psychiatric Research*, 12(1), pp. 3–21.

Andrews, G., Crino, R., Hunt, C., Lampe, L., and Page, A., 1994, *The Treatment of Anxiety Disorders: A Clinician's Guide and Patient Manuals*. Cambridge: Cambridge University Press.

Andrews, G., and Henderson, S. (eds), 2000, *Unmet Need in Psychiatry: Problems, Resources, Responses*. Cambridge: Cambridge University Press.

Anthony, W., 1993, 'Recovering from mental illness: the guiding vision of the mental health service system in the 1990s', *Psychosocial Rehabilitation Journal*, 16(4), pp. 11–23.

APA, 1994, *Diagnostic and Statistical Manual of Mental Disorders*, 4th edn (DSM IV). Washington DC: American Psychiatric Association.

APA, 2000, *Diagnostic and Statistics Manual of Mental Disorders*, (4th edn), Text Revision. Washington DC: American Psychiatric Association.

Atkinson, P.A., Coffey, A., and Delamont, S., 2001, 'A debate about our canon', *Qualitative Research*, 1(1) pp. 5–21.

Aust, R., Sharp, C., and Goulden, C., 2002, 'Prevalence of drug use: key findings from the 2001/2002 British Crime Survey' Findings 182. London: Home Office.

Banerjee, S., Clancy, C., and Crome I. (eds), 2002, *Co-existing Problems of Mental Disorder and Substance Misuse: An Information Manual*. London: Royal College of Psychiatrists Research Unit: Report to the Department of Health 2001.

Barker, P., 1992, 'Psychiatric nursing', in Butterworth, T., and Faugier, J. (eds), *Clinical Supervision and Mentorship in Nursing*. London: Chapman & Hall.

Barker, P., 2000, 'The construction of mind and madness: from Leonardo to the Hearing Voices Network', in Barker, P., and Stevenson C. (eds), *The Construction of Power and Authority in Psychiatry*. Oxford: Butterworth-Heinemann.

Barker, P., 2002, 'Realising the promise of liaison mental health care', in Regel, S., and Roberts, D. (eds), *Mental Health Liaison: A Handbook for Nurses and Health Professionals*. Edinburgh: Baillière Tindall and Royal College Nursing, Harcourt.

Barlow, D.H., Levitt, J.T., and Bufka, L.F., 1999, 'The dissemination of empirically supported treatments: a view to the future', *Behaviour Research and Therapy*, 37, pp. 147–62.

Bastion, H., December 1994, Consumer Advocate, 'The power of sharing knowledge', consumer participation in the Cochrane Consumer Collaboration Network at www.cochraneconsumer.com

Beck, A.T., Weissman, A., Lester, D., and Trexler, L., 1974, 'The measurement of pessimism: the hopelessness scale', *Journal of Consulting and Clinical Psychology*, 42, pp. 861–5.

Beck, A.T., Rush, A.J., Shaw, B.F., and Emery, G., 1979, *Cognitive Therapy for Depression*. New York: Guilford Press.

Beck, A., and Emery, G., 1985, *Anxiety Disorders and Phobias: A Cognitive Perspective*. New York: Basic Books.

Beck, A., and Steer, R., 1990, *Beck Anxiety Inventory*. San Antonio, Texas: Psychological Corporation.

Beck, A., Freeman, A., Davis, D.D., and Associates, 1990, *Cognitive Therapy of Personality Disorder*. New York: Guilford Press.

Beck, A.T., 1983, 'Cognitive theory of depression: new perspectives', in Clayton, P.J., and Barret, J.E. (eds), *Treatment of Depression: Old Controversies and New Approaches*. New York: Raven Press.

Beck, A.T., 1996, *Beck Depression Inventory*. San Antonio: The Psychological Corporation.

Beck, J., 1995, *Cognitive Therapy: Basics and Beyond*. New York: Guilford Press.

Beck-Sander, A., and Clark, A., 1998, 'Psychological models of psychosis: implications for risk assessment', *Journal of Forensic Psychiatry*, 9(3), pp. 659–71.

Bennett-Levy, J., and Taylor, B., September 2000, 'Is there a place for qualitative research in cognitive therapy?' Paper presented at the Seventh International Congress on Constructivism in Psychotherapy, Geneva.

Bennett-Levy, J., Turner, F., Beaty, T., Smith, M., Paterson, B., and Farmer, S., 2001, 'The value of self-practice of cognitive therapy techniques and self-reflection in the training of cognitive therapists', *Behavioural and Cognitive Psychotherapy*, 29, pp. 203–20.

Bennett-Levy, J., Lee, N., Travers, K., Pohlman, S., and Hamernik, E., 2003, 'Cognitive therapy from the inside: enhancing therapist skills through practising what we preach', *Behavioural and Cognitive Psychotherapy*, 31, pp. 143–58.

Benson, A., Secker, J., Balfe, E., Lipsedge, M., Robinson, S., and Walker, J., September 2003, 'Discourses of blame for aggression and violence on an acute mental health inpatient unit', *Social Science and Medicine*, 57(5), pp. 917–26.

Bentall, R. (ed.), 1990, *Reconstructing Schizophrenia*. London: Routledge.

Bentall, R.P., Kaney, S., and Dewey, M.E., 1991, 'Persecutory delusions and socical judgement: an attribution theory analysis', *British Journal of Clinical Psychology*, 30, pp. 13–23.

Blackburn, I-M., and Moorhead, S., 2000, 'Update in cognitive therapy for depression', *Journal of Cognitive Psychotherapy*, 14(3), pp. 537–49.

Bloch, S., and Kissane, D., 2000, Psychotherapies in psycho-oncology: an exciting new challenge', *British Journal of Psychiatry*, 177, pp. 112–16.

Blumenthal, S., and Lavender, T., 2000, *Violence and Mental Disorder: A Critical Aid to the Assessment and Management of Risk*. London: Jessica Kingsley.

Bolsover, N., 2002, 'Commentary: the "evidence" is weaker than claimed', *British Medical Journal*, 324, pp. 288–94.

Brennan, G., 2004, 'Stress vulnerability model of serious mental illness', in Gamble, C., and Brennan, G. (eds), *Working with Serious Mental Illness*, 2nd edn. London: Baillière Tindall.

Brooker, C., Gournay, K., O'Halloran, P., Bailey, D., and Saul, C., 2002, 'Mapping training to support the implementation of the National Service Framework for mental health', *Journal of Mental Health*, 11(1), pp. 103–16.

Burgess, M., and Chalder, T., 2001, 'Telephone cognitive behaviour therapy for chronic fatigue syndrome in secondary care: a case series', *Behavioural and Cognitive Psychotherapy*, 29, pp. 447–56.

Burns, D.D., 1989, *The Feeling Good Handbook: Using the New Mood Therapy in Everyday Life*. New York: Morrow.

Butler, G., 1989, 'Phobic disorders', in Hawton, K., Salkovskis, P.M., Kirk, J., and Clark, D.M. (eds), *Cognitive Behaviour Therapy for Psychiatric Problems: A Practical Guide*. New York: Oxford University Press.

Cascalanda, N., Perry, C.J., and Looper, K., 2002, 'Remission in major depressive disorder: a comparison of pharmacotherapy, psychotherapy and controlled trials', *American Journal of Psychiatry*, 159, pp. 1354–60.

Castillo, H., Allen, L., and Coxhead, N., 2001, 'The hurtfulness of a diagnosis: user research about personality disorder', *Mental Health Practice*, 4(9), pp. 16–19.

Chadwick, P., and Birchwood, M., 1994, 'The omnipotence of voices: a cognitive approach to auditory hallucinations', *British Journal of psychiatry*, 164, pp. 190–201.

Chadwick, P., Birchwood, M., and Trower, P., 1996, *Cognitive Therapy for Hallucinations, Delusions, Voices and Paranoia*. Chichester: John Wiley.

Chambless, D.L., and Hollon, S.D., 1998, 'Defining empirically supported therapies', *Journal of Consulting and Clinical Psychology*, 66, pp. 7–18.

Clark, D.M., Salkovskis, P.M., Hackmann, A., Wells, A., Fennell, M., Ludgate, J., Ahmad, S., Richards, H.C., and Gelder, M., 1998, 'Two psychological treatments for hypochondriasis', *British Journal of Psychiatry*, 173, pp. 218–25.

Clarke, L., 1999, 'Nursing in search of a science: the rise and rise of the new nurse brutalism', *Mental Health Care*, 21(8), pp. 270–2.

Clements, K., and Turpin, G., 1992, 'Vulnerability models and schizophrenia: the assessment and prediction of relapse', in Birchwood, M., and Tarrier, N. (eds), *Innovations in the Psychological Management of Schizophrenia*. Chichester: John Wiley.

Coker, A.L., Davis, K.E., Arias, I., Desai, S., Sanderson, M., Brandt, H.M., and Smith, P.H., November 2002, 'Physical and mental health effects of intimate partner violence for men and women', *American Journal of Preventitive Medicine*, 23(4), pp. 260–8.

Coleman, R., 1999, *Recovery: An Alien Concept*. Gloucester: Handsell Publishing.

Coleman, R., 2000, 'The politics of the illness', in Barker, P., and Stevenson, C. (eds), *The Construction of Power and Authority in Psychiatry*. Oxford: Butterworth-Heinemann.

Cormac, I., Jones, C., Campbell, C., and Silveira da Mota Neto, J., 2003, 'Cognitive behaviour therapy for schizophrenia (Cochrane Review)', in *The Cochrane Library*, Issue 3. Oxford: Update Software.

Craske, M., 1999, *Anxiety Disorders*. Oxford: Westview Press.

Davidson, J., 1996, *Davidson Trauma Scale (DTS)*. New York: MHS.

Davidson, K., 2002, *Cognitive Therapy for Personality Disorders: A Guide for Therapists*. London: Arnold.

Davidson, D., and Lowe, J., 2001, *Putting Assertive Outreach into Practice*. Brighton: Pavillion Publishing.

Davies, W., 2000, *Overcoming Anger and Irritability. A Self-help Guide using CB Techniques*. London: Constable Robinson.

Dcale, A., and Chalder, T., 2002, 'Chronic fatigue syndrome: a cognitive behavioural approach', in Regel, S., and Roberts, D. (eds), *Mental Health Liaison: A Handbook for Nurses and Health Professionals*. London: Baillière Tindall and Royal College Nursing, Harcourt.

Denzin, N.K., and Lincoln, Y.S., 2000, *Handbook of Qualitative Research*, 2nd edn. Thousand Oaks, California: Sage.

Department of Health (DoH), 1998, *Modernising Mental Health Services: Safe, Sound and Supportive*. London: The Stationery Office.

Department of Health, 1999, *National Service Framework for Mental Health: Modern Standards and Service Models*. London: Department of Health.

Department of Health, 2001a, *Treatment Choice in Psychological Therapies and Counselling: Evidence Based Clinical Practice Guideline*, brief version. London: Department of Health (also available from website, at www.doh.gov.uk/PublicationsAndStatistics/Publications/PublicationsPolicyAndGuidance/fs/en).

Department of Health, 2001b, *The Mental Health Policy Implementation Guide*. London: The Stationery Office.

Derricott, J., Preston, A., Hunt, N., and Speed, S., 1999, *The Safer Injecting Briefing*. Liverpool: HIT.

Duncan-Grant, A., 1999, 'Misrepresentation, stereotyping, and acknowledging bias in science: responses to Liam Clarke', *Mental Health Care*, 21(10), pp. 336–7.

Dyer, I., January 2000, 'Cognitive behavioural group anger management for outpatients; a retrospective study', *International Journal of Psychiatric Nursing Research*, 5(3), pp. 602–21.

Eastwick, Z., and Grant, A., in press for 2004, 'Deliberate self-harmers and accident and emergency departments: rescuing the emotional agenda', *Mental Health Practice*,

Edelman, S., and Kidman, A.D., 2000, 'Application of cognitive behaviour therapy to patients who have advanced cancer', *Behaviour Change*, 17(2), pp. 103–10.

Engel, G.L., 1980, 'The clinical application of the biopsychosocial model', *American Journal of Psychiatry*, 137, pp. 535–43.

Evans, K., Tyrer, P., Catalan, J., Schmidt, U., Davidson, K., Dent, J., Tata, P., Thornton, S., Barber, J., and Thompson, S., 1999, 'Manual-assisted cognitive behaviour therapy (MACT): a randomised controlled trial of a brief intervention with bibliotherapy in the treatment of recurrent deliberate self-harm', *Psychological Medicine*, 29, pp. 19–25.

Falsetti, S., 1997, 'The decision-making process of choosing a treatment for patients with civilian trauma-related PTSD', *Cognitive and Behavioral Practice*, 4, pp. 99–121.

Fawzy, F.I., Fawzy, N.W., and Wheeler, J.G., 1996, 'A post-hoc comparison of the efficiency of a psycho-educational intervention for melanoma patients delivered in-group versus individual formats: an analysis of data from two studies', *Psycho-oncology*, 5, pp. 81–9.

Fee, D. (ed.), 2000, *Pathology and the Postmodern: Mental Illness as Discourse and Experience*. London: Sage.

Fennell, M., 1989, 'Depression', in Hawton, K., Salkovskis, P.M., Kirk, J., and Clark, D.M. (eds), *Cognitive Behaviour Therapy for Psychiatric Problems: A Practical Guide*. New York: Oxford University Press.

Fennell, M.J., 1997, 'Low self-esteem: a cognitive perspective', *Behavioural and Cognitive Psychotherapy*, 25, pp. 1–25.

Field, H.L., and Waldfogel, S., 1995, 'Severe ocular self-injury', *General Hospital Psychiatry*, 17, pp. 224–7.

Fineman, S. (ed.), 1996a, *Emotion in Organizations*. London: Sage.

Fineman, S., 1996b, 'Organizations as emotional arenas', in Fineman, S. (ed.), *Emotion in Organizations*. London: Sage.

Fisher, S., and Tunmore, R., 2002, 'Cardiac rehabilitation: assessment and intervention strategies', in Regel, S., and Roberts, D. (eds), *Mental Health Liaison: A Handbook for Nurses and Health Professionals*. London: Bailliére Tindall and Royal College Nursing, Harcourt.

Foa, E., Keane, T., and Friedman, M., 2000, *Effective Treatments for PTSD*. New York: Guilford Press.

Fowler, P., Garety, P., and Kuipers, L., 1995, *Cognitive Behaviour Therapy for Psychosis: A Clinical Handbook*. Chichester: John Wiley.

Fox, J., and Conroy, P, 2000, 'Assessing clients' needs: the semistructured interview', in: Gamble, C., and Brennan, G. (eds), *Working with Serious Mental Illness: A Manual for Clinical Practice*. London: Ballière Tindall in association with the Royal College of Nursing, Harcourt.

Fox, J.A., and Zawitz, M.W., 1999, *Homicide Trends in the United States*. Washington DC: Bureau of Justice Statistics, United States Department of Justice.

Frame, L., and Morrison, A.P., 2001, 'Causes of PTSD in psychosis', *Archives of General Psychiatry*, 58(3), pp. 305–6.

Freyne, A., and O'Connor, A., 1992, 'Post-traumatic stress disorder symptoms in prisoners following a cellmate's death', *Irish Journal of Psychological Medicine*, 9(1), pp. 42–4.

Gamble, C., and Brennan, G. (eds), 2000, *Working with Serious Mental Illness: A Manual for Clinical Practice*. London: Ballière Tindall in association with the Royal College of Nursing, Harcourt.

Garety, P., and Hemsley, D., 1994, *Delusions: Investigations Into the Psychology of Delusional Reasoning*. Hove: Psychology Press.

Garland, A., and Scott, J., May 2002, 'Using homework in therapy for depression', *Journal of Clinical Psychology*, pp. 489–98.

Geddes, J., 2002, 'Evidence-based practice in mental health', in Trinder, L., and Reynolds, S. (eds), *Evidence-based Practice: A Critical Appraisal*. Oxford: Blackwell Science.

Gelder, M., 1997, 'The scientific foundations of cognitive behaviour therapy', in Clark, D.M., and Fairburn, C.G., *Science and Practice of Cognitive Behaviour Therapy*. New York: Oxford University Press.

Georgiades, N.J., and Phillimore, L., 1975, 'The myth of the hero-innovator and alternative strategies for organizational change', in Kiernan, C.C., and Woodward, F.P. (eds), *Behavioural Modification with the Severely Retarded*. London: Associated Scientific Publishers.

Gergen, K.J., 1999, *An Invitation to Social Construction*. London: Sage.

Gilbert, P., 2002, 'Evolutionary approaches to psychopathology and cognitive therapy', *Journal of Cognitive Psychopathology: An International Quarterly*, 16(3), pp. 263–94.

Goffman, E., 1969, *The Presentation of Self in Everyday Life*. Reading: Pelican.

Goldberg, D., and Hillier, V., 1978, 'A scaled version of the General Health Questionnaire', *Psychological Medicine*, 9, pp. 139–46.

Goleman, D., 1985, *Vital Lies, Simple Truths: The Psychology of Self-deception*. New York: Touchstone, Simon & Schuster.

Goleman, D., 1996, *Emotional Intelligence: Why It Can Matter More Than IQ*. London: Bloomsbury.

Good, M.I., 1997, 'Lethal interaction of clozapine and buspirone?', *American Journal of Psychiatry*, 154, pp. 1472–3.

Gore-Felton, C., and Spiegel, D., 2000, 'Group therapy for medically ill patients', in Stodemire, A., Fogel, B.S., and Greenberg, D.B. (eds), *Psychiatric Care of the Medical Patient*. Oxford. Oxford University Press.

Gossop, M., 2000, *Living with Drugs*. London: Ashgate.

Gournay, K., 2000, 'Nurses as therapists (1972–2000), *Behavioural and Cognitive Psychotherapy*, 28(4), pp. 369–78.

Graham, H.L., Copello, A., Birchwood, M.J., and Mueser, K.T. (eds), 2002, *Substance Misuse in Psychosis: Approaches to Treatment and Service Delivery*. Chichester: John Wiley.

Grant, A., 2001, *Clinical Supervision Activity Among Mental Health Workers: A Critical Organizational Ethnography*. Portsmouth: Nursing Praxis International.

Grant, A., and Mills, J., 2000, 'The great going nowhere show: structural power and mental health nurses', *Mental Health Practice*, 4(3), pp. 14–16.

Greenberger, D., and Padesky, C.A., 1995, *Mind over Mood: A Cognitive Therapy Treatment Manual for Clients*. New York: Guilford Press.

Greenwood, D.J., and Levin, M., 2000, 'Reconstructing the relationships between universities and society through action research', in Denzin, N.K., and Lincoln, Y.S., *Handbook of Qualitative Research*, 2nd edn. Thousand Oaks, CA: Sage.

Grey, S.J., 2002, 'Editorial: If psychological therapy makes such good sense why isn't everybody doing it?', *Journal of Mental Health*, 11(5), pp. 465–8.

Hall, D.C., Lawson, B.Z., and Wilson, L.G., 1981, 'Command hallucinations and self-amputation of the penis and hand during a first psychotic breakdown', *Journal of Clinical Psychiatry*, 42, pp. 322–4.

Hall, W., Teeson, M., Lynskey, M., and Degenhardt, L., 1999, 'The 12-month prevalence of substance use and ICD-10 substance use disorders in Australian adults: findings from the National Survey of Mental Health and Well-being', *Addiction*, 94, pp. 1541–50.

Hambridge, J.A., 1990, 'The grief process in those admitted to regional secure units following homicide', *Journal of Forensic Sciences*, 35, pp. 1149–54.

Hawton, K., and Kirk, J., 1989, 'Problem solving', in Hawton, K., Salkovskis, P. M., Kirk, J., and Clark, D.M. (eds), *Cognitive Behaviour Therapy for Psychiatric Problems: A Practical Guide*. New York: Oxford University Press.

Hawton, K., Salkovskis, P.M., Kirk, J., and Clark, D.M. (eds), 1989, *Cognitive Behaviour Therapy for Psychiatric Problems: A Practical Guide*. New York: Oxford University Press.

Heery, G., 2001, *Preventing Violence in Relationships: A Programme for Men who Feel They Have a Problem with Their Use of Controlling Violent Behaviour*. London: Jessica Kingsley.

Hellerstein, D., Frosch, W., and Koenigsberg, H.W., 1987, 'The clinical significance of command hallucinations', *American Journal of Psychiatry*, 144, pp. 219–21.

Hemming, M., Morgan, S., and O'Halloran, P., 1999, 'Assertive Outreach: Implications for the Development of the Model in the United Kingdom', *Journal of Mental Health*, 8(2), pp. 141–7.

Henry, J.L., Wilson, P.H., Bruce, D.G., Chisholm, D.J., and Rawling, P.J., 1997, 'Cognitive behavioural stress management for patients with non-insulin-dependent diabetes mellitus', *Psychological, Health and Medicine*, 2(2), pp. 109–18.

Herbert, C., 1995, *Understanding Your Reactions to Trauma: A Booklet for Survivors of Trauma and Their Families*. Witney, Oxfordshire: The Oxford Stress and Trauma Centre.

Hiller, W., Rief, W., and Fichter, M., 1997, 'How disabled are patients with somatoform disorders?', *General Hospital Psychiatry*, 19, pp. 432–8.

Hofman, S., Moscovitch, D., and Heinrichs N., 2002, 'Evolutionary mechanisms of fear and anxiety', *Journal of Cognitive Psychotherapy: An International Quarterly*, 16(3), pp. 317–34.

Holliday, A., 2002, *Doing and Writing Qualitative Research*. London: Sage.

Holmes, J., 2002, 'All you need is cognitive behaviour therapy?', *British Medical Journal*, 324, pp. 288–94.

Holt, L., 1993, 'The adolescent in accident and emergency', *Nursing Standard*, 8, p. 8.

Home Office Drugs Strategy Directorate, 2002, *Updated Drug Strategy (03/12/2002)*. London: The Stationery Office.

Hubble, M.A., Duncan, B.L., and Miller, S.D., 1999a, 'Directing attention to what works', in Hubble, M.A., Duncan, B.L., and Miller, S.D., *The Heart & Soul of Change: What Works in Therapy*. Washington DC: American Psychological Association.

Hubble, M.A., Duncan, B.L., and Miller, S.D., 1999b, *The Heart & Soul of Change: What Works in Therapy*. Washington DC: American Psychological Association.

Huckle, P.L., 1995, 'Male rape victims referred to a forensic psychiatric service', *Medicine, Science and the Law*, 35, pp. 187–92.

Iwamasa, G.Y., 1996, 'On being an ethnic minority cognitive behavioral therapist', *Cognitive and Behavioral Practice*, 3, pp. 235–54.

James, I.A., 2001, 'Schema therapy: the next generation, but should it carry a health warning?', *Behavioural and Cognitive Psychotherapy*, 29, pp. 401–7.

Johansson, C., Dahl, J., Jannert, M., Melin, L., and Andersson, G., 1998, 'Effects of a cognitive behavioural pain-management programme', *Behaviour Research and Therapy*, 36, pp. 915–30.

Johnstone, L., 2000, *Users and Abusers of Psychiatry: A Critical Look at Psychiatric Practice*. London: Routledge.

Jones, C., Cormac, I., Mota, J., and Campbell, C., 2000, 'Cognitive behaviour therapy for schizophrenia (Cochrane review)', in *The Cochrane Library*, Issue 3. Exford: Update Software.

Kane, S., 2000, *4:48 Psychosis*. London: Methuen.

Karp, J.G., Whitman, L., and Convit, A., 1991, 'Intentional ingestion of foreign objects by male prison inmates', *Hospital and Community Psychiatry*, 42, pp. 533–5.

Keefer, L., and Blanchard, E.B., 2001, 'The effects of relaxation response meditation on the symptoms of irritable bowel syndrome: results of a controlled treatment study', *Behaviour Research and Therapy*, 39, pp. 801–11.

Kemp, R., Kirov, G., Everitt, B., Hayward, P., and David, A., 1998, 'Randomised controlled trial of compliance therapy', *British Journal of Psychiatry*, 172, pp. 413–19.

Kenardy, J., McCafferty, K., and Rosa, R., 2003, 'Internet delivered indicated prevention for anxiety disorders: a randomised controlled trial', *Behavioural and Cognitive Psychotherapy*, 31, pp. 279–90.

Kennerley, H., 2000, *Overcoming Childhood Trauma*. London: Robinson.

Kingdon, D.G., and Turkington, D., 1991, 'A role for cognitive–behavioural strategies in schizophrenia?', *Social Psychiatry and Psychiatric Epidemiology*, 26, pp. 101–3.

Kingdon, D., and Turkington, D., 1994, *Cognitive Behavioural Therapy of Schizophrenia*. Hove: Lawrence Erlbaum Associates.

Kingdon, D., and Turkington, D., 2002, *The Case Study Guide to Cognitive Behaviour Therapy of Psychosis*. Chichester: John Wiley.

Kirk, J., 1989, 'Cognitive behavioural assessment', in Hawton, K., Salkovskis, P.M., Kirk, J., and Clark, D.M. (eds), *Cognitive Behaviour Therapy for Psychiatric Problems: A Practical Guide*. New York: Oxford University Press.

Kitchiner, N., 1999, 'Freeing the imprisoned mind', *Mental Health Care*, 21(12), pp. 420–4.

Kitchiner, N., 2000, The use of cognitive behaviour therapy to treat a patient with hypochondriasis', *Mental Health Practice*, 3(7), pp. 15–20.

Kruppa, I., Hickey, N., and Hubbard, C., 1995, 'The prevalence of post-traumatic stress disorder in a special hospital population of legal psychopaths', *Psychology, Crime & Law*, 2, pp. 131–41.

Laing, R.D., 1960, *The Divided Self*. Middlesex: Pelican.

Leahy, R.L., and Holland, S.J., 2000, *Treatment Plans and Interventions for Depression and Anxiety Disorders*. New York: Guilford Press.

Leahy, R.L., 2001, *Overcoming Resistance in Cognitive Therapy*. New York: Guilford Press.

Leahy, R.L., 2002, 'Pessimism and the evolution of negativity. *Journal of Cognitive Psychopathology: An International Quarterly*, 16(3), pp. 263–94.

Lehman, A.F., Meyers, C.P., and Corty, E., 1989, 'Classification of patients with psychiatric and substance abuse syndromes', *Hospital and Community Psychiatry*, 40(10), pp. 1019–25.

Leibbrand, R., and Hiller, W., 2002, 'Functional gastrointestinal disorders: cognitive behaviour treatment', *Current Opinion Psychiatry*, 15, pp. 649–52.

Lewis, D.M., February 2002, 'Responding to a violent incident: physical restraint or anger management as therapeutic interventions', *Journal of Psychiatric and Mental Health Nursing*, 9(1), pp. 57–63.

Liberman, R.P., and Corrigan, P.W.L., 1994, 'Implementing and maintaining behavior therapy programs', in Corrigan, P.W.L., and Liberman, R.P. (eds), *Behavior Therapy in Psychiatric Hospitals*. New York: Springer.

Lincoln, Y.S., and Guba, E.G., 2002, 'Paradigmatic controversies, contradictions and emerging confluences', in Denzin, N.K., and Lincoln, Y.S. (eds), *Handbook of Qualitative Research*, 2nd edn. Thousand Oaks, CA: Sage.

Lindsay, W.R., Allan, R., MacLeod, F., Smart, N., and Smith, A.H., February 2003, 'Long-term treatment and management of violent tendencies of men with intellectual disabilities convicted of assault', *Mental Retardation*, 41(1), pp. 47–56.

Linehan, M.M., 1987, 'Dialectical behavior therapy for borderline personality disorder: Theory and method', *Bulletin of the Menninger Clinic*, 51, pp. 261–76.

Linehan, M.M., 1993, *Cognitive Behavioural Treatment of Borderline Personality Disorder*. New York: Guildford Press.

Linkh, D.J., and Sonneck, S.M., June 2003, 'An application of cognitive behavioural anger management training in the military occupatuional setting: efficacy and demographic factors', *Military Medicine*, 168(6), pp. 475–8.

Lustman, P.J., Griffith, L.S., Freeland, K.E., Kissel, S., and Clouse, R.E., 1998, 'Cognitive behaviour therapy for depression in type 2 diabetes mellitus: a randomised controlled trial', *Annals of Internal Medicine*, 129, pp. 613–21.

Lyddon, W.J., and Weill, R., 1997, 'Cognitive psychotherapy and postmodernism: emerging themes and challenges', *Journal of Cognitive Psychotherapy*, 11(2), pp. 75–90.

McNeil, D.E., Eisner, J.P., and Binder, R.L., April 2003, 'The relationship between aggressive attributional style and violence by psychiatric patients', *Journal of Consultative Clinical Psychology*, 71(2), pp. 399–403.

McNutt, L.A., Carlson, B.E., Rose, I.M., and Robinson, D.A., February 2002, 'Partner violence intervention in the busy primary care environment', *American Journal of Preventative Medicine*, 22(2), pp. 84–91.

Maione, P.V., Chenail, R.J., 1999, 'Qualitative inquiry in psychotherapy: research on the common factors', in Hubble, M.A., Duncan, B.L., and Miller, S.D. *The Heart & Soul of Change: What Works in Therapy*. Washington DC: American Psychological Association.

Marks, I.M., 1978, *Living with Fear*. Maidenhead: McGraw-Hill.

Marks, I.M., and Mathews, A.M., 1979, 'Brief standard self-rating for phobic patients', *Behaviour Research and Therapy*, 17, pp. 59–68.

Marks, I.M., 1986, *Behavioural Psychotherapy: Maudsley Pocket Book of Clinical Management*. Bristol: Wright.

Marks, I.M., and Nesse, R.M., 1997, 'Fear and fitness: an evolutionary analysis of anxiety disorders', in Baron-Cohen, S. (ed.), *The Maladapted Mind: Classic Readings in Evolutionary Psychopathology*. Hove: Psychology Press.

Marlatt, G.A., and Gordon, J.R., 1985. *Relapse Prevention: Maintenance Strategies in the Treatment of Addictive Behaviours*. New York: Guilford Press.

Mathews, A., 1997, 'Information processing biases in emotional disorders', in Clark, D., and Fairburn, C. (eds), *Science and Practice of Cognitive Behaviour Therapy*. Oxford: Oxford University Press.

Mayou, R., Bass, C., and Sharpe, M., 1995, 'Overview of epidemiology, classification, and aetiology', in Mayou, R., Bass, C., and Sharpe, M. (eds), *Treatment of Functional Somatic Symptoms*. Oxford: Oxford University Press.

Meddings, S., and Perkins, R, 2002, 'What getting better means to staff and users of a rehabilitation service: an exploratory study', *Journal of Mental Health*, 11(3), pp. 319–25.

Meichenbaum, D., 1994, *Treating Post-traumatic Stress Disorder: A Handbook and Practice Manual for Therapy*. Chichester: John Wiley.

Miller, W.R., and Rollnick, S., 2002, *Motivational Interviewing: Preparing People to Change Addictive Behaviour*, 2nd edn. New York: Guilford Press.

Mills, J., 2000, 'Dealing with voices and strange thoughts', in Gamble, C., and Brennan, G. (eds), *Working with Serious Mental Illness: A Manual for Clinical Practice*. London: Ballière Tindall in association with the Royal College of Nursing, Harcourt.

Mills, J., 2003, *Psychosocial Interventions and Other Tales. Competing Accounts of Mental Health Practice*. Portsmouth: Nursing Praxis International.

Milne, D., and Gracie, I., 2001, 'The role of the supervisee: 20 ways to facilitate clinical supervision', *Clinical Psychology*, 5, pp. 13–15.

Mooney, K.A., and Padesky, C.A., 2000, 'Applying client creativity to recurrent problems: constructing possibilities and tolerating doubt', *Journal of Cognitive Psychotherapy: An International Quarterly*, 14(2), pp. 149–61.

Moorey, S., and Greer, S., 2002, *Cognitive Behaviour Therapy with People with Cancer*. Oxford: Oxford University Press.

Morgan, G., 1997, *Images of Organization*, 2nd edn. Thousand Oaks, CA: Sage.

Morley, S., Eccleston, C., and Williams, A., 1999, 'Systematic review and meta-analysis of randomised controlled trials of cognitive behaviour therapy and behaviour therapy for chronic pain in adults, excluding headache', *Pain*, 80, pp. 1 13.

Morrall, P., 2000, *Madness and Murder*. London: Whurr.

Morrison, A. (ed.), 2002, *A Casebook of Cognitive Therapy for Psychosis*. Hove: Brunner-Routledge.

Morrison, A., 2003, 'Trauma and psychosis', keynote address at the BABCP Annual Conference, York.

Morse, S.B., 2002, 'Letting it go: using cognitive therapy to treat borderline personality disorder', in Simos, G. (ed.), *Cognitive Behaviour Therapy: A Guide for the Practising Clinician*. Hove: Brunner-Routledge.

Morton, J., 2002, 'California mental health centre provides telepsychiatry to rural clients', *Mental Health Weekly*, 12(38), pp. 3–4.

Mueser, K.T., Drake, R.E., and Wallach, M.A., 1998, 'Dual diagnosis: a review of etiological theories', *Addictive Behaviours*, 23(6), pp. 717–34.

Muir Gray, J.A., 1997, *Evidence-based Healthcare: How to Make Health Policy and Management Decisions*. New York: Churchill Livingstone.

Muir Gray, J.A., 2000, 'Evidence-based public health', in Trinder, L., and Reynolds, S. (eds), *Evidence-based Practice: A Critical Appraisal*. Oxford: Blackwell.

Nathan, P.E., Gorman, J.M., and Salkind, N.J. 1999, *Treating Mental Disorders: A Guide to What Works*. New York: Oxford University Press.

National Institute for Clinical Excellence (NICE), 2002, *Schizophrenia: Core Interventions in the Treatment and Management of Schizophrenia in Primary and Secondary Care*. Available from www.nice.org.uk.

Newell, R., 2002, 'Psychological approaches to body image disturbance', in Regel, S., and Roberts, D. (eds), *Mental Health Liaison: A Handbook for Nurses and Health Professionals*. London: Baillière Tindall and Royal College Nursing, Harcourt.

Newell, R., and Gournay, K., 1994, 'British nurses in behavioural psychotherapy: a 20-year follow-up', *Journal of Advanced Nursing*, 20, pp. 53–60.

Newell, R., and Gournay, K. (eds), 2000a, *Mental Health Nursing: An Evidence-based Approach*. London: Churchill Livingstone.

Newell, R., and Gournay, K., 2000b, 'Preface', in Newell, R., and Gournay, K. (eds), *Mental Health Nursing. An Evidence-based Approach*. London: Churchill Livingstone.

Newell, R., and Marks, I., 2000, 'Phobic nature of social difficulty in facially disfigured people', *British Journal of Psychiatry*, 176, pp. 177–81.

Newman, C.F., 1994, 'Understanding client resistance: methods for enhancing motivation to change', *Cognitive and Behavioural Practice*, 1, pp. 47–69.

Nezu, C.M., and DelliCarpinni, L., 1998, 'An interview with Jeremy Safran', in Safran, J.D., *Widening the Scope of Cognitive Therapy: The Therapeutic Relationship, Emotion, and the Process of Change*. Northvale, NJ: Jason Aronson.

NHS Executive, 1996, *NHS Psychotherapy Services in England*. London: Department of Health.

NHS Centre for Reviews and Dissemination, August 2000, 'Psychosocial interventions for schizophrenia', *Effective Health care* bulletin on the effectiveness of health service interventions for decisionmakers, 6, p. 3. Available from: www.york.ac.uk/inst/crd/ehc63warn.htm

Novaco, R.W., 1994, 'Anger as a risk factor for violence among the mentally disordered', in Monaghan, H., and Steadman, H.J. (eds), *Violence and Mental Disorder: Developments in Risk Assessment*. Chicago: University of Chicago Press.

Osher, F.C., and Kofoed, L.L., 1989, 'Treatment of patients with psychiatric and psychoactive substance abuse disorders', *Hospital and Community Psychiatry*, 40, pp. 1025–30.

Ost, L-G., Hellstrom, K., and Kaver, A., 1992, 'One versus five sessions of exposure in the treatment of injection phobia', *Behaviour Therapy*, 23, pp. 263–82.

Overall, J., and Gorham, D., 1962, 'The brief psychiatric rating scale', *Psychological Reports*, 10, pp. 799–812.

Padesky, C.A., September 1993, 'Socratic questioning: Changing minds or guiding discovery?', keynote address presented at the meeting of the European Congress of Behavioural and Cognitive Therapies, London.

Padesky, C.A., 1994, 'Schema change processes in cognitive therapy', *Clinical Psychology and Psychotherapy*, 1(5), pp. 267–78.

Padesky, C.A., 1996a, *Guided Discovery Using Socratic Dialogue*. Newport Beach, CA: New Harbinger Publications and Center for Cognitive.

Padesky, C.A., 1996b, 'Developing cognitive therapist competency: teaching and supervision models', in Salkovskis, P.M. (ed.), *Frontiers of Cognitive Therapy*. New York: Guilford Press.

Padesky, C., 2–3 October 1998, 'When there's not enough time: innovation in cognitive therapy', workshop handout, Imperial College, London.

Padesky, C.A., 16–17 June 2003, 'Cognitive therapy unplugged: fine-tuning essential therapist skills, two-day workshop by Cognitive Workshops (www.cognitiveworkshops.com), Institute of Education, London.

Pam, A., and Rivera, J.A., 1995, 'Sexual pathology and dangerousness from a thematic apperception test protocol', *Professional Psychology, Research and Practice*, 26, pp. 72–7.

Persons, J., 1989, *Cognitive Therapy in Practice: A Case Formulation Approach*. New York: Norton.

Pfeffer, J., 1981, *Power in Organizations*. Marshfield, MA: Pitman.

Phipps, A., and Turkington, D., 2001, 'Psychiatry in the renal unit', *Advances in Psychiatric Treatment*, 7, pp. 426–32.

Pretzer, J., 1990, 'Borderline personality disorder', in Beck, A.T., Freeman, A., Davis, D.D., and associates, *Cognitive Therapy of Personality Disorders*. New York: Guilford Press.

Prochaska, J.O., 1999, 'How do people change, and how can we change to help many more people?', in Hubble, M.A., Duncan, B.L., and Miller, S.D., *The Heart & Soul of Change: What Works in Therapy*. Washington DC: American Psychological Association.

Prochaska, J.O., and DiClemente, C.C., 1986, 'Toward a comprehensive model of change', in: Miller, W.R., and Heather, N. (eds), *Treating Addictive Behaviours: Processes of Change*. New York: Plenum.

Purser, R.E., and Cabana, S., 1998, *The Self-managing Organization: How Leading Companies are Transforming the Work of Teams for Real Impact*. New York: Free Press, Simon & Shuster Inc.

Quirk, A., 2003, Research Fellow, Royal College of Psychiatrists' Research Unit, London, personal communication with Grant (Mental Health Qualitative Research Network).

Rachman, S.J., 1996, 'Trends in cognitive and behavioural therapies', in Salkovskis, P.M. (ed.), *Trends in Cognitive and Behavioural Therapies*. Chichester: John Wiley.

Rachman, S., 1997, 'The evolution of cognitive behavioural therapy', in Clark, D.M., and Fairburn, G. (eds), *Science and Practice of Cognitive Behavioural Therapy*. Oxford: Oxford University Press.

Rachman, S.J., and Hodgson, R., 1974, 'Synchrony and desynchrony in fear and avoidance', *Behaviour Research and Therapy*, 12, pp. 311–18.

Rachman, S., and De Silva, P., 1978, 'Abnormal and normal obsessions', *Behaviour Research and Therapy*, 16, pp. 233–48.

Raine, R., Haines, A., Sensky, T., Hutchings, A., Larkin, K., and Black, N., 2002, 'Systematic review of mental health interventions for patients with common somatic symptoms: can research evidence from secondary care be extrapolated to primary care?', *British Medical Journal*, 325, pp. 1082–5.

Rassool, G.H. (ed.), 1998, *Substance Use and Misuse: Nature, Context and Clinical Interventions*. Oxford: Blackwell

Rassool, G.H. (ed.), 2002, *Dual Diagnosis: Substance Misuse and Psychiatric Disorders*. Oxford: Blackwell.

Raue, P.J., and Goldfred M.R., 1994, 'The therapeutic alliance in cognitive behaviour therapy', in Horvath, A.O., and Greenberger, L.S., *The Working Alliance: Theory, Research, and Practice*. New York: John Wiley.

Regel, S., and Roberts, D., 2002, *Mental Health Liaison: A Handbook for Nurses and Health Professionals*. London: Baillière Tindall and Royal College of Nursing, Harcourt.

Regier, D.A., Farmer, M.E., and Rae, D.S., 1990, 'Comorbidity of mental disorders with alcohol and other drug abuse: results from the Epidemiological Catchment Area (ECA) Study', *Journal of the American Medical Association*, 264, pp. 2511–18.

Richards, D., and Lovell, K., 2000a, 'Multiple access points and level of entry (MAPLE) ensuring choice, accessibility and equity for CBT services', *Behavioural and Cognitive Psychotherapy*, 28, pp. 379–92.

Richards, D., and Lovell, K., 2000b, 'Behavioural and cognitive behavioural interventions in the post-traumatic stress disorder', in Yule, W. (ed.), *Post-traumatic Stress Disorders: Concepts and Therapy*. Chichester: John Wiley.

Roberts, D., 2002a, 'Working models for practice', in Regel, S., and Roberts, D. (eds), *Mental Health Liaison: A Handbook for Nurses and Health Professionals*. London: Baillière Tindall and Royal College Nursing, Harcourt.

Roberts, D., 2002b, 'Mental health liaison in cancer care', in Regel, S., and Roberts, D. (eds), *Mental Health Liaison: A Handbook for Nurses and Health Professionals*. London: Baillière Tindall and Royal College Nursing, Harcourt.

Rogers, P.A., 1997a, 'Behaviour nurse therapy service in forensic mental health', *Mental Health Practice*, 1(4), pp. 22–6.

Rogers, P., 1997b, 'Post-traumatic stress disorder following male rape', *Journal of Mental Health*, 6(1), pp. 5–9.

Rogers, P., Vidgen, A., 2000, 'Working with people with serious mental illness who are angry', in Gamble, C., and Brennan, G. (eds), *Working with Serious Mental Illness: A Manual for Clinical Practice*. London: Baillière Tindall in association with the Royal College of Nursing, Harcourt.

Rogers, P., Gray, N.S., Kitchiner, N., and Williams, T., 2002, 'Behavioural treatment of PTSD in a perpetrator of manslaughter', *Journal of Traumatic Stress*, 13, pp. 511–19.

Rogers, R., Gillis, J.R., Turner, R.E., and Frise-Smith, T., 1990, 'The clinical presentation of command hallucinators in a forensic population', *American Journal of Psychiatry*, 147, pp. 1304–7.

Rolfe, G., 2000, 'Taking the postmodern turn', in Rolfe, G., *Research, Truth & Authority: Postmodern Perspectives on Nursing*. London: Macmillan.

Rollnick, S., Mason, P., and Butler, C., 1999, *Health Behavior Change: A Guide for Practitioners*. London: Churchill Livingstone.

Romme, M., 1998, *Understanding Voices: Auditory Hallucinations and Confusing Realities*. Runcorn: Handsell.

Romme, M., and Escher, S., 2000, *Making Sense of Voices: A Guide for Health Professionals Working with Voice Hearers*. London: Mind.

Roth, A.D., and Fonagy, P., 1996, *What Works for Whom?: A Critical Review of Psychotherapy Research*. New York: Guilford Press.

Rowan, A.B., and Malone, R.P., 1997, 'Tics with risperidone withdrawal', *Journal of the American Academy of Child and Adolescent Psychiatry*, 36, pp. 162–3.

Royal College of Physicians and Royal College of Psychiatrists, March 1995, *The Psychological Care of Medical Patients: Recognition of Need and Service Provision*. London: Royal College of Physicians.

Royal College of Physicians and Royal College of Psychiatrists, 2003, *The Psychological Care of Medical Patients: A Practical Guide*. London: Royal College of Physicians.

Rudd, M.D., and Joiner, T.J., 1997, 'Countertransference and the therapeutic relationship: a cognitive perspective', *Journal of Cognitive Psychotherapy: An International Quarterly*, 11(4), pp. 231–50.

Russell Ramsay, J., 1998, 'Postmodern cognitive therapy: cognitions, narratives, and personal meaning-making', *Journal of Cognitive Psychotherapy: An International Quarterly*, 12(1), pp. 39–55.

Ryan, P., 1999, *Assertive Outreach in Mental Health*. London: Nursing Times Books.

Safran, J.D., 1998, *Widening the Scope of Cognitive Therapy: The Therapeutic Relationship, Emotion, and the Process of Change*. Northvale, NJ: Jason Aronson.

Salkovskis, P.M., and Kirk, J., 1989, 'Obsessional disorders', in Hawton, K., Salkovskis, P.M., Kirk, J., and Clark, D.M., *Cognitive Behaviour Therapy for Psychiatric Problems: A Practical Guide*. New York: Oxford University Press.

Salkovskis, P.M., 1991, 'The importance of behaviour in the maintainance of anxiety and panic: a cognitive account', *Behavioural Psychotherapy*, 19, pp. 6–19.

Salkovskis, P., and Campbell, P., 1994, 'Thought suppression induces intrusion in naturally occurring intrusive thoughts', *Behaviour Research and Therapy*, 32, pp. 1–8.

Salkovskis, P.M., 1996, 'The cognitive approach to anxiety: threat beliefs, safety-seeking behaviour and the special case of healthy anxiety and obsessions', in Salkovskis, P. (ed.), *Frontiers of Cognitive Therapy*. New York: Guilford Press.

Scaife, J., 2001, *Supervision in the Mental Health Professions: A Practitioner's Guide*. Hove: Brunner-Routledge.

Schwandt, T.A., 2000, 'Three epistemological stances for qualitative inquiry: interpretivism, hermeneutics and social constructionism', in Denzin, N.K., and Lincoln, Y.S., Handbook of Qualitative Research, 2nd edn. Thousand Oaks, CA: Sage.

Scott, J., Paykel, E., Teasdale, J., and Hayhurst, H., March 2003, 'Use of cognitive therapy for relapse prevention in chronic depression: a cost-effectiveness study', *British Journal of Psychiatry*, 182, pp. 221–7.

Segal, Z.V., Williams, J.M.G., and Teasdale, J.D., 2001, *Mindfulness-based Cognitive Therapy for Depression: A New Approach to Preventing Relapse*. New York: Guilford Press.

Seivewright, N., 2000, *Community Treatment of Drug Misuse: More than Methadone*. Cambridge: Cambridge University Press.

Sharp, L.K., and Lipsky, M.S., September 2002, 'Screening for depression across the lifespan: a review of measures for use in primary care settings. *American Family Physician*, 66(6), pp. 952–5.

Sharpe, L., Sensky, T., Timberlake, N., Allard, S., and Brewin, C.R., 2001, 'The role of cognitive–behavioural therapy in facilitating adaptation to illness in rheumatoid arthritis: a case series', *Behavioural and Cognitive Psychotherapy*, 29, pp. 303–9.

Sheffield Hallam University, 1997, *BA (Hons) Adult Behavioural Psychotherapy ENB650 Definitive Document*, Sheffield: Sheffield Hallam University.

Short, N., and Kitchiner, N.J., 2003, 'Implementing cognitive behaviour therapy in routine clinical practice', *Journal of Psychiatric and Mental Health Nursing*, 10, pp. 484–93.

Short, N., Kitchiner, N., and Curran, J., 2004, 'Unreliable evidence', *Journal of Psychiatric and Mental Health Nursing*, 11(1), pp. 106–11.

Snyder, C.R., Michael, S.T., and Cheavens, J.S., 1999, 'Hope as a psychotherapeutic foundation of common factors, placebos, and expectancies', in Hubble, M.A., Duncan, B.L., and Miller, S.D., *The Heart & Soul of Change: What Works in Therapy*. Washington DC: American Psychological Association.

Spencer, C., Castle, D., and Michie, P.T., 2002, 'Motivations that maintain substance use among individuals with psychotic disorders', *Schizophrenia Bulletin*, 28(2), pp. 233–47.

Spiegel, D., Bloom, J.R., Kraemer, H.J.C., 1989, 'Effect of psychosocial treatment on survival in patients with metastatic breast cancer', *Lancet*, 14, pp. 881–91.

Sullivan, J., and Rogers, P., 1997, 'Cognitive Behavioural nursing therapy in paranoid psychosis', *Nursing Times*, 93(2), pp. 28–30.

Tait, L., Birchwood, M., and Trower, P., 2002, 'A new scale (SES) to measure engagement with community mental health services', *Journal of Mental Health*, 11(2), pp. 191–8.

Tanaka-Matsumi, J., and Seiden, D.Y., 1996, 'The culturally enformed functional assessment (CIFA) interview: a strategy for cross-cultural behavioral practice', *Cognitive and Behavioral Practice*, 3, pp. 215–33.

Tang, M., October 2001, 'Clinical outcome and client satisfaction of an anger management group program', *Canadian Journal of Occupational Therapy*, 68, pp. 228–36.

Tarrier, N., and Barrowclough, C., Haddock, G., and McGovern, J., 1999, 'The dissemination of innovative cognitive behavioural psychosocial treatments for schizophrenia', *Journal of Mental Health*, 8(6), pp. 569–82.

Tarrier, N., and Calam, R., 2002, 'New developments in cognitive-behavioural case formulation – epidemiological, systemic and social context: an integrative approach', *Behavioural and Cognitive Psychotherapy*, 30(3), pp. 311–28.

Teasedale, J.D., Moore, R.G., Hayhurst, H., Pope, M., Williams, S., and Segal, Z.V., April 2002, 'Metacognitive awareness and prevention of relapse in depression: empirical evidence', *Journal of Consulting and Clinical Psychology*, 70(92), pp. 275–87.

Tooby, J., and Cosmides, L., 1992, 'The psychological foundations of culture', in Barkow, J., and Cosmides, L. (eds), *The Adapted Mind: Evolutionary Psychology and the Generation of Culture*. New York: Oxford University Press.

Townend, M., Iannetta, L., and Freeston, M.H., 2002, 'Clinical supervision in practice: a survey of UK cognitive – behavioural psychotherapists accredited by the BABCP', *Behavioural and Cognitive Psychotherapy*, 30, pp. 485–500.

Townsend, W., Boyd, S., Griffen, G., Larkins, G., and Hicks, P., 2000, *Emerging Best Practices in Mental Health Recovery*. Columbus, OH. Ohio Department of Mental Health.

Trenoweth, S., May 2003, 'Perceiving risk in dangerous situations: risks of violence among mental health inpatients', *Journal of Advanced Nursing*, 42(93), pp. 278–87.

Trinder, L.A., 2002, 'Critical appraisal of evidence-based practice', in Trinder, L., and Reynolds, S. (eds), *Evidence-based practice: A Critical Appraisal*. Oxford: Blackwell.

Trinder, L., and Reynolds, S. (eds), 2000, *Evidence-based Practice: A Critical Appraisal*. Oxford: Blackwell.

Waddington, L., 2002, 'The therapy relationship in cognitive therapy', *Behavioural and Cognitive Psychotherapy*, 30(2), pp. 179–91.

Wanigaratne, S., Wallace, W., Pullin, J., Keaney, F., and Farmer, R., 1990, *Relapse Prevention for Addictive Behaviours: A Manual for Therapists*. Oxford: Blackwell.

Watts, F., Powell, E., Austin, S., 1973, 'The modification of abnormal beliefs', *British Journal of Medical Psychology*, 46, pp. 359–63.

Webster, C., Harris, G., Rice, M., Cormier, C., and Quinsey, V., 1995, *The HCR-20 Scheme: The Assessment of Dangerousness and Risk*. Vancouver: Simon Fraser University and British Columbia Forensic Psychiatric Services Commission.

Wells, A., 1997, *Cognitive Therapy of Anxiety Disorders: A Practice Manual and Conceptual Guide*. Chichester: John Wiley.

Wells, A., 2000, *Emotional Disorders and Metacognition: Innovative Cognitive Therapy*. Chichester: John Wiley.

White, J., 2000, *Treating Anxiety and Stress: A Group Psycho-educational Approach Using Brief CBT*. Chichester: John Wiley.

White, C.A., 2001, *Cognitive Behaviour Therapy for Chronic Medical Problems: A Guide to Assessment and Treatment in Practice*. Chichester: John Wiley.

Whitehead, L., and Royles, M., 2002, 'Deliberate self-harm: assessment and treatment interventions', in Regel, S., and Roberts, D. (eds), *Mental Health Liaison: A Handbook for Nurses and Health Professionals*. London: Baillière Tindall and Royal College Nursing, Harcourt.

Whittal, M.L., Rachman, S., and McLean, P.D., 2002, 'Psychosocial treatments for OCD: combining cognitive and behavioural treatments', in Simos, G. (ed.), *Cognitive Behaviour Therapy: A Guide for the Practicing Clinician*. Hove: Brunner-Routledge.

WHO, 2001, *World Health Organization Report on the Burden of Disease*. Geneva: World Health Organization.

Williams, C., 2001, *Overcoming Depression: A Five-area Approach*. London: Arnold.

Williams, J.E., Nieto, F.J., Sanford, C.P., Couper, D.J., and Tyroler, H.A., January 2002, 'The association between trait anger and incident stroke risk: the Atherosclerosis Risk in Communities (ARIC) study', *Stroke*, 33(1), pp. 13–9.

Worthless, I.M., Competent, U.R., and Lemonde-Terrible, O., 2002, 'Cognitive therapy training stress disorder: a cognitive perspective', *Behavioural and Cognitive Psychotherapy*, 30(3), pp. 365–74.

Wright, S., 1994, 'Culture in anthropology and organizational studies', in Wright, S. (ed.), *Anthropology of Organizations*. London: Routledge.

Wright, J.H., and Davis, D., 1994, 'The therapeutic relationship in cognitive behavioural therapy: patient perceptions and therapist responses', *Cognitive and Behavioural Practice*, 1, pp. 25–45.

Wright, L., and Lavery, A., 2002, 'Liaison mental health nursing and HIV and AIDS', in Regel, S., and Roberts, D. (eds), *Mental Health Liaison: A Handbook for Nurses and Health Professionals*. London: Baillière Tindall and Royal College Nursing, Harcourt.

Wright, S., Gournay, K., Glorney, F., and Thornicroft, G., 2000, 'Dual diagnosis in the suburbs: prevalence, need and inpatient service use', *Social Psychiatry and Psychiatric Epidemiology*, 35, pp. 297–304.

Wu, L.T., Ringwald, C.L., and Williams, C.E., March 2003, 'Use of substance abuse treatment services by persons with mental health and substance use problems', *Psychiatric Services*, 54(3), pp. 363–9.

Yates W.R., and Bowers, W.A., 2000, 'Cognitive therapy in the medical-psychiatric patient', in Stoudemire, A., Fogel, B.S., and Greenberg, D.B. (eds), *Psychiatric Care of the Medical Patient*, Oxford: Oxford University Press.

Young, J., 1990, *Cognitive Therapy for Personality Disorders: A Schema-focused Approach*, 3rd edn. Sarasota, FL: Professional Resource Exchange.

Yusupoff, L., and Tarrier, N., 2000, 'Coping strategy enhancement for persistent hallucinations and delusions', in Haddock, G., and Slade, P. (eds), *Cognitive Behavioural Interventions with Psychotic Disorders*. London: Routledge.

Zisook, S., Byrd, D., Kuck, J., and Jeste, D., 1995, 'Command hallucinations in outpatients with schizophrenia', *Journal of Clinical Psychiatry*, 56, pp. 462–5.

Zubin, J., and Spring, B., 1997, 'Vulnerability: a new view of schizophrenia', *Journal of Abnormal Psychology*, 86, pp. 260–6.

Other sources

Barker, P., 2000, personal communication to Short.

Bennett-Levy, J., 2003, personal communication to Grant.

Padesky, C.A., 1996a, *Guided Discovery Using Socratic Dialogue*. Newport Beach, CA: New Harbinger Publications and Center for Cognitive Therapy (video available from www.padesky.com).

Padesky, C.A., 2003b, personal communication to Grant.

Index